CORPORATE SOCIAL RESPONSIBILITY AND THE WELFARE STATE

T0303964

To Andrew and Nick

Corporate Social Responsibility and the Welfare State
The Historical and Contemporary Role of CSR in the Mixed Economy of Welfare

JEANETTE BREJNING
University of Bristol, UK

Routledge
Taylor & Francis Group

LONDON AND NEW YORK

First published 2012 by Ashgate Publishing

Published 2016 by Routledge
2 Park Square, Milton Park, Abingdon, Oxfordshire OX14 4RN
711 Third Avenue, New York, NY 10017, USA

First issued in paperback 2016

Routledge is an imprint of the Taylor & Francis Group, an informa business

British Library Cataloguing in Publication Data
Brejning, Jeanette.
 Corporate social responsibility and the welfare state : the historical and
contemporary role of CSR in the mixed economy of welfare.
 1. Social responsibility of business--Europe, Western.
 2. Industries--Social aspects--Europe, Western.
 3. Welfare state--Europe, Western. 4. Business and
politics--Europe, Western. 5. Social responsibility of
business--Europe, Western--History. 6. Social
responsibility of business--Political aspects--Europe,
Western. 7. Social responsibility of business--England.
 8. Social responsibility of business--Denmark. 9. Social
policy--Cross-cultural studies.
 I. Title
 306.3'094-dc23

Library of Congress Cataloging-in-Publication Data
Brejning, Jeanette.
 Corporate social responsibility and the welfare state : the historical and
contemporary role of CSR in the mixed economy of welfare / by Jeanette
Brejning.
   p. cm.
 Includes bibliographical references and index.
 ISBN 978-1-4094-2451-2 (hbk) -- ISBN 978-1-4094-2452-9 (ebk)
 1. Social responsibility of business. 2. Welfare state. 3.
Social policy. 4. Globalization--Social aspects. I. Title.
 HD60.B74 2011
 658.4'08--dc23

2011035634

ISBN 13: 978-1-138-25510-4 (pbk)
ISBN 13: 978-1-4094-2451-2 (hbk)

Contents

List of Figures

Acknowledgements

I would like to thank the interviewees in England, Denmark and the European Commission for participating in this book's case study. I am grateful for the time they took out of their working hours to share with me their knowledge, experience, views and thoughts, and also for their general kindness and helpfulness.

I would also like to thank Professor Hartley Dean, Dr Kevin Farnsworth, Professor Bent Greve and Dr Simon Pemberton for encouraging and supporting the publication of this book, and Dr Patricia Kennett and Dr Ranji Devadason for useful advice and encouragement during the process. Thank you also to Commissioning Editor Claire Jarvis at Ashgate Publishing Group. Finally, special thanks to my family, especially Nick, both our parents, and Andrew.

List of Abbreviations

ALMP	Active Labour Market Policy
CSR	Corporate Social Responsibility
HI	Historical Institutionalism
MEOW	Mixed Economy of Welfare
MESP	Mixed Economy Sectoral Paradigm
MUD	Moral Underclass Discourse
NGO	Non-Governmental Organization
NPM	New Public Management
RED	Redistributionist Discourse
SID	Social Integrationist Discourse

Chapter 1

Introduction:
Examining the Social Dimension
of Corporate Social Responsibility

> While there is more than 40 years of research on what effects CSR initiatives
> may or may not have on the corporate bottom line we know very little about the
> outcomes of these initiatives for society. (Banerjee, 2010: 266)

Since the 1990s, the issue of corporate social responsibility (CSR) has gained
increasing currency on both national and international policy agendas. The
notion of CSR is now applied to a wide range of social issues, ranging from
environmental sustainability to human rights and labour market inclusion. CSR is
also being employed by several governments to address social problems such as
social exclusion (EU-COM, 2007). This recent turn of events has made it clear that
the idea of CSR and its associated activities are relevant not just to the sphere of
business but to society as a whole. Yet, as Banarjee points out in the quote above,
CSR has remained a subject area which is predominantly studied from a business
perspective. As a result, very little is known about the impact of CSR on society.
This is in spite of the fact that researchers within business schools recognize that
the theme and practices of corporate social responsibility are relevant beyond their
own disciplinary boundaries. Indeed some have called for the CSR research agenda
to move beyond the (mostly quantitative, correlational) preoccupation with the
business benefits of CSR towards more qualitative explorations of what they call
'the social returns of CSR' (McWilliams et al., 2006: 9). The aim of this book is to
redress this imbalance in what is known about corporate social responsibility by
investigating CSR's 'social' rather than 'corporate' dimension. More specifically,
the area of interest here is the relationship between CSR and the welfare state.

Why CSR is Relevant to Welfare State Politics and Research

The range of activities which are today known as CSR practices frequently take
the shape of businesses or employers providing some form of welfare, whether
for employees or for social stakeholders outside the organization. As such CSR
represents the production of welfare by welfare actors other than the state. This
raises questions about the social significance of the recent increase in CSR activity,
in particular in relation to the welfare state. Is there a trade-off, for instance,
between CSR and state-provided welfare? Does CSR, in other words, constitute a

rolling out of the commercial sector and a rolling back of the welfare state? This is a core concern of this book. However, the aim is not to take a predetermined critical stance against corporate social responsibility. Instead, the investigation remains open to the possibility that CSR could be perceived from a more benign perspective, as a positive development promising new and innovative approaches to addressing persistent social problems such a social exclusion. The question then becomes whether CSR should be interpreted as an endeavour to roll back the state or instead as an additional undertaking to roll out new solutions to social problems.

By exploring the relationship between CSR and the welfare state this book not only addresses the under-researched issue of what McWilliams et al. referred to earlier as the 'social returns' of CSR. The book also contributes to central debates in the politics and study of welfare states. The notion of responsibility is a recurring and increasingly topical theme within welfare state research. Early comparative social policy writing, from the 1950s and into the 1970s, was largely preoccupied with the expansion of state responsibility for social welfare in advanced industrial nations. In the mid-1970s and 1980s, the assumption that state responsibility would inevitably continue to extend was undermined by economic, political and ideological developments. The 'welfare state crisis' of those decades dampened welfare state expansion in many countries and challenged the generally taken-for-granted value of state responsibility for welfare. The notion of responsibility was central to the political debate as arguments were put forward about the economic, political and sometimes moral advantages of shifting welfare responsibilities to non-state providers such as the commercial sector, the non-profit sector and the informal sector. Since then both social policy and comparative social policy research have paid more attention to the role of welfare producers other than the state and have also become interested in the ways in which welfare responsibilities are distributed and redistributed within the whole of the mixed economy of welfare (Rose, 1986, Evers, 1993, Mayo, 1994, Lewis, 1995, Fridberg, 1997, Johnson, 1999, Cochraine et al., 2001, Esping-Andersen, 2002, Hill, 2007).

The political discussion about the appropriate allocation of responsibilities within the mixed economy carried on into the 1990s and continues today. There is an overall trend of governments of welfare states being increasingly in favour of extending the welfare responsibilities of both the commercial and non-profit sectors. In England, for example, the family is repeatedly being presented as a particularly important locus of welfare provision and social responsibility. The policies of both New Labour's 'Third Way' and the current Conservative–Liberal Democrat Coalition's 'Big Society' include an emphasis on individual responsibility. The political rhetoric has been particularly explicit in arguing that welfare state citizenship entails not only social rights but also moral and social responsibilities. In an increasing number of welfare states, the social right of receiving unemployment compensation has over the last decades been made conditional upon what is considered the social responsibility of individuals to contribute to society by working. In addition, state measures aimed at overcoming poverty are increasingly being reframed in the language of social exclusion and inclusion. Now the onus is as much on those agencies set up to tackle social exclusion as it is on the individuals themselves to take responsibility for their own inclusion, preferably by taking up employment (see for example Torfing, 1999, Lødemel and Trickey, 2001, Taylor-Gooby, 2001, MacGregor, 2003, Levitas, 2005, Aust and Arriba, 2005).

These developments have been covered extensively and critically in welfare state research. When it comes to the commercial sector, however, it seems that only some of the changes taking place have been considered relevant. Attention has been given to issues around privatization, outsourcing, private financing of public services, occupational welfare and marketization of the public sector. And, more recently, social policy analyses have considered the effects of globalization upon the balance of power between businesses and governments, expressing concerns about the growing ability of transnational corporations to influence national social policy agendas – mainly in the direction of dismantling social policy measures and minimizing state responsibilities (Macleod and Lewis, 2004, Bridgen and Meyer, 2005, Farnsworth and Holden, 2006). Yet the aspect of the development which is of interest in this book – corporate social responsibility ('CSR') – has generated little, if any, interest. Comparative studies of CSR are particularly sparse. This is an oversight because, as this book will be demonstrating, CSR is an integral part of the changing perceptions and conceptualizations of responsibilities within the mixed economy of welfare.

It is the recognition of these gaps in our knowledge – about the social dimension of CSR and about the significance of CSR for welfare state politics and research – which has motivated the writing of this book. The overarching objective of this book is therefore to fill this knowledge gap by furthering our understanding of the relationship between corporate social responsibility and the welfare state.

There are two main questions driving the inquiry at the heart of this book. These two questions are also two sides of the same coin. They are, firstly: to what extent do historical and institutional (welfare state) contexts influence the ways in which CSR is interpreted, applied and linked to social exclusion? And secondly: to what degree do the ideas and practices of CSR influence the institutional structures of welfare states? Or to put this latter question more specifically: is CSR, when applied to addressing social exclusion, a vehicle for rolling back the state, or does CSR constitute a roll-out of a new type of solution to persistent social problems?

Investigating the Relationship between CSR and the Welfare State

The question of the relationship between CSR and the welfare state will be approached from three angles, corresponding to the three sections of this book. Firstly, in Part I, the conceptual relationship will be explored between the notion of corporate social responsibility and social issues such as social change and social exclusion. Secondly, in Part II, the historical evolution of CSR in the mixed economy of welfare will be investigated. And thirdly, in Part III, the findings from a case study will be presented exploring how CSR is interpreted and applied in the two welfare states of England and Denmark. The case study will compare the experiences of CSR practitioners in Denmark and England, exploring their perspectives on the social impacts of CSR and on the wider relationship between CSR and the welfare state. It is important to point out, however, that Parts I and II are not based exclusively on the cases of England and Denmark. Part I stays on the general level, and in Part II, historical insights from authors who have studied the emergence and development of CSR in other countries are also integrated into the analysis, including the countries of Sweden, Norway, France and Germany. Throughout the sections in this book CSR will be considered both at the general level and more specifically when CSR is applied to the issue of social exclusion.

The cross-national comparative perspective of this book is important because it is through comparative inquiries that insights can be gained into the ways in which a social phenomenon such as CSR comes to expression in different ways in different national settings. It is, in other words, in order to understand the relationship between CSR and the welfare state in general that this book sets out to explore the extent to which varying national approaches to CSR are affected by historically, institutionally and/or culturally specific ideas about the appropriate relationship between business and society. The theoretical approach chosen for the analysis is Historical Institutionalism, which has been integrated here with the analytical framework of the mixed economy of welfare.

Both qualitative and quantitative studies are important in relation to the separate research fields of CSR and welfare state studies. However, the investigation undertaken in this book warrants qualitative research methods as these are suitable for exploring the as yet unidentified and multiple possible relevant connections between CSR and the welfare state. The data from the CSR practitioners has been extracted by conducting 34 semi-structured interviews with a range of key political, policy and social actors working with CSR in different parts of the mixed economy and on multiple levels of governance: the international level of the European Commission; the national 'central levels' in England and Denmark; and the national 'local levels'. Interviewees include: policy makers in both countries and from the European Commission; people working with CSR in industry; and practitioners working to implement local CSR programmes.

Conducting the interviews with CSR practitioners has been an integral part of carrying out the research for this book. The view here is that comparing how people who work with CSR perceive and experience CSR is a central part of understanding the extent to which the historical and institutional contexts of welfare states influence the ways in which CSR is interpreted, applied and linked to social exclusion. Understandings of CSR amongst people engaged with CSR are in themselves part of the relationship between CSR and its social context.

The idea behind interviewing CSR practitioners on three different spatial scales is to gain insights about CSR as it is being employed and experienced on multiple levels of governance. On the national levels, the goal has been to learn from the knowledge and experiences of people who have been central to national

CSR agendas in recent years. The reason for including the international level is as a means of taking into account that CSR not only takes on different shapes and forms depending on its national context, but that there is also a separate CSR agenda on the international level. The aim of carrying out interviews on the local level has been to explore how being involved with CSR 'at ground level' shapes people's views and perceptions of CSR. It was thought that people practising CSR locally could offer particularly interesting perspectives on what is considered to be the 'social impacts' of CSR.

The issue of the many shapes and forms which corporate social responsibility can take both conceptually and in practice is addressed in the conceptual and historical chapters of this book. For the purpose of the interviews on the local levels, however, an exclusive focus on just one type of CSR practice was adopted. The focus was on projects where CSR is employed explicitly to overcome social exclusion and to promote social inclusion. In both England and Denmark, the local CSR projects chosen have in common that they offer work placements and other labour market preparation activities for people considered socially excluded, either because they are homeless (in the English projects) or because they are recent immigrants with insufficient knowledge of the spoken language in their country of residency (in the Danish projects). More detail on these projects will be provided in the introduction to Part III.

Although it is in Part III of this book that the focus will turn specifically to the contexts of England and Denmark, findings from the case studies will also be drawn on in other chapters of this book. In the historical analysis of Part II, for example, the arguments made regarding the historical development in England and Denmark will be supported with quotes from English and Danish respondents.

One of the most important influencing factors in selecting England and Denmark for this book's cross-national comparison is based on these two countries' similar characteristics as 'welfare states'. Yet England and Denmark also represent two different welfare state types, at least when seen from the vantage point in the comparative social policy literature which considers welfare states as belonging to different qualitative clusters or regimes (this will be explained in more detail in Chapter 2). These differences are important in the context of this book's historical institutionalist theoretical standpoint, where national institutional contexts are considered important mediators of similar social phenomena and thereby also important variables for understanding and explaining similarities and differences. England and Denmark also present particularly fruitful contexts within which to explore CSR, because both England and Denmark are decided European front runners in developing CSR, an observation which is frequently confirmed in the literature on CSR (Albareda et al., 2006, Eberhard-Harribey, 2006). The reason for focusing on England rather than Britain is based on the recognition of the significant variations between social policy traditions and mixed economies in England, Scotland and Wales (see for example Taylor-Gooby, 2008b). The choice of additional countries for the historical analysis has again been informed by the theoretical allegiance with welfare typologies. Including Sweden and Norway thus serves to expand the scope for making assertions about any particularly Scandinavian, 'social democratic' approaches to CSR. Similarly, the inclusion of Germany and France serves the purpose of including into the historical analysis a third 'conservative' welfare state type (see Chapter 2).

The Content of this Book

Part I of this book (Chapters 2 and 3) starts at the theoretical and conceptual level. Chapter 2 presents this book's theoretical framework. This framework consists of an integration of the mixed economy of welfare approach to social policy analysis and the theoretical stance of Historical Institutionalism. The chapter highlights the value of this integrated framework for the purpose of investigating corporate social responsibility within different welfare institutional settings.

Chapter 3 considers CSR conceptually. The first issue dealt with is the matter of the many co-existing but often conflicting definitions of corporate social responsibility found in the academic literature on CSR. In Chapter 3 these conceptual contradictions are explained by illustrating how the varying CSR definitions are situated within different ideological and normative discourses. These discourses differ not only in their descriptions of CSR but also in their implications for broader themes such as the appropriate relationship between business and the wider mixed economy, and the extent to which CSR should be employed as a vehicle for social change. Chapter 3 thus maps out the range of CSR discourses available to CSR practitioners and other CSR stakeholders. The following section of this chapter links these CSR discourses with different discursive approaches to social inclusion and exclusion. The final section of Chapter 3 presents an overview of CSR definitions used by people who are engaged in CSR in their working lives. The connection between these practitioners' definitions and the ideological CSR discourses will be explored. For the purpose of this exercise, findings from the interviews with English and Danish CSR practitioners will be used as examples.

Part II moves on to present an historical analysis of CSR which focuses on how CSR emerged and developed in different West European welfare states. These are England, Denmark, Sweden, Norway, France and Germany. The chapters in Part II explore the history of CSR within these mixed economies of welfare as a way of gaining an insight into why CSR takes both different and similar forms in different social contexts. The focus is on institutional developments which have influenced and shaped CSR throughout its history and which continue to affect the ways in which CSR is interpreted and applied today. As part of this historical investigation, the changing and varying links between CSR and social exclusion are also explored.

In Part III the emphasis is on the findings from the comparative case study of CSR in England and Denmark. Chapter 7 concentrates on the question of the social impacts of CSR. Drawing on respondents' accounts and views of the positive and negative social impacts of CSR, this chapter presents a detailed analysis of CSR when it is applied to addressing issues around social exclusion. Chapter 8 discusses the extent to which CSR can be considered a vehicle for, or a contribution to, institutional change within the two English and Danish mixed economies. Employing the study's integrated mixed economy and historical institutionalist framework, this question is investigated by exploring the local CSR projects, both in terms of how they operate at the various formal institutional levels to the broader levels of ideational regulation. The chapter concludes by considering the past, present and future of CSR, both in relation to social exclusion and in relation to the mixed economy of welfare. It also discusses the various drivers and mechanisms of institutional change and continuity emerging from the historical analysis and from respondents' predictions for the future. Overall, although the chapters of Part III are based on the empirical study of England and Denmark, these chapters also address some of the core questions of this book on the more general level.

The concluding chapter, Chapter 9, draws together the various parts of this book to reflect on what has been achieved overall. This chapter finishes with a discussion of the future of CSR in the light of changes that have occurred in recent years, in particular taking into account issues relating to the current economic climate.

PART I
Theory and Concepts

Chapter 2

Theoretical Framework: Integrating Historical Institutionalism and the Mixed Economy of Welfare Approach

Introduction

This chapter outlines the theoretical framework of the book. This consists of an integration of the mixed economy of welfare analytical approach and the theoretical framework of Historical Institutionalism. The chapter will outline the perspectives of each approach in turn and then highlight the value of combining the two frameworks.

The Mixed Economy of Welfare

The idea of a 'mixed economy of welfare' ('MEOW') emerged in the 1980s in the context of what was widely considered a welfare state crisis. This crisis was accompanied by substantial political criticism of the welfare state. The criticism was directed in particular against the welfare state's extensive public sector. The critical voices ranged from the New Right, with its preference for a wider role for the market, to the libertarian left and its arguments about the virtues of the 'community sector'. Within welfare state research, the term 'mixed economy of welfare' also appeared in the 1980s and gained grounds steadily throughout the 1990s, but less in support of any of the contemporary political rhetoric and more as a recognition of the field's long-term neglect of welfare providers other than the state (Lewis, 1992, Evers, 1993, Mishra, 1990, Rose, 1986). Today, the existence alongside the state of a range of welfare providers is taken for granted within welfare state analysis to the extent that references to the mixed economy can no longer be interpreted as a bias towards any particular mix (Kennett, 2004, Cochraine et al., 2001, Alcock, 2001, Evers et al., 2005).

Employing the mixed economy of welfare as an analytical framework entails conceptualizing the welfare state as a 'welfare society' or a 'welfare economy' consisting of different 'sectors' of welfare producers. Most contemporary MEOW analyses work on the basis of four sectors all of which are referred to with various labels. In this book the four sectors are labelled as follows: the public sector, the commercial sector, the non-profit sector and the informal sector. By way of

Sector	Public	Commercial	Non-profit	Informal
Agents	• Central and Local Government • Non-departmental Public Bodies • Public Service Providers	• Commercial Enterprises • Commercial Service Providers	• Campaign Groups • Self-help Groups • Faith Groups • Charities • Social Enterprises • NGOs • Non-profit Service Providers	• Family/ Household • Friends • Neighbours • Extended Social Networks

Figure 2.1   The Four Sectors of the Mixed Economy of Welfare and its Agents

illustration, Figure 2.1 gives an overview of these four sectors and provides (non-exhaustive) examples of the types of agents operating within each sector.

Viewing the welfare state as comprising of these four sectors brings to attention the many spaces in which welfare in a 'welfare state' is produced beyond the realm of the state (the public sector). As the MEOW analytical framework has developed since the 1980s, additional valuable insights have followed not only about the various sectors but also about the different levels on which welfare can be carried out. Instead of seeing welfare purely in its final form, as a delivered outcome, researchers using the MEOW approach have divided their analysis into the separate welfare operations of regulating, funding and provisioning (Johnson, 1999). This adds a second dimension to the analysis because now it is not only a question of there being four different sectors which each produce different forms of welfare. The same form of welfare outcome can be produced by several welfare sectors in combination.

The conceptualization of welfare societies as strictly divided into four welfare producing sectors is an analytical device rather than an accurate depiction of the reality of welfare states. Not only is the relationship between welfare sectors mostly fluid and the boundaries between them therefore permeable and ambiguous (Powell, 2007), but the whole idea of a mixed economy is also ultimately a social construct. Yet, the MEOW analytical framework is useful for taking into account forms of welfare that are produced outside the realm of the public sector; for drawing out cross-national differences in mixed economies; and for the analysis of welfare state change. The MEOW framework is not, however, an explanatory theoretical framework. It does not offer any explanations of what causes welfare mixes to change over time, nor does it explain why different national mixed economies change in different or similar directions over time and have different welfare mixes at any given time. For the purpose of understanding and explaining the relationship between corporate social responsibility and the mixed economy of welfare, the MEOW framework outlined above will therefore be integrated with the theoretical framework of Historical Institutionalism. Historical Institutionalism offers perspectives on the relationship between social structure and agency and on how and when these dynamics either foster social changes or continuities.

Historical Institutionalism

Historical Institutionalism ('HI') is a branch of New Institutionalism which emerged in the social sciences in the 1980s as a reaction against decades of domination by Behaviouralism (Peters, 2001). Against Behaviouralism's focus on individual agency, New Institutionalism represented a reintroduction of structure to political analysis, in the form of institutions (Peters, 2001). Within New Institutionalism, those academics credited with having established the Historical Institutionalist branch, such as Thelen and Steinmo, explicitly position Historical Institutionalism between what they consider the structural determinism of institutional neo-Marxism and the non-empirical theorizing of institutional Rational Choice (Thelen and Steinmo, 1992).

Within the field of welfare state studies, HI has become increasingly influential over the last two decades. Historical institutionalists started contributing to comparative social policy debates when they joined in the 'welfare state crisis' debate. Whereas most other welfare state theories have taken for granted the perception that welfare states throughout the Western world found themselves in crisis in the 1970s and 1980s and that economic and political, external and internal pressures forced politicians to undertake drastic cutbacks on state welfare (Tanzi, 2002), historical institutionalists have questioned the extent of this crisis and the degree to which welfare states were actually 'rolled back' in those decades (Green-Pedersen, 2004, Starke, 2006, Starke et al., 2008). This position made HI a new and distinct position in the crisis debate. Historical institutionalists argue that the welfare state has proved itself change-resistant against external and internal, economic and political pressures for change thanks to the resilience of its institutional design (Pierson, 1996).

Another important contribution of HI to the field of welfare state studies relates to the field's long-running debates regarding whether welfare states will eventually all converge around the same social model, or whether national divergences will remain. Authors writing from a historical institutionalist perspective have widely united in arguing against convergence. Most recently, historical institutionalists have taken positions against the globalization thesis' convergence prediction. The globalization thesis is based on a perception of globalization as an external force driving all welfare states and all welfare regimes into a 'race to the bottom' towards the same neo-liberal welfare state model with low tax rates and low levels of public social expenditure (Teeple, 2000, Mishra, 1999). Historical institutionalist authors argue instead that welfare state differences will remain because the different institutional structures of welfare states give nation-states the strength to take different stances in reaction to global pressures (Wilding, 1997, Geyer, 1998, Blank and Burau, 2006) and thus will continue to mediate external influences such as globalization (Hattam, 1992, Thelen and Steinmo, 1992, Carroll, 2002, Hay and Rosamond, 2002).

Finally, taking a historical institutionalist position entails regarding as significant for understanding cross-national differences the unique historical trajectories of different countries' institutions. In short, the theoretical starting points of an historical institutionalist analysis can be captured in the frequently referred to statements that 'history matters' and 'institutions matter'.

It is important to emphasize that HI does not constitute one coherent theoretical approach. Amongst historical institutionalists differences remain regarding how welfare state formation and development is explained and regarding how change takes place. The remainder of this chapter will present this book's position within the broad framework that is Historical Institutionalism.

Formal Institutions

Within HI, a useful distinction between different types of institutions is increasingly made between 'formal' and 'informal' institutions (Thelen, 1999) or 'material' and 'ideational' institutions (Skocpol, 1992).[1] Earlier historical institutionalist studies tend to focus on 'formal' or 'material' institutions such as governments and political party systems (Dunleavy, 1992, King, 1992), constitutional structures (Hattam, 1992) and legal systems (Hattam, 1992).

Formal institutions are important to historical institutionalist analysis because they have been found to explain why similar policy ideas or programs have been adopted and developed differently – or not adopted at all – in different countries (Immergut, 1992, Bonoli, 2001). In comparing countries such as England and Denmark, for example, a significant formal institutional difference includes the need for governments in a corporatist country such as Denmark to include social partners in negotiations concerning the labour market. These social partners can impose constraints upon government reforms in Denmark, by acting as so-called 'veto players' (Immergut, 1992). In contrast, in a pluralist country such as England, governments operate under fewer such formal institutional restraints (Schmidt, 2002).

---

1   To avoid confusion with the notion of the 'informal sector' in the mixed economy of welfare, from now on this category of institutions shall only be referred to as 'ideational'.

More recently, and of particular interest here, historical institutionalists are broadening their definitions of formal institutions to encompass wider 'governance arrangements' (Lieberman, 2002). Researchers with a specific interest in the welfare state are arguing that the definition of formal institutions should also include the formal institutions and rules related to the welfare state (Palier, 2002, Starke, 2006). In the area of social security, for example, Palier argues that the mode of access to benefits, the benefit structure and the financing mechanisms all constitute formal institutional rules (Palier, 2002). It is, in other words, possible to conceptualize the mixed economy of welfare as a formal institution on the basis that it is a governance arrangement governed by institutional rules relating to welfare provision and welfare funding. Moreover, these institutional rules are to a large degree formally regulated by governments through their social policies, particularly in relation to the public, commercial and non-profit sectors whilst arguably less in relation to the informal sector.

Ideational Institutions

Over the last 15 years historical institutionalist authors have increasingly taken into account those social structures which are generally conceptualized as 'ideational institutions' (Beland, 2005, Berman, 2001, Campbell, 2002, Hall, 1993, Lieberman, 2002, McNamara, 1998, Surel, 2000). Ideational institutions are different from formal institutions in the sense that they exist on the more intangible level of 'ideas'. The notion of ideational institutions is heavily inspired by the Sociological Institutionalist perspective where individuals and their behaviour are shaped by social structures such as cognitive maps, morals, symbols, scripts, routines and identities (see Hall and Taylor, 1996). Early integration of this conceptualization of institutions into a New Institutionalist framework can be seen in March and Olsen's definition of institutions as collections of norms, rules, understandings and routines (March and Olsen, 1989) and in their subsequent thesis that institutions can influence individuals to act at times against their self-interest and instead guided by a 'logic of appropriateness' derived from their institutional surroundings. Within Historical Institutionalism, researchers have highlighted the significance of elements that are part of the ideational institutions of society such as paradigms (Hall, 1992), norms (Katzenstein, 1996), 'shared understandings' (Thelen, 1999), culture and belief structures (Berman, 2001), identities (Torfing, 2001), values (Cox, 2004), tradition (Bevir and Rhodes, 2004), ideologies such as communism or neo-liberalism (Lieberman, 2002, Beland, 2005), policy principles, such as universalism (Lindbom, 2001, Cox, 2004), theories and conceptual models (Campbell, 2002) and discourse (Schmidt, 2002, Hay and Rosamond, 2002, Taylor-Gooby, 2005a).

Amongst those authors that are developing the historical institutionalist framework by emphasizing the role of ideas there is as yet no clear consensus around questions such as how the notion of 'ideas' should be defined more precisely, or how different conceptions of ideas interrelate. It is also unclear which types of ideas are part of the ideational institutional framework and which exist independently from this structural level. Instead, different authors' frameworks point in different directions where several different conceptions of 'ideas' are sometimes considered synonymous (Campbell, 2002), sometimes divided into separate but equal groups (Hansen and King, 2001) and at other times categorized according to more hierarchic systems (Taylor-Gooby, 2005a, Lynggard, 2007). This absence of a coherent theory regarding the role of ideas is widely recognized within the literature itself (Starke, 2006). The ideational framework proposed here focuses on the three main concepts of paradigms, discourses and also what will be referred to here as 'free-floating ideas'. Inspired by Berman's distinction between ideas as either dependent or independent variables (Berman, 2001), free-floating ideas are notions and concepts that are not part of or fully ingrained into the ideational institutional structures. This is in contrast to paradigms and discourses, which make up the ideational institutional structure.

Paradigms   Perhaps the most influential development of the paradigm concept within the historical institutionalist framework is Hall's analysis of the shift from Keynesianism to monetarism in the United Kingdom in the 1970s (Hall, 1993). In this analysis Hall likens ideational institutions to worldviews or 'gestalts'. Policymakers will derive from such worldviews their interpretive frameworks and these interpretive frameworks are applied to address policy problems. Hall argues that particular policy fields are often dominated by one interpretive framework at a time, comparable to the dominance of Kuhn's (1970) notion of scientific paradigms (Hall, 1993). This analogy between the natural sciences and the social world has since been widely disputed. Yet Hall's proposition that paradigms are important components of the institutional framework (on the ideational level) and that paradigms influence the policy process continues to gain currency. Within comparative social policy researchers are increasingly widening the original application of the paradigm concept to specific policy sectors to now also relating paradigms to the whole of national social policy contexts or, even more broadly, to welfare state regions or clusters (Cox, 2004, Taylor-Gooby, 2008a). Commenting on the relationship between narrower and broader paradigms, Merrien distinguishes between 'sectoral' and 'general' paradigms and argues that sectoral paradigms tend to be embedded within a general paradigm, whereas general paradigms, determining for example a collective's ideas about gender roles, will tend to cut across all policy sectors (Merrien, 2001).

Discourse   Paradigms are mostly taken for granted rather than explicitly articulated. This is one of the main aspects distinguishing paradigms from discourses in the theoretical framework of this book. Discourses are defined here as the articulated interpretation of concepts, ideas and the general complexities of the social world. As such they are on a par with Hall's 'interpretive frameworks' (1993), or to Hay and Rosamund's 'cognitive filters' and 'conceptual lenses' through which actors render intelligible the social world (Hay and Rosamond, 2002). In contrast to free-floating ideas, discourses are made up of broader 'systems of meaning' (Lynggard, 2007) in which often several concepts and notions are tied together (Beland, 2007). And in contrast to paradigms, discourses are not deeply ingrained and taken-for-granted. Discourses mostly exist alongside alternative versions and competing interpretations of the same idea (Taylor-Gooby, 2005a). Discourses are therefore also often contested rather than widely agreed. In the framework applied here discourses are the link between free-floating ideas and paradigms. Free-floating ideas are embedded in discourses, whilst discourses are heavily influenced by the paradigms of the context in which they are articulated. As argued by Hay and Rosamund, discourses are created by actors, and in this creation process actors will largely draw on the repertoire of discursive resources available to them, such as already existing narratives and understandings (Hay and Rosamond, 2002). Discourses can also influence or change paradigms if new ideas are articulated by actors in ways which successfully render change legitimate. As pointed out by Schmidt (2003), discourses can be employed both as passive accompaniments to continuity or as active enablers of change (Schmidt, 2003).

Institutions and Continuity: Path-dependency

A key component of the historical institutionalist theoretical framework is the idea that institutions have an inbuilt tendency to sustain continuity in the short term, and to constrain frequent and far-reaching changes. In the longer term only incremental changes take place. This bias towards continuity is supported through the mechanism of 'path-dependency'. Path-dependency describes the propensity of initial and often random choices to create a pattern which will persist. In HI the concept is used to explain how the policy choices made when an institution is being formed, or when a policy is initiated, will have a continuing and largely determinate influence over policy far into the future (Skocpol, 1992, King, 1992). The general argument is that early historical policy decisions set any development upon a specific trajectory. From then on the development will be 'locked in' (Krasner, 1984) and have an inbuilt bias towards continuing along the given path rather than changing direction. Moreover, the original policy choices – also known as policy legacies (Weir and Skocpol, 1983) – determine the extent and type of change possible (Pierson, 1994, Pierson, 2004, Mahoney, 2000). Over time it is more likely that a policy pathway changes incrementally, in an evolutionary rather than a revolutionary manner, seeing change happening within rather than of the institutional framework (Starke, 2006).

Another way in which institutions are seen to support continuity more often than change relates to historical institutionalism's fundamentally structuralist perception of the relationship between structure and agency. When HI was founded, one of its defining positions was the argument that institutions shape the behaviour of individuals and structure their relationships. Contrasting itself explicitly to agency-oriented theoretical standpoints such as Rational Choice, HI represented the outlook that preferences, interests and objectives of individuals are not exogenous to social structures but are rather defined by the institutional context (Hay and Wincott, 1998, Thelen, 1999). At the formal institutional level, institutions are regarded as distributors of power between individuals and groups (Hall and Taylor, 1996) and mediators of political conflict (Thelen, 1999). Within the area of policy, formal policy institutions create constraints and opportunities for those involved in policymaking (Beland, 2005). Actors operating within these constraints and opportunities can be expected to reinforce path-dependency. Actors will generally experience the benefits of continuity over change as they will have increasingly adapted their behaviour to the unique 'logic' of well-established institutions (Thelen, 1999). Over time this logic is increasingly likely to be reproduced and thereby reinforced (Beland, 2005). The same argument can be taken to the ideational institutional level. Here ideational structures influence actors towards continuity not only by dictating appropriate behaviour through the 'logic of appropriateness' (March and Olsen, 1989) but also by linking preferences with ideas about identities, culture and norms. As pointed out by Mahoney, actors reproduce institutions through the mechanism of path-dependency in various ways based on different motivations, from individually orientated utilitarian calculations to more socially grounded beliefs about the need to uphold what is perceived as legitimate institutions (Mahoney, 2000).

The introduction of the notion of path-dependency into the area of welfare state analysis is one of Historical Institutionalism's most significant contributions. It is important, however, not to equate HI exclusively with path-dependency. Firstly because the concept of path-dependency is open to the criticism that it is less of a theoretical explanation than a 'post-dicting' narration, which draws eclectically on historical events from a present-day vantage point to form the almost functionalist impression that 'what happened happened because it had to' (Peters, 2001: 75). Indeed, if one goes back far enough in time, any contemporary situation could be interpreted as path-dependent. These points of criticism are recognized by historical institutionalists. Yet once taking the position that 'history matters' it also becomes necessary to accept that any historical explanation can be accused of having an arbitrary starting point (Mahoney, 2000). The other reason why path-dependency should not be seen as the full representation of HI has to do with the criticism directed against HI – not just from its opponents but also from within HI itself – that HI is mostly appropriate for explaining continuity whilst it struggles to explain change (Thelen, 1999, Lieberman, 2002, Beland, 2005, Andersen, 2002). This perception is misleading. HI offers a variety of ways of understanding change once attention is given to concepts other than path-dependency and once the analysis broadens to focus not only on institutions as resilient, agency-shaping, path-dependent social structures but also on the various sources of dynamics in and amongst institutions.

Explaining Change

In HI change does take place. Firstly, within path-dependency change happens albeit predominantly in incremental and evolutionary ways and rarely in revolutionary manners. To explain how an institutional path is initiated, historical institutionalists point to founding or 'formative moments' (Rothstein, 1992) and to explain what makes an existing path go in a new direction authors have pointed to 'critical junctures'. Frequently used examples of such events are state formation, nation-building (Gal and Bargal, 2002), economic crises or military conflicts (Hall and Taylor, 1996). These founding moments set different countries on different development paths. The paths should not be seen as predetermined, however, as institutions do continue to evolve, both in response to changing environmental conditions and to internal political dynamics. But from a historical institutionalist perspective this evolution happens in ways that are constrained by past trajectories (Thelen, 1999).

The above examples of change-inducing events reveal that, in general, the most commonly considered sources of change within traditional HI can all be regarded as what Pierson terms 'exogenous shocks' (Pierson, 2000) or what Thelen and Steinmo call 'external influences' (Thelen and Steinmo, 1992). The widely researched impact of globalization upon national institutions is a contemporary example one such external influence (Swank and Steinmo, 2002, Carroll, 2002). Institutions play the important role in relation to external influences that they mediate the impacts of these external influences, thereby upholding a greater degree of institutional continuity than predicted in other welfare state theories. However, amongst those historical institutionalists interested in the ideational institutional level, the notion of external influences has been challenged. According to authors such as Cox and Goul-Andersen, external influences are not objectively 'out there', exogenous to institutions. Instead they argue that the significance of phenomena like economic crises depends on the ways in which institutional actors interpret them and the extent to which those actors translate their interpretations into actions for change. 'Problem pressures' are not exogenous to the policy process but must be understood as defined by actors. In that sense they are socially constructed by actors, particularly those actors involved in solving the problems (Cox, 2001, Andersen, 2002). This social constructivist perspective on the idea of external influences, which is also embraced in this book, calls to attention the role of agency in relation to change.

Agency and Change The types of actors most commonly included in historical institutionalist analyses are typically classified as either political, policy or social actors. These three categories of actors have in common that they are important because they wield certain degrees of influence within the formal institutional system. In the majority of historical institutionalist analyses, however, the underlying perception is that this influence does not derive from their individual agency. On the contrary, the influencing capacity of agents is mostly seen as derived from their formal institutional positions.

An alternative perspective on the capacity of individuals to influence structures is presented in Kingdon's notion of 'policy entrepreneurs' (Kingdon, 1995). Policy entrepreneurs do not necessarily derive their influence from their institutional positions. Rather, policy entrepreneurs can operate both from within the formal political structures or outside the formal policy process, only they do need to be taken seriously by other actors, for example as authoritative experts, leaders or decision-makers. The influencing role of policy entrepreneurs is more importantly defined by their unusually ambitious, skilled and persistent personalities combined with a personal interest and investment in certain ideas. Kingdon's notion of policy entrepreneurs has been integrated into historical institutionalist frameworks, particularly amongst authors interested in the role of ideas for bringing about change (Cox, 2001, Corbett, 2003, Beland, 2005). Other researchers have used different terms but similar ideas when highlighting the significance of particular types of individuals in bringing about change, that is not just individuals in institutional powerful positions but also individuals who are 'enthusiastic' about particular ideas (Hansen and King, 2001) or who can be seen as 'carriers' or 'champions' of ideas (Berman, 2001). Such 'influencing individuals', as they could also be called, have in common that they can champion ideas in ways that might influence or possibly change the institutional fabric.

Framing   The notion that ideas can play a significant role as a way for actors to bring about institutional change has gained considerable currency within Historical Institutionalism in recent years (Clemens and Cook, 1999, King and Hansen, 1999, Hansen and King, 2001, Cox, 2001, Lieberman, 2002, Cox, 2004, Beland, 2005, Taylor-Gooby, 2005a). Of particular interest has been a mechanism through which such a process of change can happen known as 'framing' (Cox, 2001, Taylor-Gooby, 2005a, Lynggard, 2007, Slothuus, 2007, Steensland, 2008). This notion turns the attention once again back to the concept of discourse. As explained earlier discourse is the link between free-floating ideas and paradigms. Discourses are created by actors as they attempt to make sense of emerging ideas and social developments in their environments. In this creation process, discourses are often aligned with the existing institutional paradigms, ensuring that new ideas are incorporated into and adjusted to the established ideational structure. Actors can, for example, link new ideas to national values (see for example Taylor-Gooby, 2005b). In those circumstances discourse upholds the status quo. But discourse can also be actively employed to change institutions, for example through framing. Framing is a way for influencing individuals to link new ideas to a coherent ideological repertoire, complete with shared cultural and political symbols, from which the new idea can be presented to the policy community or the wider public as a viable policy alternative. By framing, influencing individuals embed an idea within a specific discourse, and this serves the purpose of legitimizing the idea to the necessary, specifically identified group of people (Beland, 2005).

An important part of the process of framing is not only identifying an idea as a solution to a problem. It can also involve constructing a particular situation as a social problem in order to facilitate the presentation of the new idea as a solution (Beland, 2005, Cox, 2001, Andersen, 2002). To legitimize welfare state cutbacks, for example, policymakers can construct a new 'burden problem' or draw on the already existing 'crisis discourse' related to ageing populations or enhanced global competitiveness (Andersen, 2002).

Conflict Emphasizing ideas and agency does not entail rejecting altogether the explanatory value of path-dependency. But the problem with an analysis that over-emphasizes path-dependency is that it obscures the reality of conflict, political opposition and underlying tensions of interests which tend to always exist in policy contexts as well as in the social world in general. As pointed out by Thelen (1999), actors may adapt to new paths that were taken against their interests, but that does not mean that they will embrace and reproduce the new institutions wholeheartedly. Rather they are likely to be biding their times until conditions shift, or they might work within the new system but in subversive ways (Thelen, 1999). Similarly, on the ideational level, several authors have argued against the suggestion by Hall that policy paradigms are hegemonic and path-dependent in the same way as Kuhn's scientific paradigms (Cox, 1998a, Schmidt, 2002, Taylor-Gooby, 2005a). As pointed out by Schmidt (2002), whilst a policy programme may be dominant at one given time, there are likely always to be other 'minority discourses' waiting in the wings that might one day become the dominant paradigm (Schmidt, 2002).

Windows of Opportunity The final question to consider when acknowledging both path-dependency and potential for change is the issue of when change happens. To explain this, historical institutionalists have pointed firstly to the broader structural level, to occasions when 'points of friction' (Lieberman, 2002) occur between or within institutional orders (Thelen, 1999). Friction can for example arise when different institutional contexts clash, such as between domestic and EU policy (Pierson, 1996), or when different social models collide within institutions, such as in Eastern Europe (Stark and Bruszt, 1998). Another angle on the possibilities for change incorporates the role of agency and is based on Kingdon's thoughts on policy entrepreneurs (Beland, 2005). According to Kingdon, policy entrepreneurs only achieve change successfully when there is a 'window of opportunity' for such change. Such opportunities arise in 'moments of political opportunity', such as when a government changes or a new powerful interest group emerges. It is under such circumstances that policy entrepreneurs can get their idea onto the policy agenda by framing their idea as a viable policy alternative to a situation which is either already considered a problem or which the policy entrepreneurs can construct as a problem (Beland, 2005). Overall, the different propositions regarding when change takes place are widely compatible with more traditional historical institutionalist ideas about firstly institutions as mostly durable yet not resistant to forces for change, and secondly about the importance of timing in relation to change. Yet, by drawing attention to the role of ideas, conflict and individual agency as important drivers of change, this more recent development of historical institutionalist theory has shifted the balance of this framework away from the overemphasis on continuity and institutional constraints and towards change and opportunities for agency.

Integrating the Mixed Economy Approach and Historical Institutionalism

Ideational Regulation

Applying the theoretical ideas of HI to the MEOW framework provides an opportunity to expand the somewhat underdeveloped conception of how the mixed economy is regulated. Where 'regulation' in the MEOW literature means mostly governmental ruling, HI offers a more complex account of how institutions such as the mixed economy are 'regulated', not just by formal political systems and processes but also by the ideational structures of an institutional context.

Figure 2.2 below demonstrates that the governmental regulation which takes place on the formal institutional level is just one of many ways in which the mixed economy is regulated. On the ideational level, the mixed economy is regulated by four different 'layers' of paradigms: policy area; mixed economy sectoral; welfare state; and international paradigms.

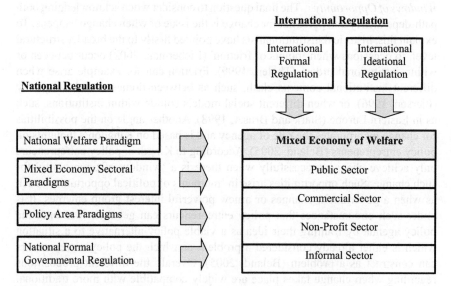

Figure 2.2   Types of Regulation in the Mixed Economy of Welfare

Policy Area Paradigms   'Policy area paradigms' are influential within specific welfare policy areas. As such they are on a par with what Merrien called 'sectoral paradigms' (Merrien, 2001). An example here could be the paradigm currently favouring labour market activation within the area of unemployment in many welfare states around the world (Lødemel and Trickey, 2001).

Mixed Economy Sectoral Paradigms   Above the policy area, this framework also incorporates a layer which has been named 'mixed economy sectoral paradigms'. This type of paradigm is important because welfare sector paradigms contain often unarticulated ideas about each individual welfare sector. That could be ideas about the distinctive purposes of each sector and about the appropriate and expected behaviour of the agencies within them. Such perceptions are frequently reinforced in the academic literature, for example in the debate about the 'marketization' of the public sector, which is centred around notions of distinctive characteristics and values of the public and commercial sectors and disagreements about the appropriateness of transferring values and goals from one sector to the other (Le Grand, 1991, Taylor-Gooby, 1999, Drakeford, 2007). Some authors have also explicitly argued that the different welfare sectors each have their own 'logic' which motivates the agents within them in different ways. In this way, 'mixed economy sector paradigms' regulate the agencies in each of the welfare sectors on the ideational level.

Welfare State Paradigms   Above the mixed economy sectoral paradigms we find national paradigms such as the different welfare state regimes identified by Esping-Andersen (1990). Esping-Andersen elaborated on Titmus's (1974) idea that the spectrum of different welfare states can be organized into a few categories of similar welfare state 'types'. Esping-Andersen claimed that the welfare states of the developed industrialized countries under his investigation clustered around three welfare state 'regimes': a Nordic 'social democratic'; an Anglo-American 'liberal'; and a continental 'conservative' regime. What makes these regimes distinct from each other are the different degrees to which social policy measures enable individuals to exist independently of the labour market. Countries within each regime, meanwhile, share similar degrees of 'de-commodification' (Esping-Andersen, 1990).

Esping-Andersen's typologies have been criticized from a variety of angles: for being gender-blind by for example overlooking differences in the extent of gender inequality on the labour market (Langan and Ostner, 1991, Orloff, 1993, O'Connor, 1993) or overlooking the underlying labour market variable of unpaid (mostly female) welfare provision in the family (Taylor-Gooby, 1991, Antonnen and Sipilä, 1996, Lewis, 2000); for missing out a large number of welfare states around the world such as Southern Europe (Leibfried, 1993, Ferrera, 1996), the European ex-communist states (Deacon, 1993) and Asian welfare states (Jones, 1993, Walker and Wong, 1996, Peng, 2000); for being Eurocentric, for example when predominantly using Britain's residual social policy approach as the template for the liberal welfare regime, hereby ignoring nationally unique welfare values in both the United States (Marmor et al., 1990, Rose, 1991) and Australia (Castles and Mitchell, 1992); and for being normatively biased towards the social democratic, Scandinavian model (Baldwin, 1996). Yet the 1990 publication is still a major reference point for comparative social policy and the notion of welfare state regimes remains a defining characteristic of the field.

As national level paradigms, welfare state regimes have an influence upon the mixed economy because such paradigms contain culturally ingrained and path-dependent ideas about the appropriate balance of the overall mixed economy.

International Paradigms Considering the widely acknowledged influence of international and supranational governance structures in relation to national welfare states (Jessop, 2004, Kennett, 2004, Yeates, 2006), this book's analytical framework also incorporates the regulatory influences of formal international institutions such as the EU, UN and OECD. International ideational structures are also significant, particularly in a context where international formal agreements are unenforceable, but also in relation to ideas and unwritten rules about the appropriate behaviour of governments, businesses and non-profit organizations, whether in the international system or in national contexts.

Applying the HI/MEOW Framework to Explore Welfare State Change

Retrenchment The question of welfare state change is important in this book because of the interest in exploring whether corporate social responsibility might be a vehicle for changing the balance in the mixed economy – pushing back the public sector and rolling out the commercial sector. In order to apply the combined MEOW/HI framework to explore welfare state change it is necessary to consider how change can be investigated. The notion of change is an amorphous concept which is difficult to operationalize, especially in a way that enables the researcher to precisely 'measure' change let alone produce undisputable evidence of either change or continuity. Within HI, a large body of literature has approached this issue by focusing on investigating instances of welfare state 'retrenchment' (for an overview see Starke, 2006), that is, situations where the public sector can be said to have retreated whilst in some way or other transferred its welfare responsibilities to other sectors in the mixed economy of welfare. The problem with the retrenchment approach, as highlighted by Green-Pedersen (2004), is that the concept of retrenchment has become almost as nebulous as the notion of change. Different studies have evidenced retrenchment on the basis of widely different definitions and conceptualizations of the term. Whilst some studies focus on instances of cutbacks of welfare entitlements within specific social policy areas (Starke et al., 2008), others have adopted a broader perspective and considered retrenchment in relation to the overall institutional structures including ideational elements such as the particular, regime-dependent welfare state principles and values (Pierson, 2001b, Cox, 2004). In this book, the broader definition of retrenchment will be applied. The advantage of applying the broader retrenchment perspective is the ability to consider the wider social, institutional implications of the emergence of the social phenomena of CSR. For this undertaking, Hall's framework for exploring institutional change will be employed (Hall, 1993).

Hall's Framework of Institutional Change   Hall (1993) distinguishes between three degrees of institutional change. A change can be considered only a 'first order change', the lowest degree of change, when all that has been changed is the exact 'setting' of a policy provision, such as for example the funding level of a social security transfer. Second order change is a stronger degree of change, when both settings and 'instruments' have changed, such as perhaps a withdrawal of a type of welfare provision. The most profound form of change is third order change. This is when not just the 'settings' and the 'instruments' but also the 'overarching goals' of a policy area or a welfare state regime have changed in a way that can be considered paradigmatic change (Hall, 1993). Hall's framework for considering change on three levels is a useful way of linking the formal institutions of the mixed economy of welfare with the broader formal and ideational institutions. 'Settings' can be paralleled to the funding level in the mixed economy, 'instruments' can be understood as encompassing both welfare provision and formal government regulation and finally, the 'overarching goals' provides a way of taking into account the various levels of ideational regulation accounted for in the HI framework but not usually considered in MEOW analyses.

Welfare State Change: Change from What?

The final issue that needs addressing before the exploration of welfare state change can begin is the question of what the countries under investigation in this book might (or might not) be changing away from. What kinds of mixed economies make up the welfare states of England, Denmark, Sweden, Norway, Germany and France?

Welfare State Paradigms: Liberal, Conservative and Social Democratic   Starting at the ideational institutional level of national welfare paradigms it is first of all clear that, according to Esping-Andersen's analysis (1990), the countries explored in this book belong to different types of welfare regimes. Whereas England represents a liberal welfare state, the Scandinavian countries of Denmark, Sweden and Norway belong to the social democratic welfare state type, whilst France and Germany represent conservative welfare states. In relation to the mixed economy of welfare, the implications of these paradigms are that the public sector plays a much bigger role in providing and funding welfare in the social democratic and conservative welfare countries than it does in England. In Scandinavia in particular, welfare services are comparatively more widely available and relatively generously funded by the public sector, based on the paradigmatic welfare principle of universalism. In Germany and France, the public sector plays a large role in some welfare areas whilst other areas, especially that of care, are predominantly the responsibility of (women in) the informal sector. In England, access to public welfare services – social security benefits in particular – is more restricted and less generously funded. As a result of these different institutional constellations, social equality is the highest in the Scandinavian social democratic welfare states and the lowest in liberal England (Esping-Andersen, 1990).

Mixed Economy Sectoral Paradigm: Liberal and Coordinative   Moving down to the level of the mixed economy sectoral paradigms the focus in this book is on the commercial sector. For this, a useful framework is provided by Hall and Soskice's identification of different commercial sector paradigms within liberal and coordinative 'varieties of capitalism' (2001). Reflecting an explicitly stated overlap with Esping-Andersen's welfare regimes England is once again placed in the liberal category by the authors whilst social democratic and conservative welfare states belong this time jointly to the coordinative category. The main difference is that in England, the commercial sector is governed by market forces to a much higher degree than in coordinative market economies. That is because the English liberal paradigm prescribes as little public sector intervention as possible, whereas in European Continental countries, firms need to 'coordinate' their activities with the social partners. This makes English firms more dependent on profitability and being able to constantly demonstrate this profitability to investors, whilst firms in coordinated market economies can survive longer on the trust they have built up through the coordinative networks. These two different institutional contexts also influence the social behaviour of English and European Continental firms. Whilst firms in the latter category are more likely to contribute to collective institutions, for example in the area of vocational training, English firms are more likely to focus entirely on being competitive, shying away from contributing to collective institutions for fear of free riders that will in turn undermine their own competitiveness. This has led to the conclusion that firms in coordinated market economies are more socially embedded than their liberal counterparts (Hall and Soskice, 2001).

Policy Area Paradigms: Active Labour Market Policy   Finally, on the level of policy area paradigms, a policy domain relevant to the analysis in this book is the area of labour market policy. Here authors have argued for the emergence in later years of a 'hybrid' paradigm cutting across the liberal, social democratic and conservative welfare state regimes and seeing instead countries like England, Denmark, Sweden, France, Germany and also the Netherlands pursuing very similar policy goals based on shared convictions of the benefit of labour market activation (Lødemel and Trickey, 2001, Lindsay and Mailand, 2004, Aust and Arriba, 2005, Taylor-Gooby, 2008a).

Conclusion

The integrated MEOW/HI framework presented in this chapter constitutes the framework within which the relationship between corporate social responsibility and the welfare state will be explored in this book. This framework is useful for several reasons. Firstly, the broad perspective on welfare, which takes into account welfare produced beyond the state, makes it possible to consider CSR from the position that it is a form of welfare and part of the mixed economy rather than merely a business activity. Secondly, the differentiation of the production of welfare into the levels of funding, provision and regulation will facilitate the understanding of how, more precisely, CSR operates as a form of welfare in the mixed economy. This aspect will be given particular attention in Chapter 8. Thirdly, the MEOW/HI framework is well suited for investigating the extent to which the historical and institutional national contexts of welfare states influence the ways in which CSR is interpreted, applied and linked to social exclusion. Part II of this book sets out to uncover how the historical development of CSR has been interwoven with the historical trajectories of the different mixed economies under investigation in this book. The role of 'influencing individuals' in championing the idea of CSR shall be considered as will the role of conflict in relation to CSR's development. Yet at the same time, the many formal and ideational ways in which path-dependency has at times constrained the scope for CSR will also be taken into account.

Finally, the MEOW/HI framework is useful for exploring the extent to which CSR might be a vehicle for welfare state change. In relation to this question, ideas from HI about institutional change and continuity can be constructively applied. To understand the concept of CSR, for example, CSR will be considered a 'free-floating idea', which has yet to become embedded in the formal or ideational institutions of any of the welfare states under investigation here. Instead CSR is currently articulated within various different and often conflicting ideological discourses, from where the notion of CSR is framed to legitimize various degrees of institutional change or continuity. This particular application of the MEOW/HI framework will be the focus of the next chapter (Chapter 3).

Corporate Social Responsibility: Making Sense of a Contested Concept

Introduction

This chapter concentrates on the meaning of the term 'corporate social responsibility' ('CSR'). The chapter begins with the recognition that CSR cannot be considered one coherent idea. Rather, CSR is a contested concept, defined in diverse and often conflicting manners. Therefore, to make sense of the many meanings of CSR it is necessary to look beyond the various definitions and to investigate the different ideological and normative discourses within which different definitions are embedded. The first section of this chapter maps out a continuum of such 'CSR discourses'. This analysis will emphasize differences and similarities in the discourses' views about the appropriate relationship between business and society, the commercial sector and the public sector. The second section of the chapter goes on to consider the social impacts of CSR. Staying on the conceptual level, this part of the analysis reflects on the question of whether any links can be established between the discourses of CSR and different discursive approaches to social exclusion.

Theoretically, the concept of CSR will be approached from the position that it is a 'free-floating' idea. As was explained in Chapter 2, free-floating ideas are ideas that cannot be considered part of the ideational structures of an institutional context. Instead they can be conceptualized as existing independently within institutions; less institutionalized norms and more free-floating, conceptual notions. As such these ideas can have the potential to challenge the existing institutional status quo – if 'activated' and employed successfully by influential, entrepreneurial actors who choose to champion them. It is this potential to challenge – or indeed defend – the current social order which makes it important to understand the idea of CSR. And in order to gain a thorough understanding of the idea of CSR it is necessary to start at the conceptual level. This is the level at which to establish and become familiar with the various different meanings applied by different actors to the term 'corporate social responsibility'.

Discourses of Corporate Social Responsibility

The corporate social responsibility (CSR) construct describes the relationship between business and the larger society. An exact definition of CSR is elusive

since beliefs and attitudes regarding the nature of this association fluctuate with
the relevant issues of the day. (Hill et al., 2003: 340)

It is widely acknowledged within the literature on corporate social responsibility
that there is a distinct lack of consensus or even broad agreement about how to
define the concept of CSR (Hill et al., 2003, Pedersen, 2006, McWilliams et al.,
2006, Doh and Guay, 2006, Crowther and Rayman-Bacchus, 2004, Whitehouse,
2003, Windsor, 2006). This is in spite the fact that the idea that companies and
their managers have responsibilities to society is mentioned in literature dating
back as far as the 1930s (Berle and Means, 1932, Barnard, 1938, Clark, 1939).
Also, the actual term 'corporate social responsibility' has been used since the
1960s to describe, prescribe and discuss the role of business in society (for a
detailed overview of the evolution of the concept of CSR see Carroll, 1999). Yet
even after 50 years of expanding research into the notion of CSR, CSR researchers
and practitioners alike can only agree that CSR is a contested concept and that
a definition of CSR remains elusive. Apart from having varying meanings in
different national institutional settings, as most concepts have, CSR is also
contested within national contexts. Even in countries that to the outside world
appear to have a coherent national CSR policy, CSR stakeholders typically
disagree about how to interpret the idea of corporate social responsibility and how
to legitimately translate CSR into practice. To phrase this in theoretical terms,
there is no 'paradigmatic' notion of what CSR is and what it should be within
national institutional contexts. In order to gain a deeper understanding of the many
co-existing meanings of corporate social responsibility found around the world, a
number of competing discourses on CSR has been identified and will be presented
in this chapter. Such discourses are important because CSR stakeholders use them
not only to make sense of CSR but also to formulate and legitimize their particular
CSR strategies in the political arena.

The various arguments for and against CSR, the opinions about what CSR can
do and should do and the suggestions as to how the objectives may best be achieved
all reflect fundamental ideological stances. These stances are spread along the
traditional right to left political continuums where proponents are split between
being for and against state responsibility for social problems, for and against state
intervention in matters of trade and business, for and against wealth redistribution
and, ultimately, for and against capitalist society as a whole. In countries that
consider themselves welfare states, attitudes towards CSR also reflect perceptions
of and attitudes towards the welfare state and its mixed economy. Except where
positions are taken against the notion of CSR, the dominant sense throughout the
different discourse is an awareness of being in a transitory phase where contracts
of all sorts are up for negotiation, whether this is an idea of the contract between
business and society or the 'social contract' as a whole. The CSR discourses have
been labelled so as to reflect their attitude to social change; from a 'conservative'
extreme end, which is very averse to change; to 'liberal' and 'social democratic'
discourses, each one more open to ideas of change than the other; and finally

to 'radical' and 'sceptical' positions which advocate more far-reaching social changes. The remainder of this section will deal with each CSR discourse one at a time moving along the traditional right-left political ideological continuum. An overview of all the CSR discourses is presented in table form on page 40.

The Conservative CSR Discourse

Starting from the political right on the continuum, a CSR discourse has been identified and positioned here and given the label the 'conservative CSR discourse'. In the conservative CSR discourse, the idea of corporate social responsibility is fundamentally rejected. Not even a minimalist definition of CSR is considered acceptable. A classic basic definition of CSR still quoted widely today holds that:

> The idea of corporate social responsibility supposes that the corporation has not only economic and legal obligations, but also certain responsibilities to society which extend beyond these obligations. (McGuire, 1963: 144)

Authors and stakeholders associated with the conservative CSR discourse object to the idea that a company has responsibilities extending beyond its economic obligations. The most widely quoted representative of the conservative CSR discourse is Milton Friedman, who already in the 1960s and 1970s argued that a company's only responsibilities are to their shareholders. Friedman held that businesses contribute to society by creating wealth and jobs, but fundamentally 'the business of business is business'. Social issues such as wealth redistribution or solving social problems are entirely the government's job (Friedman, 1979). The social contract between business and society is, in other words, one which clearly distinguishes between the business sphere and the social sphere, and between the commercial sector and the public sector. Although the conservative CSR discourse is perhaps ideologically more neoliberal than 'Conservative' in the party-political sense of the term, the conservative label applies in as much as there is a clear view that no contracts of any sorts are up for negotiation. Society and business must carry on as they are. This position also implies that in the mixed economy of welfare, the institutional boundaries between the commercial sector and the governmental sector – both the formal and the ideational boundaries – must be upheld. For that reason, developments such as the growing popularity of CSR are undesirable and must be opposed.

The conservative CSR discourse continues to inform scholarly thinking on CSR (Jensen, 2000, McWilliams and Siegel, 2001, Henderson, 2001) although the ideological position is mostly known under the labels of 'shareholder theory' or 'stockholder theory' (Smith and Hasnas, 1999). The views of the conservative CSR discourse can also be found in the (right-leaning) financial press such as the *Financial Times* (Wolf, 2002) and the *Economist* (*Economist*, 2005). In recent years, however, there are some signs that the conservative CSR discourse has developed so that a minimum of CSR is now acceptable, albeit only when individual businesses are at risk if they do *not* adopt some form of CSR strategy. This latest variant of the conservative CSR discourse, which can be termed the 'reluctantly supportive' conservative CSR discourse, reflects a social context where CSR is gaining so much grounds that it is becoming a basic standard in the mainstream of businesses rather than an exceptional form of behaviour amongst a minority. In the words of some commentators, CSR is being increasingly institutionalized (Moon, 2002: 393). Yet in the reluctantly supportive conservative CSR discourse the emphasis is firmly on strategic rather than ethical motivations, and on minimizing business risks – such as reputational risk – rather than seeking to achieve any other social objectives (Husted and Salazar, 2006). From a theoretical perspective, the reluctantly supportive conservative CSR discourse emerges as an example of a 'minority discourse' (see Chapter 2). By reluctantly accepting a minimum of CSR, the conservative CSR discourse has adapted to an emerging institutional consensus or 'path' in which the majority of other CSR discourses have embraced the idea of CSR even if there is still disagreement over its exact meaning and social implications.

The Liberal CSR Discourse

Moving along the continuum, away from resistance to more openness towards social change, the next position identified here has been labelled 'the liberal CSR discourse'. Here the attitude is that CSR is a good thing as long as there remains a clear advantage for businesses when they engage with CSR. Known as 'the business case for CSR', the list of often quoted business benefits of CSR include strengthening a company's brand; attracting the best new staff; improving employee relations; building trust between the business and its consumers; spurring innovation within the company; and achieving cost savings from energy efficiency measures (see for example Dean, 2001, Moon, 2002, Joseph and Parkinson, 2002). Within business studies researchers have sought to test these claims, and findings have included evidence of a positive relationship between CSR and company reputation (Brammer and Millington, 2005) and between CSR and a company's financial performance (Margolis and Walsh, 2000).

The liberal CSR discourse is heavily influenced by and also widely known in the literature as stakeholder theory (e.g. Smith and Hasnas, 1999, Hendry, 2001, Doh and Guay, 2006). Pioneered within business studies in the 1980s by Freeman (1984), this theory argues for the business benefits of companies conducting their business not only focusing on satisfying their shareholders but also conducting their business in a way which takes into account a wider range of people and places with a 'stake' in the company. Freeman defined stakeholders as 'any group or individual who can affect or is affected by the achievement of the organization's objectives' (Freeman, 1984: 46). The more precise identification of a company's stakeholders is yet another point of debate, and the length of the lists of included stakeholder nominees varies between authors. Whilst some consider mainly groups such as shareholders, investors, employees, customers, the local community and suppliers, others also regard as stakeholders entities such as the government, social pressure groups, the natural environment and future generations (for the perhaps most exhaustive list of proposed stakeholders see Wheeler and Sillanpaa, 1997). The point of all stakeholder theory is that it makes long-term business sense for companies to consider stakeholders beyond merely their shareholders when planning their business strategy. Spending money and/or time beyond a company's core business does not have to be against the company's own interest. Rather it can be detrimental to a company's future if its management is *not* stakeholder orientated (Clarkson, 1995). Stakeholder theory continues to gain ground within business studies (Maclagan, 1999, Hendry, 2001, Doh and Guay, 2006, Pedersen, 2006) and studies have also evidenced an increasing influence of the ideas of stakeholder theory upon CSR-practicing businesses (Collings, 2003, Brammer and Millington, 2004).

The liberal aspect of the liberal CSR discourse is recognized firstly in the un-conservative openness towards a new idea like CSR. In this openness, authors and stakeholders associated with the liberal discourse show themselves receptive to the idea of some degree of institutional change; to a renegotiation of the relationship between business and society; or to a reconsideration of the balance in the mixed economy of welfare. Unlike the conservative CSR discourse, the liberal CSR discourse can accommodate the idea of businesses becoming more involved in social matters. Yet it is also a characteristic utilitarian feature that a company's CSR efforts have to be compatible with its own self-interests.

Another characteristically liberal feature of the liberal CSR discourse is the opposition to government involvement in CSR. Stakeholders associated with the liberal CSR discourse strongly resist calls for government legislation on CSR, and they are also likely to be suspicious of other forms of government involvement in CSR, such as monitoring or setting formal standards. Instead, CSR is emphasized as a voluntary activity (Pedersen, 2006, Trillingsgaard and Holbech Jespersen, 2003, Brammer and Pavelin, 2006). CSR is seen as a business matter and, equally important, as a discretionary concern for each individual business. From a characteristically liberal-libertarian outlook, stakeholders will argue that businesses should have the freedom to choose if they want to get involved in CSR or not and, if they do, it should also be up to each business to decide exactly how it will integrate CSR into its strategy. The position that 'one size doesn't fit all' when it comes to CSR (CBI, 2004) is also supported in academia, where studies highlight the importance of matching CSR initiatives to an organization's core business (Brammer and Pavelin, 2006, Collings, 2003). If CSR is to be promoted at all it must be done purely within the business community itself. Acceptable methods include positive example setting made visible through high profile reporting, and rewarding initiatives such as the Per Cent Club and the FTSE4GOOD index (Secretan, 1998).

Authors and stakeholders associated with the liberal CSR discourse do not put much emphasis on the question of the social benefits of CSR. Whatever the social impacts of CSR might be, they remain secondary spill-over effects. At its most socially engaged, the liberal CSR discourse can be employed to frame a business case for CSR in terms of business benefits at the collective level. In this way, CSR measures which are seemingly designed with social benefits in mind can be argued to have collective business benefits. Contributing towards education and training outside the workplace, for example, is not just a benefit to society but also to businesses as it improves the quality of the workforce and the pool of potential future employees (Moon, 2002). The emphasis in the liberal CSR discourse's justification of CSR is in other words strictly on the rational, strategic interests of business actors. Unlike in some of the discourses positioned further along the continuum, there are no arguments made here about CSR as morally important for firms and the actors within them.

The Social Democratic CSR Discourse

Moving further along on the right-left continuum, the next position identified here has been labelled 'the social democratic CSR discourse'. As in the liberal CSR discourse, the social democratic CSR discourse represents a welcoming of the idea of CSR. Authors and stakeholders associated with the social democratic CSR discourse see in CSR an opportunity to renegotiate the contract between business and society. But in contrast to the liberal CSR discourse, the focus in the social democratic CSR discourse is on the benefits of CSR to society rather than to business.

Other authors considering different positions on CSR have used alternative names for the social democratic CSR discourse, one of which is the 'social contract' position (Smith and Hasnas, 1999). This label refers to the discourse's fundamentally contractarian outlook (Locke, 1988 [1689], Rousseau, 1998 [1762], Hobbes, 1998 [1651]), that is the belief that a social contract exists between business and society. This contract grants companies the rights to be formed, to own and use land and natural resources, to operate and to hire the members of society as employees (Smith and Hasnas, 1999). However, the argument is also that with rights come responsibilities, and companies have in return for their rights the responsibility to not only remain within the bounds of the law, but also to (solely) pursue profits in ways which contributes to the welfare of society overall (Cannon, 1992). Amongst proponents of the social democratic CSR discourse companies are seen to have social responsibilities just like all other agents operating in the mixed economy of welfare, from the government to non-profit organizations and individuals (Holt, 1998).

Contemporary contractarian perceptions of a reciprocal relationship between business and society (Etzioni, 1993) are generally associated politically with social democratic parties. In the English context, for example, New Labour's party policies have since the 1990s been explicitly founded on the Communitarian-inspired principle that rights – whether that of businesses or individuals – must be balanced with social responsibilities (Giddens, 1998). As part of this political discourse, New Labour thinkers have also championed the idea of a 'stakeholder society'. Suggested as an alternative to the existing social model, the stakeholder society is built on capitalism but expects companies to be morally informed and socially engaged rather than narrowly focused on short-term profit-making (Hutton, 1996). Although the idea of the stakeholder society is directly inspired by the stakeholder theories developed within businesses schools (see Levitas, 2005), the stakeholder notion is taken one step further in the stakeholder society concept. Whereas stakeholder theory is about businesses identifying those groups that have stakes in the company apart from their shareholders, the stakeholder society is about companies operating on the basis of the fundamental understanding that business and society have a mutual stake in each other.

A key idea of the social democratic CSR discourse is the concept of partnership. The partnership approach to CSR promotes more involvement of businesses in society and in social problems in particular. Involvement is encouraged through partnerships between businesses, the public sector and often also the non-profit sector. The partnership idea is based on the view that the current social model is too stringently based on the public sector solving social problems on its own. What is needed instead is more 'flexible cooperation' (Abrahamson, 2003: 19), that is a better balance of responsibilities between the sectors in the mixed economy of welfare, especially when it comes to addressing social problems. The argued advantage of the partnership approach is that the various partners are seen to bring to the table different types of competencies and abilities. Ideally this new model of cooperation will then lead to new and innovative ways of solving social problems, to the benefit of society overall (Abrahamson, 2003, Lund, 2003, Albareda et al., 2006, Edwards et al., 2001).

Unlike the liberal and conservative CSR discourses, the social democratic CSR discourse does not represent a stance against government involvement with CSR. On the contrary, government involvement is seen as important for getting businesses to commit to taking more social responsibility. How far governments should go to get businesses on board is an open question, however. Legislating on CSR is never ruled out, but it is not seen as the preferred form of action either (Hutton, 2002). In the social democratic CSR discourse, the prescribed role of governments in relation to CSR is more in line with New Public Management thinking, where governments do the steering and not the rowing (Osborne and Gaebler, 1992). The partnership approach in particular is seen by many as a CSR model inspired by New Public Management ideas (Evers, 2003). On the national and international levels, the role of governments is to facilitate, encourage and promote CSR to businesses all the while providing the optimum institutional environment – economic, legal and social – to ensure the future growth of CSR. Within this loose framework provided by the government, stakeholders associated with the social democratic CSR discourse expects businesses to explore CSR on their own and to develop best practices, which will work towards spreading the enthusiasm and support for CSR within the business community. In this respect, the social democratic CSR discourse resembles the liberal CSR discourse in favouring methods of example setting through indices and prizes.

With ideas such as the stakeholder society and the partnership approach to CSR, social democratic CSR is clearly about advocating more far-reaching social change than both the conservative and the liberal CSR discourse. Social change is seen as necessary on two counts. Firstly, there is a perception that businesses have taken the capitalist paradigm too far and used it to legitimize one-dimensional, profit-seeking behaviour at the cost of society. In this context CSR is the inevitable result of the 'overarching necessity to redefine the role and behaviour of organizations in post-industrial society' (McIntosh, 1993: 3). Secondly, CSR is also seen as a solution to the perceived welfare state crisis of public sector overload (Albareda et al., 2006, Abrahamson, 2003). Within the social democratic CSR discourse, CSR is a means by which welfare state governments can get the assistance of businesses in the increasingly difficult tasks of providing welfare and solving social problems.

In theoretical terms, an important difference between the social democratic CSR discourse and the other two discourses discussed so far is the use of CSR by the social democratic CSR discourse to seek to institute change not just at the formal institutional level but also at the ideational level. The social democratic CSR discourse challenges those 'mixed economy sectoral paradigms' which contain ideas about the distinctive roles and responsibilities of individual mixed economy sectors and about the necessity of upholding strict boundaries between them (see Chapter 2). Stakeholders who campaign for CSR by using the social democratic CSR discourse are seeking to renegotiate current perceptions of mixed economy responsibilities, particular of the commercial and the public sector. When appealing to firms, these stakeholders do not just emphasize the business benefits of CSR, they also try to appeal to the moral outlook of business leaders. Proponents of the social democratic CSR discourse seek to engender in businesses a sense that social problems are also their problems and that they therefore have an interest in contributing to their prevention and solution.

The Radical CSR Discourse

The next position on the continuum has been given the name 'the radical CSR discourse' because proponents of this discourse use CSR to advocate far-reaching social change. What characterizes the radical CSR discourse is the belief in the social benefit of CSR when employed as a vehicle for bringing about fundamental social changes. CSR is seen as an opportunity to renegotiate not just the contract between business and society, and not just national mixed economies, but the global social contract as a whole. In particular, the radical CSR discourse relates CSR to global issues such as third world poverty, human rights, global social justice and environmental sustainability (Coleman, 2000) – issues that go beyond that of national welfare states. The global social contract needs renegotiating because the current capitalist paradigm is seen to have institutionalized and legitimized not only global social inequalities but also corporate greed and 'vice' (Moore, 2003) and in some cases outright corporate misbehaviour (Crowther and Rayman-Bacchus, 2004). Hence in an ideal world, the current capitalist world system would be replaced by better, more socially just and equitable alternatives. But in the short term, the radical CSR discourse is employed by those wishing to challenge the basic values of neo-liberalism.

Ideologically the radical CSR discourse is informed by a socialist perspective. CSR practitioners whose views of CSR are informed by the radical CSR discourse are typically grass-root activists, for example working for international NGOs. Likeminded academic researchers tend to conduct 'action research', which advocates social change through research (Prieto, 2002). The opposition to neo-liberalism situates the radical CSR discourse in the broader social context of the anti-globalization movement (Sadler, 2004). From within this movement, proponents of the radical CSR discourse employ their version of CSR as one way of challenging the hegemonic, paradigmatic status of neo-liberalism, particularly in the international sphere. From a theoretical point of view, the radical CSR discourse emerges as embedded within the wider 'minority discourse' that is the anti-globalization movement.

In the radical CSR discourse, the involvement of national as well as supranational governments in matters of CSR is desirable (Crowther and Rayman-Bacchus, 2004). However, in recognition of the fact that in the global governance system the power of governments to legislate businesses is limited, proponents of the radical CSR discourse support instead any types of CSR measure which will facilitate institutional changes, whether formal or ideational.

An often championed CSR approach in the radical CSR discourse is 'codes of conduct'. CSR campaigners using the radical CSR discourse argue for the importance of governments and NGOs putting pressure businesses to follow certain codes of business conduct. These codes should apply to any dimension of a business' operation, and they should be particularly adhered to when companies conduct their business in countries where regulatory standards are very low or absent (Coleman, 2000, Whitehouse, 2003, Logsdon and Wood, 2005). In this approach to practicing CSR, proponents of the radical CSR discourse clearly aim at instituting change at the ideational level. Like in the social democratic CSR discourse, campaigners using the radical CSR discourse are seeking to change certain mixed economy sectoral paradigms. In the case of the radical CSR discourse, the sectoral paradigms being targeted are those which have made being virtuous institutionally irreconcilable with being a business (Raiborn and Payne, 1990, Sarre et al., 2001, Moore, 2003). The underlying argument that businesses should consider themselves moral actors rather than merely economic entities explains why there is within this discourse a particularly prevalent tendency to use the notion of 'corporate citizenship' as a synonym for CSR and sometimes as a preferred replacement term for CSR (Whitehouse, 2003).

Radical CSR proponents also promote the importance of companies reporting about their CSR efforts. Social reporting holds companies accountable to those stakeholders whom proponents of the radical CSR approach see as the most important: the environment and the global community. Supporters of CSR reporting see this CSR practice as a way of achieving more long-term social objectives rather than just settling for short-term, easily measurable achievements. The long-term benefits of reporting could also be that the reporting exercise itself forces businesses to reflect on their effects on the societies and environments around them. In this way, it could be hoped that reporting will over time bring about the desired change in the fundamental attitudes of business leaders (Ruggie, 2002) and in turn make the proposed codes of conduct take precedence over the existing global social contract.

The Sceptical CSR Discourse

The final CSR discourse on the continuum has been labelled 'the sceptical CSR discourse' and is positioned as the discourse advocating the most far-reaching degree of social change. Like the radical CSR discourse, people taking a sceptical approach to CSR are likely to be sympathetic to different variants of socialist ideology. Their basis for being sceptical about CSR is their view of CSR as nothing but a disguised vehicle for sustaining the current neo-liberal global social contract, which allows corporate, economic interests to increasingly overrule social concerns. Authors writing from within the sceptical CSR discourse are often concerned about the growing influence of business over governments in matters of social policy (Farnsworth, 2004, Monbiot, 2001). The very concept of corporate social responsibility is considered a contradiction in terms as, in the words of one prominent CSR sceptic, 'the corporation, like the psychopathic personality it resembles, is programmed to exploit others for profit' (Bakan, 2004: 69). CSR is just another means through which businesses are upholding a status quo which purely serves business' own interests whilst guiltlessly sacrificing society's welfare. Therefore, rather than promoting CSR, the CSR sceptics only engage in the topic of CSR to reveal its business-serving nature, for example by exposing the frequent insincerity of CSR reports (Crowther, 2004), contradictions between rhetoric and action (Manokha, 2004) or the direct abuse of CSR by companies wanting to 'buy' better reputation (Caulkin, 2002).

In terms of contract renegotiation, the sceptical CSR discourse shares with the liberal, social democratic and radical CSR discourses the conviction that the business-society contract needs renegotiating. However, for the sceptics it is a question of avoiding the involvement of businesses in social matters and minimizing rather than expanding the commercial sector's role in the mixed economy. Unlike any of the other CSR discourses, authors associated with the sceptical CSR discourse would prefer governments to introduce more legislation restricting the power of businesses, particularly transnational corporations, instead of encouraging companies to adopt CSR strategies (Bakan, 2004, Macleod and Lewis, 2004).

The sceptical CSR discourse shares with the radical CSR discourse the opposition to the broader international institutional paradigm of neo-liberalism.

Yet unlike the radical CSR discourse, the sceptical CSR discourse cannot reconcile embracing CSR with resistance to neo-liberalism. In this fundamental rejection of the very idea of CSR, the sceptical CSR discourse emerges as a minority discourse in a context where the majority of CSR discourses have all come to accept CSR albeit in different ways and to different degrees. Even the conservative CSR discourse, which would be the only other discourse opposed to CSR, is in the process of adapting to the emerging undeniable presence of CSR by reluctantly conceding a minimum of CSR. This leaves the sceptical CSR discourse the only CSR discourse which continues to fully oppose the idea of CSR. The five CSR discourses are summarized in Figure 3.1.

The range of CSR discourses identified in this chapter makes it clear that corporate social responsibility is an idea which is not only perceived and conceptualized differently depending on the national context in which it is articulated. Any analysis of the differences and similarities between understandings and practices of CSR in different national institutional contexts must first appreciate the many ways in which CSR can be understood *within* each national context. CSR is not an idea which forms part of any country's ideational institutional structures. Instead, various interpretations of CSR exist and compete alongside each other within countries, and each interpretation represents a distinct ideological worldview with a particular perspective on the appropriate relationship between business and society. Only when these ideological differences have been fully understood is it possible to grasp the complex interplay of CSR positions and national institutions. This dynamics, which determines the unique national CSR agenda of any given country at any given time, will be the focus of the next section of the book (Part II).

The CSR Discourses and Social Impacts

Whilst the various CSR discourses have reasonably clear views on the extent to which they envisage a change in the relationship between business and society, it is less evident what kinds of social impacts the CSR discourses would like to achieve with CSR, if any. This uncertainty is partly the outcome of the fact that CSR can be practiced in a variety of ways. Therefore, different CSR measures will inevitably have different kinds of social impacts. Ascertaining in a more detailed manner the social impacts implied by the different CSR discourses is also made complicated by the situation that each CSR discourse does not necessarily advocate a specified set of CSR practices, nor can any CSR measure be unambiguously accredited to one particular CSR discourse. Therefore, in order to get an idea of the social impacts of CSR, it is necessary to consider each type of CSR practice in its own right. In this book the focus is on CSR measures explicitly designed to overcome social exclusion. Like CSR, social exclusion is a contested concept in its own right. And just as with the concept of CSR, the controversy over social exclusion policies and measures is evident also at the conceptual level. Therefore, as a first step towards understanding the social implications of CSR, the remainder

	Conservative	Liberal	Social democratic	Radical	Sceptical
For / against CSR	Against/ Reluctantly for	For	For	For	Against
CSR Objectives	None	Business gains. Aligning business and stakeholder interests	Social gains. Involving businesses in social issues including solving social problems.	Bring about global fundamental change. Eliminate global poverty. Justice & sustainability.	None. CSR is a scam, a disguised way of continuing business exploitation of society.
Contract negotiation	None	Role of business in mixed economy	Role of business in mixed economy	Global social contract	Global social contract
Acceptable level of governmental involvement in CSR	None	None. CSR should be a voluntary matter	Some. Main role: to encourage, facilitate rather than legislate.	As much as possible. Legislation where practical, otherwise: governmental pressure.	None. Instead the power of corporations should be restricted by law.
Non-governmental means of promoting CSR	None	Example setting within business community through indices and prizes	Example setting within business community through indices and prizes	NGO activism Academic action-research.	None. The media, NGOs and academics must instead expose business misconduct and abuse of CSR for business gains.
Means of putting CSR into practice	None	No universal CSR model. Each company must match its CSR efforts with its business profile	Partnerships between business, public sector and/or non-profit sector	Internationally agreed codes of conduct. CSR reporting	None.
Theoretical foundation	Neo-liberal economics	Stakeholder theory	Social contract, Communitarianism, New Public Management	Critical theory, Neo-Marxism, Action-research	Critical theory, Neo-Marxism
Ideological foundation	Neo-liberal	Liberal	Social democratic	Socialist	Socialist

Figure 3.1   Mapping the CSR Discourses

of this chapter will explore the conceptual relationship between CSR and social exclusion. The emphasis will be on developing an understanding of the connection between the different CSR discourses and conceptualizations of social exclusion.

Discourses of Social Exclusion

The Concept of Social Exclusion

> An exclusion discourse is possible from many political perspectives. It can be a call for radical restructuring of society, but it can also be a way of rendering major social problems innocuous by breaking them down, so that unemployment becomes not a problem for society as a whole, but a problem for the underskilled, for the handicapped, for migrants and for other specific groups. (Rodgers, 1995: 53)

The term 'social exclusion' is widely acknowledged to have originated in France where it was used in the 1980s as a reference to people considered on the margin of society due to their lack of social insurance. At first the socially excluded counted disabled people, lone parents and uninsured unemployed people, but later the main marginalized groups of concern were disaffected youths and socially isolated individuals. In the early and mid-1990s commentators note the adoption of the social exclusion term by the European Union as the concept came to replace the concept of poverty in what was the EU's poverty programme. Social exclusion became the EU's main social policy focus and this shift trickled down, via National Action Plans on social inclusion, to all EU member states (for historical overviews see for example Levitas, 2006, Gore et al., 1995, Burchardt et al., 2002, Percy-Smith, 2000, Lister, 2004, Walker and Walker, 1997, Silver, 1995). In the UK, for example, a 'social exclusion unit' was set up by the incoming New Labour government in 1997. In Denmark, a similar 'Council for Socially Excluded' was established in 2002.

As the quote above by Rodgers illustrates, the meaning of social exclusion is a contested issue, and much of the debate concerns the relationship between social exclusion and the concept and realities of poverty. Analysts have asked whether social exclusion constitutes a new empirical phenomenon or whether social exclusion reflects a human experience no different from poverty. Questions have also been raised regarding the value of introducing a novel concept such as social exclusion in the place of poverty, and different commentators have taken different views on the exact conceptual relationship between the two concepts. Those taking a favourable view of the social exclusion term typically argue that it constitutes an improvement from the focus on poverty because social exclusion introduces more dimensions than merely the material deprivation, income-related aspect of the poverty experience. Social exclusion also encompasses social, political and cultural inequalities (Rodgers, 1995) inadequate social participation

(Larsen, 2004), lack of social integration, lack of power (Room, 1995), the denial of citizenship rights (Berghman, 1995, Walker, 1997) and discrimination based on health, geographic location, cultural identification (Burchardt et al., 2002) as well as gender, race, ethnicity, sexuality and age (Lister, 2004). Furthermore, analysts have argued that social exclusion introduces a more dynamic aspect to the social analysis. Social exclusion is seen as a process whereas poverty is merely an outcome, and considering social exclusion in this way enables the analysis to illuminate not just the people who are excluded but also those agents and structures doing the excluding (e.g. Room, 1995, Rodgers, 1995, Berghman, 1995).

Critics of the social exclusion concept, on the other hand, claim that the new term serves the normative and political purpose of euphemizing and camouflaging poverty (Øyen, 1997). The dual terms of social exclusion and social inclusion are seen to set discriminating boundaries between different forms of social being, making the socially included represent normality, morality, responsibility, independence and competitiveness whilst the socially excluded represent difference, redundancy, pathology, immorality and obsolescence (Bauman, 1998). Overall, many analysts feel that social exclusion analyses are predominantly focused on the victims of exclusion and their shortcomings as social agents. Meanwhile, not enough attention is given to the excluding structures (Cameron, 2006, Bowring, 2000). Critics of the social exclusion concept also tend to be critical of the social inclusion concept, which is seen to signify the simplistic assumption that social inclusion is the positive, desirable opposite and solution to social exclusion. Users of this value-laden dichotomy thereby draw attention away from the inequalities and differences among the included (Levitas, 2005). Furthermore, in practice, the more specific route to social inclusion that the socially excluded are expected to take tends to go through paid work. But the demand to participate in the labour market overlooks the potential experiences of inequality, discrimination, marginalization and poverty which may just as well take place inside the labour market as outside of it (Rodgers, 1995, Levitas, 2005, Labonte, 2004, Søndergård, 2002).

In many welfare states, and especially in European Union member states, perceptions of social exclusion are central to many CSR stakeholders and practitioners. In comparison, the concept of poverty is very rarely seen in corporate or policy documents on CSR, nor was the notion of poverty drawn on or even alluded to by the respondents interviewed for this study. That is why, despite the many angles from which the notion of social exclusion can be critiqued, in this book the concept of social exclusion has been chosen over poverty or other concepts whenever the issue of the social implications of CSR is being considered.

Putting the concept of social exclusion into a comparative, cross-national context raises the immediate question of whether the interpretation and articulation of social exclusion varies depending on the national, institutional contexts in which it is addressed. This idea has attained some support amongst social exclusion analysts, perhaps most notably in the form of Silver's social exclusion paradigms (1995). Silver distinguishes between three ideologically distinct approaches to social exclusion, each of which is associated with its own geography and/or culture; from a French republican tradition; to Anglo-American liberalism; and finally to a social democratic approach to social exclusion attributed to 'the European Left' (Silver, 1995: 69). Although Silver's paradigms are widely recognized as a valuable contribution to the understanding of the variety of ways in which social exclusion is addressed (Burchardt et al., 2002, Gore et al., 1995, Levitas, 2005, Lister, 2004, Rodgers, 1995), the favoured perspective in this book is one which considers the plurality of co-existing discourses at play *within* national institutional contexts. As with the idea of corporate social responsibility, the view taken here is that the concept of social exclusion cannot be at the same time considered both a contested concept and a paradigm, even when different paradigms are associated with separate institutional contexts, and even when those contextual paradigms are acknowledged as ideal types. On this basis, the analysis draws instead on Levitas's analysis of the range of social exclusion discourses which she finds within the contemporary political context of England (2005). Although Levitas's analysis is confined to England, her identification of social exclusion discourses has been widely acclaimed as well as acknowledged as applicable to most European welfare states (see for example Aust and Arriba, 2005, Beland, 2007).

MUD, SID and RED: Levitas's Discourses of Social Exclusion

In *The Inclusive Society*, originally published in 1998, Levitas examines critically the new political language of social exclusion and inclusion in Britain (2005). With a view to unveiling the ideological foundations and the policy implications of these new terms Levitas carries out discourse analyses on a range of relevant policy documents and publications. As a result, Levitas identifies three ideal typical discourses of social exclusion. As with the CSR discourses, the co-existing and competing social exclusion discourses are significant because they constitute the discursive repertoire available to those political, policy and social actors participating in the political debate on social exclusion within a given institutional context. In the particular context of this book, Levitas's typologies are relevant because they provide an opportunity to link social exclusion conceptually to CSR.

Starting with Levitas's 'Moral Underclass Discourse', which she shortens with the mnemonic acronym 'MUD', this discourse is ideologically located within New Right thinking. MUD grew out of concern amongst Neo-Conservatives about rising social security spending in the 1980s following this decade's growing unemployment. Inspired by US right-wing social commentators such as Murray (Murray, 1990), the MUD discourse is permeated by notions of 'underclass' and 'dependency culture'. There is a perception of an underclass having emerged consisting of welfare dependent individuals. Made up mostly of lone workless mothers and young workless men, this underclass is seen as dominated by a 'culture of dependency'. The dependency culture is seen as a pathological moral and psychological condition, which rejects the values of work and the family and embraces instead illegitimacy, crime, delinquency and general antisocial behaviour. Furthermore, the moral underclass is seen as a product of the benefit system of the welfare state. Too generous benefits are seen to have created dependency and eroded the incentive to work and save. The preferred policy solution to social exclusion is therefore to tighten benefit eligibility and restrict its generosity, thereby giving back to the moral underclass the incentive to become self-sufficient.

The second social exclusion discourse, the 'Social Integrationist Discourse', is shortened to SID. Central concepts in the social integrationist discourse include 'social exclusion', 'social inclusion', 'integration' and 'social cohesion'. The development of SID is part of the history of the social exclusion term. The application of SID originated within the French policy context of the 1980s and was later used more widely in European Union social policy. Levitas sees SID as rooted in French Republican contractarian social thinking (Rousseau, 1998 [1762]). It presents a worldview in which moral integration, solidarity and social 'insertion' are considered the antidotes to social exclusion. Here social exclusion is understood as the breakdown of the structural, cultural and moral ties which bind individuals to society. But SID has also been shaped by the Anglo-Saxon liberal version of contractarianism, which found expression in British politics when New Labour re-launched itself in the 1990s with a party programme heavily inspired by Communitarian thinking (Etzioni, 1993). Communitarianism shares with Republicanism the emphasis on moral integration, social order and reciprocity. Levitas describes how SID, when developed at the European Union level, came to increasingly move the agenda away from alleviating poverty and towards a narrow focus on social exclusion as the exclusion from paid work with policy solutions centring round labour market integration.

Finally, Levitas identifies a third social exclusion discourse, which she labels the 'redistributionist discourse' and shortens to RED. Concepts core to RED include poverty, deprivation, citizenship and also social exclusion. Levitas traces the origins of the redistributionist discourse to the late 1970s and to British critical social policy. She attributes RED's initial development to Peter Townsend's groundbreaking research on poverty (Townsend, 1979). Instead of perceiving poverty as an absolute condition characterized by a lack of material resources, Townsend redefined the notion of poverty so that it came to encompass a relative condition, defined by whether people have sufficient resources to participate in the customary life of society and to fulfil what is expected of them as members of it (Levitas, 2005: 9). In this context, the idea of social exclusion is not considered synonymous with poverty but is rather seen as an aspect of poverty where deprivation has led to a reduction in the extent of social participation or a withdrawal from the community's style of living. In RED redistribution is seen as the best policy solution to poverty and social exclusion. According to Levitas, policy activists informed by RED promotes redistributive measures such as tax-funded benefits (although not means-tested benefits) and public services, the minimum wage, a minimum income for those unable to work and a form of financial recognition of unpaid work. Levitas goes on to describe how RED was developed further in the

1990s by critical social policy research such as that carried out by the Childhood Poverty Action Group (Walker, 1997). In its more recent expression, the concept of social exclusion has become more prominent within RED, as has the notion of citizenship, which is used in RED as a euphemism for equality. In the British policy context, RED represents the recasting of the social democratic agenda in the new language of exclusion and citizenship (Levitas, 2005: 13).

MUD, SID and RED thus differ in terms of how they present the relationship between inclusion, exclusion and inequality, how they differentiate between people as included or excluded and in their preferred solutions to social exclusion. MUD addresses the inequalities between the underclass and the rest of society, SID addresses the inequality between paid workers and unemployed people, whilst RED addresses both the social, political, cultural and economic dimensions of inequality. MUD differentiates between the socially excluded and the socially included on the basis of the kinds of morals held by the two groups, in SID the line is drawn between those in work and those out of work, and in RED money is seen as the key indicator of who the socially excluded and included are. In terms of causes and solutions, in MUD social exclusion is perceived a lifestyle chosen by the socially excluded, and this lifestyle is encouraged by the generous benefit system. Proponents of MUD are therefore against increasing social benefits. This stands in contrast to RED where social exclusion is considered a condition arising from material poverty, which in turn is considered a structurally created situation. Proponents of RED therefore advocate increasing social benefits and generally enhancing redistributive, tax-funded measures. In between those two options, SID leaves space for acknowledging (like RED) that the market has failings, produces inequalities and thus requires regulation and management. However, like in MUD, in SID current levels of welfare provision are considered excessive and therefore proponents of SID do not favour increasing social benefits. Instead the policy solution preferred by SID is to use paid work as a means to foster more solidarity and better social integration, social inclusion and social cohesion. MUD shares with SID the conviction that paid work is the solution to social exclusion, but MUD's perspective favours paid work as a means of disciplining the excluded. Only in RED is unpaid work acknowledged by suggesting it should be valorized in some financial form.

Levitas herself is particularly critical of SID and MUD for seeing paid work as the main route to social inclusion. Levitas sees the focus on paid work as problematic because it ignores problems of low pay and gender segregation in the labour market. It also devalues the important welfare providing work carried out outside the labour market, particularly in the informal sector, where women are often engaged full time in child caring. This makes RED the more preferable option to Levitas compared with SID or MUD. However, RED too has its shortcomings, most fundamentally in that it is too weak a challenge of the dominant culture and norms of capitalist society. What is needed is a much more radical break from market distribution than is possible within an inclusion/exclusion paradigm (Levitas, 2005). This critique of the available social exclusion discourses in contemporary politics is backed up by other analysts. Bowring, for example, sees RED as too closely related to SID in its emphasis on social inclusion (2000). Moreover, RED only extends its social critique to material class divisions. Bowring calls instead for what could be considered here a fourth social exclusion discourse as he demands a much more radical and imaginative social alternative to any of the social exclusion discourses identified by Levitas. Bowring believes in the need for an approach which is critical of the very dominant rules, norms and practices from which poor people are excluded. Taking a Marxist position, Bowring's ultimate social ideal includes overthrowing the capitalist social system and replacing it with a society which could offer properly funded programmes of social provision and a guaranteed social income. These measures would meet people's real social needs by increasing their disposable time rather than merely their material resources (Bowring, 2000).

Levitas's analysis has been highly influential not just in a British social policy context but also in comparative social policy research. Levitas demonstrates through her discourse analysis that social exclusion is a multifaceted concept whose still widening political acceptance can be attributed to its ability to mean different things to different people. Levitas emphasizes, however, that the three discourses are ideal types. Therefore they are most likely to be used interchangeably in the public discourse. Levitas concludes her analysis by applying her discourses to the most recent developments within the New Labour Party in Britain. Here Levitas identifies a shift in the party's discourse away from its traditional redistributive, RED roots towards 'an inconsistent combination of MUD and SID' (Levitas, 2005: 27). This discursive shift implies a policy transition away from a focus on poverty and redistribution and towards an increasing emphasis on paid work as the policy solution to social exclusion.

Connections between CSR Discourses and Social Exclusion Discourses?

Levitas's social exclusion discourses are interesting because they raise the question of whether any links can be made to the discourses of corporate social responsibility presented earlier. Is it possible, even, to establish a connection between specific CSR discourses and specific social exclusion discourses? These questions lead to the further question of whether there is a potential for attributing to each of the CSR discourses a particular ideological view of social exclusion and the socially excluded, and whether each CSR discourse thereby implies a specific approach to addressing social exclusion.

One way of approaching these questions is to consider whether it is possible to establish a relationship between the two continuums along which the CSR discourses and the social exclusion discourses are positioned. The continuum aligning the CSR discourses in relation to each other is explicitly political-ideological, starting from the political right and moving to the political left. Levitas's social exclusion discourses are perhaps not as overtly aligned along a continuum, yet the discourses are reasonably clearly associated with positions within the political spectrum: from

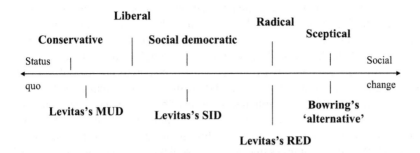

Figure 3.2 Linking up the CSR and Social Exclusion Continuums

MUD's New Right (and thereby right-wing) foundations to RED's 'old labour' or critical social policy foundations at the left end of the scale. SID arguably sits somewhere in the middle, associated with New Labour in England. It seems plausible to consider SID ideologically related to the social liberalism embraced by most modernized social democratic parties in Europe. Having found an overlap in continuums, the next question is whether any lines can be drawn between the different positions on the spectrums. Figure 3.2 shows how the CSR and social exclusion discourses might be aligned on the same continuum.

Starting at the political right side of the scale, an association between the conservative CSR discourse and the moral underclass social exclusion discourse would not seem implausible. Both are anchored in the right-wing, conservative ideologies of the closely related neo-liberalism and New Right. Both stand for opposition to the kind of social change that would shift the balance of the mixed economy of welfare. Instead, the emphasis is on preserving the existing structural, institutional boundaries and then leaving the various agents of society to take responsibility for themselves. In the conservative CSR discourse, business should be left alone by the government to do its business. And in MUD, the government should be more willing to leave socially deprived and economically dependent individuals alone as a way of teaching them to fend for themselves. The conservative CSR discourse and MUD hereby have in common a perspective on social responsibility which puts the onus for survival in the social system strictly on agency and which objects to locating responsibility at any structural level. The implied way of dealing with social exclusion in the conservative CSR discourse is in other words for businesses and government to do less rather than more. The socially excluded, meanwhile, will have to take responsibility for becoming included by themselves – or remain socially excluded.

The next position on the CSR continuum is the liberal CSR discourse. The liberal CSR discourse hovers in the space between MUD and SID. The liberal

CSR discourse seems to share its social outlook with both the moral underclass discourse and the social integrationist discourses on social exclusion. They all three emphasize agency rather than structure when it comes to social change. Both MUD and SID put the onus on the socially excluded for becoming socially included, and the liberal CSR discourse also strongly represents a rejection of any form of government involvement. When it comes to the idea of businesses engaging in social exclusion the point of departure for the liberal CSR discourse is the demand that CSR must result in some form of business benefit. This once again leaves no space for a concerted, structural redesign of the social model towards preventing and overcoming social exclusion throughout society. Instead, the liberal CSR discourse implies that achieving social results such as social inclusion with CSR is left to the individual businesses at the local level.

The next position on the social exclusion continuum is SID. The worldview inherent in this discourse arguably has quite a bit in common with the social democratic CSR discourse. Both are rooted in contractarian perceptions of society, whether Republican or Communitarian. Both are championed by modernized social democratic parties such as the New Labour Party in Britain and the Social Democratic Party in Denmark. Both discourses advocate some degree of social change, which would see both businesses and individuals taking their roles more seriously as parties to a social contract. But neither SID nor the social democratic CSR discourse point towards an embrace of government intervention in social matters, neither through the regulation of businesses, nor through monetary redistribution to the socially excluded. Instead, SID and the social democratic CSR discourse represent the belief that the role of the government is to encourage and incentivize social agents, such as businesses and individuals, to participate in society and to show solidarity with other parts of society. Both discourses are designed to appeal to the social responsibility of social agents so that social transformation can happen through agency rather than through any form of social restructuring. The beneficiaries of the changes are not merely the socially excluded but also society itself. A society where businesses are socially responsible and engaged, and where individuals take responsibility for their own integration, is also a stable and cohesive society. On the basis of these parallels it would not seem implausible to suggest that the social democratic CSR discourse implies an approach to social exclusion which sees labour market integration as the solution to social exclusion.

Moving along the social exclusion/CSR continuum, the next social exclusion discourse is RED. RED arguably has some similarities with the radical CSR discourse. Both discourses promote radical social changes towards more redistribution to the poor, and both advocate more government commitment to and involvement in achieving this goal. The radical CSR discourse, however, is more measured in its expectations. This is partly in recognition of the limited powers of international governance structures. But the pro-regulation position of the radical CSR discourse is also constantly being suppressed by the dominant neo-liberal bias towards as little regulation as possible. Therefore, in realization of its current minority position, the radical CSR discourse has embraced CSR and is seeking to define CSR according to the radical discourse's own social goals. In a similar manner RED has arguably undergone a transformation in its approach to social exclusion, from having at first dismissed the social exclusion concept in favour of the concept of poverty, to having embraced the notion of social exclusion, alongside with citizenship, as part of the recasting of the social democratic agenda. On the issue of government intervention, however, RED remains committed to the redistributive, government-regulated solution to social exclusion. In contrast, proponents of the radical CSR discourse have, at least for the moment, suspended their insistence on regulation in favour of encouraging businesses to adopt a universal set of codes of conduct. These differences are partly down to the spheres to which the two discourses apply: RED applies to a national discourse and the radical CSR discourse is mostly concerned about global issues. It would therefore seem plausible to suggest that if the radical CSR discourse was applied to the issue of social exclusion within a national context, it would advocate solutions involving redistribution and governmental intervention.

Finally, at the political left end of the continuum we find Bowring's Marxist radical alternative to Levitas's social exclusion discourses. This social exclusion discourse greatly resembles the sceptical CSR discourse. Both stand for a rejection of all the other discourses for not being radical enough and for accepting terms and ideas such as corporate social responsibility, social exclusion and social inclusion, which are essentially rooted in the same (capitalist) ideological thinking that is creating the problems they are seeking to address in the first place. If the capitalist economic system was not directly encouraging businesses to act in socially irresponsible manners, the idea of CSR would be irrelevant. Similarly, if the capitalist social system had not already created the structural inequalities leading certain groups to be socially excluded, it would not be necessary to speak in terms of social exclusion and social inclusion. Embracing the notions of CSR and social exclusion is therefore seen as submission and a failure to advocate sufficient social change.

In summary there are several angles from which some of the CSR discourses can be linked with the social exclusion discourses. Although it should be remembered that both the CSR discourses and the social exclusion discourses are ideal types and therefore unlikely to be found in their pure forms in any political or social context, it is also important to appreciate the value of taking time to reflect on the conceptual and ideological connections between CSR and social exclusion. When the idea of corporate social responsibility is promoted and debated, the question of what kinds of social impacts may be envisaged remains mostly unarticulated. Drawing out the conceptual and ideological overlaps is therefore a way of addressing the issue of the social impacts of CSR. And in relation to social exclusion more specifically, the above exercise has highlighted that each CSR discourse may imply a different approach to addressing the particular social problem of social exclusion.

Conclusion

The aim of this chapter was to understand the meaning of the term 'corporate social responsibility'. Having at first established that CSR is a contested concept whose exact definition remains elusive, the approach in this chapter was to offer an overview of the many ways in which CSR is currently understood. Five different discourses of CSR were identified within the literature on CSR. These were related to each other in terms of their attitudes to social, institutional change and their general perceptions of the appropriate relationship between business and society, the commercial sector and the public sector. Another objective of this chapter was to consider the social implications of corporate social responsibility, particularly in relation to the area of social exclusion. To this end, the CSR discourses have been related to various social exclusion discourses found in the existing sociological literature.

The analysis in this chapter will provide the conceptual background for the analysis yet to be carried out in the remaining chapters of this book. When exploring the views on the social impacts of CSR amongst the CSR practitioners interviewed for the case study in this book, the emerging perspectives will be weighed against the suggested connections made here between the different CSR discourses and social exclusion discourses (Chapter 7). But before moving on to the case study, the next part of the book (Part II) will consider how the different CSR discourses come to expression within specific national institutional contexts.

PART II
A History of Corporate Social Responsibility in the Mixed Economy of Welfare

PART II

Introduction to Part II

This section of the book concentrates on the emergence and historical development of corporate social responsibility, both as an idea but also as various types of practices. The most important aspect of the historical investigation is the relationship between CSR and the mixed economy of welfare. As the origins and evolutions of CSR are traced within a range of West European welfare states, special attention will be given to the extent to which CSR's historical development has been affected by changes and continuities within these countries' mixed economies. The countries included in the analysis are: England, Denmark, Sweden, Norway, Germany and France.

The countries of England and Denmark have for natural reasons been awarded the most space in the historical analysis. This is because it has been possible to draw not only on the CSR literature but also on the insights from the English and Danish CSR stakeholders interviewed for the comparative case study of this book (presented in Part III). Hence the arguments made regarding the historical development of CSR in England and Denmark will be supported with quotes from English, Danish and EU respondents.[1] The countries of Sweden and Norway are presented alongside each other in each chapter on the grounds that these two countries both represent the same Scandinavian, social democratic welfare state model (Esping-Andersen, 1990). As such the Swedish and Norwegian CSR histories complement the historical analysis of Denmark by bringing to light which parts of Denmark's CSR history are uniquely Danish and which parts represent a Scandinavian-wide experience. Like Sweden and Norway, the two countries of Germany and France are also presented alongside each other. The rationale for this grouping again relates to Esping-Andersen's welfare typologies in which Germany and France both belong to the conservative welfare state regime (Esping-Andersen, 1990). (For an elaboration of Esping-Andersen's welfare regimes see Chapter 2).

From a theoretical point of view, applying a historical perspective is important. In historical institutionalism, historical investigation is key to understanding contemporary cross-national differences and similarities. Hence, situating CSR within the unique historical trajectories of various European welfare institutions can help elucidate how and why the social phenomenon of CSR has developed into sometimes different and sometimes similar interpretations and applications in different countries today. Another theoretical interest is the question of what types

---

1   In order to comply with ethical research guidelines, the original names of interviewees have been changed to code names. Specific locations and organization names have also been changed where these could lead to the identification of the person interviewed.

of drivers have driven the development of CSR. In this context, consideration will be given to influences not just at the formal institutional level but also at the ideational institutional level. Consideration will also be given to the question of where in the mixed economy CSR has been driven from. Finally, an important part of the historical investigation consists in keeping an eye on the extent to which the different CSR discourses outlined in Chapter 3 are applied at different times in history to promote different forms of CSR or to push the development of CSR in any particular direction.

The historical analysis is divided into three 'historical strands'. In each historical strand CSR emerges at a different time in history and in a different part of the mixed economy. As the historical CSR strands evolve into contemporary times it will become clear in the analysis that their trajectories often interrelate, affect each other's development or co-exist in parallel. The three historical strands are dealt with separately in Chapters 4, 5 and 6. In Chapter 4, the connections between contemporary CSR and nineteenth century corporate philanthropy will be explored. Chapter 5 will focus on CSR when it has been applied by governments as a social policy tool. And Chapter 6 will take into account the growth of CSR on the international arena and the extent to which this development has influenced the national CSR contexts of the countries included in the analysis. In each of the chapters, attention will be paid to the many different ways in which CSR has been practiced throughout history. Different types of CSR activities are hereby put into a historical context. In this process a historical perspective is also acquired on CSR when it is applied to issues around social exclusion. And finally, an insight is gained into the place of social exclusion within the overall contexts of different national CSR agendas.

Chapter 4

Connections between CSR
and Nineteenth-century Philanthropy:
CSR in the Commercial Sector

Introduction

The focus in this chapter is the strand of corporate social responsibility which originated in the commercial sector and which has been developed by actors within that sector, that is, businesses and employers. This part of the history of CSR goes back as far as the nineteenth century. The analysis will throw light on the connections between CSR and philanthropy. Particular attention will be paid to the effects of changes in the mixed economy of welfare upon the development of CSR, and to the significance of the formal and ideational institutional levels. The countries under investigation are: England, Denmark, Sweden and Norway, and Germany and France.

England: Explicit Links between Contemporary and Victorian CSR

When CSR is considered in relation to the English context in the academic literature there is a widespread tendency to relate contemporary English CSR to certain business activities emerging in the nineteenth century (e.g. Cannon, 1992, Clarke, 1997, Crowther and Rayman-Bacchus, 2004, Hemingway and Maclagan, 2004). Clarke (1997), for example, introduces her analysis of the 'community contributions' of British firms by stating that this particular approach to CSR 'has its roots in the philanthropic activities of Victorian industrialists' (Clarke, 1997: 201). Similarly, Hemingway and Maclagan (2004) explain that contemporary English CSR is 'historically associated in British and American history with the Quakers' and as examples they point to philanthropic industrialists such as Rowntree, Fry and Cadbury's (Hemingway and Maclagan, 2004: 37). These particular names appear to belong to a set list of nationally recognized symbols of 'early CSR'. Crowther and Rayman-Bacchus (2004), for example, use Robert Owen, the entrepreneur who pioneered the idea of cooperatives, as their case for arguing that 'issues of socially responsible behaviour are not of course new' (Crowther and Rayman-Bacchus, 2004: 1). The sentiment that contemporary CSR constitutes a continuity rather than a novel social phenomena is also noticeable amongst the English respondents interviewed for this book's case study. Simon, who is the project manager of the local English CSR project, is just one amongst many English respondents linking contemporary CSR with Victorian practices. This extract from Simon's interview is taken from his reflections on how CSR should be defined. Having stated that CSR is about responsible business practices, Simon elaborates:

> ... you know, in the way that all the old sort of Victorian paternalists did. Cadbury's and all those other great ones. They built houses for their workers because they needed [...] you know, it was a good business practice, because that meant people had to turn up to work on time because they lived right next to the factory. But it also meant that obviously someone had somewhere to live. And, you know, times have changed, things are different, but [those businesses] are still a part of that [CSR].

As well as Simon's mentioning of Cadbury's, English respondents also use company names such as Quaker's Oats, Cadbury's, Fry's, Whitbread and Rowntree's as examples of historic CSR. When Simon expresses his opinion on what prompted nineteenth-century philanthropists to engage in CSR he touches on the theme of motivations, which is important to this analysis and will be dealt with later in this section.

In the literature, most CSR authors making the historical connection to the nineteenth century do not go beyond the more general references to Victorian industrialists and philanthropy. Similarly, when English respondents use historical examples of CSR it is mostly to point out briefly that CSR is 'nothing new'. To a wide extent, the association between contemporary English CSR and Victorian times is taken for granted within the English context. Cannon (1992) is one of few authors who offers some explanations of how nineteenth-century CSR arose in the English context and how it developed into modern forms of CSR. As illustrations of Victorian CSR, Cannon draws on the social areas of housing and education. Reiterating Simon's example, Cannon points out that some factory owners built 'model communities' for their workers, which took care of the workers' housing needs. Within the area of education, wealthy industrialists established Sunday schools, libraries, civic universities and engineering institutions.

Cannon credits the socioeconomic transformations brought about by the industrial revolution for creating an environment in which CSR as a new form of business activity could emerge. Firstly, the industrial revolution's new technologies enabled large-scale corporations of 'vast power and wealth' to materialize (Cannon, 1992: 2). Along with these new business entities a new wealthy industrial ruling class also arose. Secondly, the Victorian era was also characterized by an increasing influence of religious values and this led to a rise in philanthropic activities directed at the poor and disadvantaged. According to Cannon, the combination of new wealth and religion was central to the emergence of those activities which today are considered early forms of CSR. The pioneers of Victorian CSR – companies such as Whitbread, Truman's, Lloyds, Darbys, Barclays, Cadbury,

Rowntree's, Pilkington, Wills and Players – all had in common that they were owned and run by wealthy Quaker entrepreneurs. Cannon considers it significant that these Quakers had successfully climbed the social ladder in a society where only until recently Quakers were persecuted outsiders. Entrepreneurship had been one of the few means of social mobility open to them. These experiences were crucial in making this group of CSR pioneers particularly keen on establishing educational institutions. In what Cannon labels 'the non-conformist challenge', the newly moneyed Quakers were making education accessible to the general public, rather than to just a small elite. Hereby they also promoted social mobility within a society where conforming to one's predetermined social position was still considered a virtue. Finally, the Quaker religion challenged the Victorian capitalist worldview where poverty was considered self-imposed, emphasizing instead the responsibilities associated with wealth and success. The educational institutions were the Quakers' instruments for conveying the ethos of self-improvement and teaching the poor prudence, thrift, enterprise and abstinence (Cannon, 1992).

As Cannon charts the development of CSR in England going into the twentieth century, key moments in the historical trajectory include the Depression of the 1930s, which, according to Cannon, exposed the limitations of corporations as agents of social change and shifted instead the focus toward the government. Following this experience, the establishment and continuing expansion of the welfare state is also seen as central in phasing out CSR as a form of social provisioning. Instead, the government gradually assumed more and more responsibility for tackling issues around 'poverty, disadvantage, unemployment and social injustice' (Cannon, 1992: 224). Cannon's historical analysis is reiterated and backed up by Moon (2004), who also sees the gradual expansion of social provisioning by the state as having narrowed the scope for business to play a direct role as social providers. Moon adds that as a result, the ways in which companies carried out CSR therefore changed from around the 1930s, from the more all-encompassing forms of philanthropy to means such as charitable donations, where company chairmen would support a favourite charity unrelated to the business. Rotary clubs and Chambers of Commerce emerged as spaces for CSR activities, as these organizations enabled individual business people to engage in local social issues in a philanthropic way (Moon, 2004).

It is interesting to note how those factors cited by Cannon and Moon as significant for the origin and development of CSR interrelate with the broader institutional social fabric of the English mixed economy of welfare. The emergence of CSR as social provisioning by employers in the commercial sector coincided with a dramatic transformation of the commercial sector as it became dominated by the larger actors of corporations and as the commercial sector became the most important contributor to the financial wealth of society as a whole. This change also affected the overall balance of the mixed economy, as the actors within the commercial sector – that is, corporations and their owners – were now so wealthy that they could fund and provide new forms of welfare in response to the new social needs arising from the social changes brought on by the industrial revolution. As pointed out by Moon (2004), the philanthropic activities by Victorian businesses took place at a time in history when the public sector had not yet adapted to the task of providing assistance to the impoverished in mass urban society (Moon, 2004). The perspective that nineteenth-century CSR originated as a response to newly emerging social needs arising from the socioeconomic changes related to industrialization has much in common with the functionalist explanations of the origin of the welfare state. Here the welfare state is also considered a natural outcome of industrialization and modernization (Wilensky, 1975, Flora and Alber, 1981). But, few (if any) comparative social policy accounts consider the role of the commercial sector – or a very specific segment of the commercial sector – in meeting some of those social needs in the years before public sector provisioning became widely established. As the historical analysis of CSR in England moves on from the Victorian era and into the twentieth century a pattern emerges in which there is a direct trade-off relationship between the degree of public sector welfare provisioning available and the prominence of CSR as a form of commercial sector welfare provisioning.

On the theoretical level it is possible to reframe in mixed economy and historical institutionalist terms the influences identified by Cannon and Moon as important for the emergence of CSR. From this perspective, developments took place not only on the formal institutional level but also on the ideational institutional level (for an elaboration on the book's theoretical framework see Chapter 2). This complementary development is exemplified in the relationship between CSR and the non-profit sector. Firstly, CSR appears to have arisen in parallel with the rise of philanthropy and thereby the non-profit sector as a significant welfare provider. But apart from this change at the formal institutional level it is also already well documented in the social policy literature that this sector's growth in the nineteenth century was underpinned by changes at the ideational institutional level. Here, a new paradigmatic value-system was emerging, which blended liberalism's emphasis on self-improvement with religious ideas about the importance of philanthropy (e.g. Cochraine et al., 2001, Powell and Hewitt, 2002, Lund, 2007). By including CSR in the historical analysis it now also transpires that these values from the non-profit sector spilled over into the commercial sector and dictated the codes of conducts of some of its actors. From a theoretical point of view, the central role of religion and values to the development of CSR lends credit to the argument made by some historical institutionalists in recent years that ideational institutions are just as important as formal institutions for the understanding of historical change (Hall, 1993, Berman, 2001, Lieberman, 2002, Campbell, 2002, Beland, 2005).

In relation to the question of where in the mixed economy CSR is driven from, this particular strand of the history of CSR in England leads to the conclusion that CSR is first and foremost an activity originating in, developed by and run from the commercial sector. This observation corresponds to a widely held view in the CSR literature, and also amongst many respondents, that CSR is 'business driven' (Albareda et al., 2006). The implication of this often used phrase is that CSR is independent from governmental decrees. Yet, it is important to note that CSR as a form of business behaviour is not representative of the commercial sector as a whole, neither today nor historically. In relation to Victorian CSR, another interesting aspect of the historical perspective coming across in the literature and amongst many respondents is the importance assigned to a particular type of actors. The model communities and the educational institutions established by company owners were novel forms of welfare provisioning as well as novel forms of behaviour by actors in the commercial sector. The philanthropic industrialists were conducting social experiments rather than following the norms. It is on this basis that the Victorian CSR practitioners are frequently referred to as 'pioneers', both in the literature and by English CSR stakeholders, as reflected in the interviews. To rephrase using the book's theoretical terminology, these CSR practitioners are, as pioneers, types of actors known as 'ideas champions', or 'carriers' of novel and alternative ideas about how to approach social problems (Berman, 2001). This type of agency stands in contrast to actors that are merely executors of already institutionally dominating ideas or policies. The origin of CSR in England, in other words, appears to owe as much to changes in the social structures as it does to the efforts of particular types of social actors. The importance of 'ideas champions' or CSR champions for the further development of CSR remains relevant to contemporary debates about English CSR. Here it is a widely held view that the mantle of English CSR continues to be carried by a minority of English businesses that are all well known as CSR front runners (Pryce, 2002).

The final theme of interest here, and which is dealt with both in the literature and by many respondents, is that of the motivations behind CSR. In relation to the Victorian CSR practitioners, Cannon is not alone in emphasizing the central role of religion to this group of people. Hemingway and Maclagan, for example, in their reference to historic CSR cited earlier, also stress the association between CSR and the Quakers (Hemingway and Maclagan, 2004). The perception that Victorian CSR was motivated by philanthropic ideals is also held by others than Cannon, such as when Clarke connects contemporary forms of CSR to the 'philanthropic activities of Victorian industrialists' (Clarke, 1997: 201). Altogether there appears to be a strong sense that altruism played a major part in motivating the Victorian CSR practitioners. Yet at the same time, most analysts as well as most of the respondents making references to historic CSR will make the point that beside the altruistic motivations it is also possible to discern more self-interested incentives for the various CSR initiatives. In relation to the model communities, Cannon regards this form of Victorian CSR as having been inspired not only by religion but also by the ruling classes' fear of 'the mob'. In a context where the working class was becoming increasingly organized as a political movement for social reforms, the model communities were not just initiatives designed to improve the living condition of workers – they were also a way of containing a social movement seen as a threat. And in relation to the educational projects, Cannon emphasize their value to the Quakers as a form of challenge to a social establishment, which had until then denied the Quakers any social status (Cannon, 1992). Amongst the respondents, Simon mentions in the quote cited earlier that although the houses built for workers constituted a social contribution by meeting the workers' housing needs, they also benefited the employers as they ensured that their employees had no excuses for turning up late for work. Other respondents point out that by providing good quality housing for factory staff, the factory owners got in return a healthier work force and this again enhanced the workers' ability to work hard and generate a good profit for the factory owners.

The question of motivations, and the perception that CSR has been simultaneously motivated by altruism and self-interest, is interesting in relation to this analysis because it can help establish a link between the historical trajectory of CSR, as driven from within the commercial sector, and the discursive framework which has been 'motivating' this development. The view taken here is that commercial sector-driven CSR is mostly influenced by the discourse, which in Chapter 3 was labelled the 'liberal CSR discourse'. Like the forms of historic CSR presented above, the liberal discourse is characterized by being on the one hand in favour of CSR as a way for the commercial sector to contribute to the mixed economy of welfare, whilst on the other hand also arguing for the need for businesses to plan their CSR activities around their own self-interest. Philanthropic behaviour can be accommodated within the liberal CSR discourse on the basis that this discourse considers CSR a discretionary business activity. But in also advocating 'the business case' for CSR, and increasingly so in recent years, the liberal CSR discourse focuses on obtaining not only social but also commercial benefits from CSR. This duality is captured particularly well in Porter and Kramer's notion of 'strategic philanthropy' (Porter and Kramer, 2002).

It emerges from the historical accounts presented above as well as from the briefer historical references cited at the beginning of this section, that in the English context CSR is considered a continuity rather than a new phenomenon. Although the actions by nineteenth-century industrialists were not named 'corporate social responsibility' at the time, and although many of those types of activities carried out in the nineteenth century no longer exist in present times, there is a widespread tendency to construct the historical development of CSR in England as a continuation of a particular *idea* about the social responsibility of businesses. It is this idea, which originated in the nineteenth century. This perspective is also widespread amongst respondents. Bill, a national level CSR policy actor working for a major English union organization, is just one English respondent who regards contemporary CSR as a continuation of a long-established institutional path:

> Here [in Britain] there is a strong tradition of kind of philanthropy, charity, all
> that kind of stuff. If you go back to the industrial revolution it's peppered with
> individual do-gooders, who emerge through industrial enterprises and look at
> the suffering of society and want to give something back. So I think there's
> always been that tradition within British businesses.

Bill's perception of philanthropic CSR as a 'tradition' is reiterated by many English respondents in the context of philanthropic CSR. In evoking the notion of tradition respondents appear to be quite clearly referring to what the theory terms an 'institutional path'. Indeed, in some parts of the historical institutionalist literature these two concepts are considered synonymous (Hudson et al., 2008). Moreover, as will be apparent in the analysis of Danish philanthropic CSR, the idea of a tradition is used by Danish respondents too in relation to philanthropy, albeit in order to make an altogether different point about Danish CSR.

The continuing existence of the philanthropic tradition within English business referred to by Bill and other English respondents is embodied in particular types of business activities. These are activities, which predate the modern CSR agenda, but which are widely considered to be practical expressions of CSR today, both in the literature and by respondents. One such activity is the practice of donating money to charities or charitable causes. Alan, an English local council employee whose first-hand experience of CSR is of working with businesses offering work placements to homeless people, sums up the essence of the CSR practice of charitable giving:

> Sometimes I hear phrases like business people and representatives of significantly sized profit making companies talking about 'putting something back'. [...] I understand that they're actually talking about not simply giving 100 per cent of profits made to their shareholders and to their chief executive, but actually using a chunk of it to actually exercise some form of social responsibility. Whether that is ... I mean I understand that Orange, the mobile phone company, does that. It has a charitable fund that organizations can bid for ...

Charitable donations as a form of CSR were mentioned earlier in the historical analysis as emerging around the time of the Great Depression. But the fact that this form of CSR is still widely practiced is evident in the CSR literature, where this CSR measure is often used as a practical example of CSR within the English context (Campbell et al., 2002, Seifert et al., 2003, Brammer and Millington, 2004). Other forms of present-day CSR also widely associated with an English philanthropic 'tradition' are the practices generally referred to as 'community engagement' or 'community involvement'. Pamela, who is a CSR director for a large English business, is just one respondent who includes a reference to 'community involvement' in her portrayal of her company's approach to CSR:

> The chief executive in the UK is very, very passionate about community involvement as part of the business model. He wants his employees to be engaged and, you know, for us, the business, to be a good corporate citizen.

Pamela later goes on to provide an example of community involvement:

> ... and then in some places, I don't think all, because this isn't a universal
> phenomenon, but volunteering [is a way of practicing CSR]. In the UK and the
> US. People in branches very typically volunteered to play a role perhaps with a
> local school, or to raise funds. So that's really the tradition.

Once again, philanthropic activities such as community involvement and volunteering can be seen framed within the notion of a 'tradition'. This reflects the wide extent to which these types of CSR activities are recognized as ways in which business in England can practice CSR, both by respondents and in the literature (Clarke, 1997, Matten and Moon, 2008, de Gilder et al., 2005). It is interesting to note Pamela's perception that volunteering is unique to the English and American CSR contexts. This implies firstly that the degree to which certain forms of CSR are expressed does depend on the institutional environment. But in grouping together the UK and the US Pamela also suggests that there are connections between interpretations and applications of CSR and cultural contexts beyond the national. From a comparative social policy perspective, Pamela's analysis indicates that there is a connection between CSR and Esping-Andersen's welfare state regimes (Esping-Andersen, 1990) (for an elaboration on welfare state regimes see Chapter 2). Such indications are very much reinforced by the views of Danish CSR stakeholders. The focus of attention will therefore now shift to the analysis of philanthropic CSR in Denmark.

Denmark: Associating Philanthropy with Less Equal Societies

One of the most immediate signs that the connection between nineteenth-century philanthropy and contemporary CSR is not as explicitly and repeatedly articulated in Denmark as it is in England is the fact that almost all accounts of the origin and development of Danish CSR begin with certain governmental initiatives in the 1990s. This is the case both in the literature on Danish CSR and amongst the Danish CSR practitioners interviewed for this book's case study. This does not mean, however, that there are no examples in Denmark of the philanthropic forms of CSR found in Victorian England. As pointed out by Cannon in his analysis, firms throughout Scandinavia could be seen providing support facilities for workers ranging from medical services, which often extended beyond the immediate workforce to the wider community, to schools and colleges for workers and their families (Cannon, 1992: 19). The difference between the Danish and the English context is that in today's CSR discourse, these nineteenth-century social experiments are not considered CSR. In contrast to the English CSR authors and stakeholders, the Danish equivalents very rarely make a connection between contemporary CSR and any welfare measures provided by the commercial sector before the 1990s. One single exception emerges from the interviews. One of the Danish national business respondents goes further back in time when he considers his own company's history of conducting CSR. Bret's company is one of the leading businesses on the Danish CSR agenda today:

> Well, in terms of [Bret's company] I feel that that responsibility goes a long way back. Right back to when [Bret's company] was started, where we said: 'well, we'd like to take responsibility for [our employees'] ability to maintain a lifestyle which will enable them to give 100 per cent when they go to work'. And therefore we started out by providing housing for them. And we employed our own doctor. And that was completely new at that time. [...] That was around the turn of the century, around 1905–1910 [...] And there were special sickness insurance arrangements, you know, before it became a state responsibility to insure workers. [...] So it goes back to that time.

Bret's example has many similarities with the English examples of early CSR presented before. Bret mentions the provision of housing for workers and, like in the English analyses, he also considers the motivation for such a measure from a 'business case' perspective. In relation to the sickness insurance it is also significant that Bret points out that this practice died out as the responsibility for social insurances was gradually taken over by the public sector in Denmark (as widely documented in the social policy literature, e.g. Jensen, 1999, Korpi, 2002, Bundesen, 2003). It would appear, in other words, that although the long view of the history of CSR is rarely taken in Denmark, Danish CSR stakeholders like Bret hold perceptions similar to their English counterparts about the relationship between commercial sector-driven CSR and the public sector. CSR as a form of welfare provisioning by the commercial sector only tends to exist in an institutional context where welfare provisioning by the public sector is undeveloped or scarce.

In the Danish context it is not widespread, in other words, to regard contemporary Danish CSR as a continuation of pre-welfare state commercial sector welfare activities. The absence of such considerations only becomes apparent when comparing the Danish CSR literature to the English CSR literature. From speaking to Danish CSR stakeholders, another perspective is added to the absent connection between historical philanthropy and CSR. From the way in which many respondents discuss the theme of philanthropy it becomes clear that not only is practicing CSR as a form of philanthropy not considered relevant to the Danish CSR history, it is also considered inappropriate within the Danish context. Hanne, who works at the national level as CSR policy maker for the Danish government, is just one out of a number of respondents who expresses such a view:

> ... the whole Anglo-American tradition [...] that kind of 'community work' [pronounced in English], voluntary work and all that. Although it is a reasonably solid tradition in Denmark, we have, as the welfare state rolled out, found other ways of solving problems than through voluntary work.

Hanne's analysis is remarkably similar to all of the other Danish respondents discussing this theme. All believe that philanthropic CSR – exemplified here in contemporary practices such as community work and voluntary work – did once exist as a tradition, or an 'institutional path', within the Danish context, just like in England. However, with the expansion of the welfare state, philanthropic CSR as an approach to solving social problems has been made redundant. Whereas in England, CSR authors and stakeholder speak of a continuing tradition, Danish CSR stakeholders consider the Danish philanthropic tradition a thing of the past. Moreover, they also regard philanthropic CSR as belonging to a particular type of institutional context. Hanne's association between philanthropy and the 'Anglo-American tradition' is reiterated by several Danish respondents. Danish respondents are, in other words, reinforcing the perception already observed amongst some English respondents who associated specific expressions of CSR with not only national institutional contexts but with broader cultural contexts which also match prevailing ideas in comparative social policy about welfare state regimes (Esping-Andersen, 1990). Pelle, who works nationally for a non-profit organization advising Danish businesses on matters of CSR, is one respondent who elaborates on why Danish CSR stakeholders have a different relationship with philanthropy than their English counterparts. Pelle has just stated that philanthropy 'just isn't the done thing' in Denmark, and here he explains why:

> It's got something to do with the tax pressure and that kind of thing. [England and Denmark] are just built up in a different way, aren't we […] … of course it is cultural to a degree, but I do also think that it has something to do with England having rich people. Rich and poor people. I think it is very implicit that there is an upper class which has to help the underclass. We would claim that we don't have such an underclass. And we don't, not to the same degree. […] I'm convinced that it has something to do with that. Because we have a different tax system … which means, we have a different social division.

It is apparent not just from Pelle's comments but also from the way in which many Danish respondents speak of philanthropic forms of CSR that philanthropy is associated with more unequal societies than Denmark and with less generous or expanded welfare states than Denmark. This perception is backed up in parts of the Danish CSR literature. Here Knudsen (2004) distinguishes between two contemporary approaches to CSR; public-private partnerships and corporate philanthropy. In relation to corporate philanthropy Knudsen argues that this form of CSR is predominantly found in countries that belong to the liberal welfare state model (Knudsen, 2004). Although Danish respondents do understandably not make this explicit link to welfare state theory, their repeated references to an 'Anglo-American' tradition supports Knudsen's argument. (The public-private partnership approach to CSR will be dealt with in Chapter 5).

From the historical analyses of commercial sector-driven CSR in England and Denmark it has emerged that this strand of CSR is highly influenced by the institutional framework of the mixed economy of welfare, at both the formal and the ideational institutional levels. This finding has been supported by the historical comparison of England and Denmark. From this comparison it has become evident that philanthropic forms of CSR find very different expressions in these two different institutional contexts. These differences emanate from institutional differences, both at the formal level – in the composition of the two countries' mixed economies of welfare – and at the ideational level, where different 'logics of appropriateness' (March and Olsen, 1989) determine how CSR should fit into the contemporary social fabric. The analysis uncovered that the 'original' form of CSR, carried out as philanthropic activities and driven from within the commercial sector, is closely associated with the liberal CSR discourse. This throws light on why philanthropic CSR is widely accepted in England, a welfare state widely regarded as belonging to the liberal welfare regime, whereas philanthropic CSR is less accepted in a social democratic welfare state such as Denmark. These findings are given further strength when the perspective is widened to include insights about philanthropic CSR in countries other than England and Denmark.

Further Views from Scandinavia

Having established a strong link between the social democratic welfare institutional context of Denmark and the scarcity of philanthropic CSR found here it is interesting to look beyond Denmark and explore the prevalence of and attitudes to philanthropic CSR in other social democratic welfare states. This exercise further supports the assertions made on the basis of the Danish case. In De Geer et al's (2009) investigations into the evolution of CSR in Sweden, for example, it emerges that philanthropic business activities were as widespread here in the late nineteenth century as they were at the same time in England and Denmark. De Geer et al. mention housing, fuel and alimentary goods as examples of nineteenth-century corporate welfare provisioning and the authors explain these services as an expression of the newly emerging industrial employers taking on the *pater familias* role which was already traditionally held by employers in the disappearing agricultural society (De Geer 2009). However, unlike in the English history of CSR, the philanthropic tradition did not survive throughout the twentieth century. Instead, the Swedish story is similar to the Danish evolution of CSR. Swedish philanthropic CSR was increasingly made superfluous as the public sector was rolled out to become the domineering provider of welfare services, to a degree only matched in other social democratic welfare states (De Geer et al., 2009).

Alongside with the developments in the formal institutional composition of the Swedish mixed economy of welfare, De Geer also explains how developments on the ideational institutional level helped consolidate a certain division of labour in which the role of business in society became irreconcilable with engaging in philanthropic activities. De Geer et al. consider the Swedish context one in which business provision of welfare is not perceived as acceptable. Welfare provisioning is seen as the sole domain of the state. Instead the contribution of businesses to society is to pay tax. And, just as in Denmark, philanthropic CSR as a supplement to state welfare is not deemed acceptable either. Echoing the opinions of the Danish CSR stakeholders quoted earlier, charity is seen as an inequitable concept; voluntarism is considered unsustainable on the basis that it is arbitrary; and paternalism is rejected on the grounds that it engenders dependency (De Geer et al., 2009). The Swedish rejection of philanthropic CSR is, in other words, based on an almost identical 'logic of appropriateness' (March and Olsen, 1989) regarding the roles of the sectors in the mixed economy as that which was found in Denmark.

Another parallel between the Swedish and Danish attitudes to philanthropic CSR is found in the association between philanthropic CSR and the liberal welfare state regime. Several authors writing about the Swedish approach to CSR in general note that the modern CSR agenda came late to Sweden, despite being promoted since the 1990s by supranational institutions such as the European Union and the UN (De Geer et al., 2009, Tengblad and Ohlsson, 2009, Frostenson and Borglund, 2006). The reason for this delay is explained by a Swedish perception of CSR as being an Anglo-Saxon concept and tradition largely expressed in philanthropic activities such as provisioning of health care or community volunteering. Because of this association between CSR and philanthropy, CSR was until very recently seen as irreconcilable with the Swedish welfare state context (De Geer et al., 2009). This initial negative response to modern day CSR was also found in Norway, another social democratic welfare state. Here CSR was also until recently considered unnecessary and irrelevant to the Norwegian context on the basis that the welfare state already provides sufficient welfare (Albareda et al., 2008). Today, however, CSR is firmly on the agendas in both Sweden and Norway (EU-COM, 2007). Philanthropic CSR, however, is not. As in Denmark, the perception remains in Sweden and Norway that philanthropic CSR and the social democratic welfare state is irreconcilable. How CSR is understood and approached instead in Scandinavia will be covered in Chapter 6, when the historical analysis turns to look at the influences of globalization on the evolution of CSR.

France and Germany: Institutional Barriers in Conservative Welfare States

When considering philanthropic CSR in relation to countries commonly perceived as belonging to the conservative welfare regime, the sentiment that the philanthropic approach to CSR is unique to liberal welfare states is further reinforced. Amongst authors who have examined CSR in the contexts of France and Germany there is wide agreement that both those countries have come very late to the CSR agenda compared with the rest of the world (Blasco and Zølner, 2010, Fairbrass, 2008, Antal et al., 2009). Research into attitudes towards CSR amongst employers and scholars in Germany and France have found the prevailing attitude characterized by either indifference or scepticism and often also outright resistance towards CSR (Blasco and Zølner, 2010), particularly when CSR is carried out as philanthropic activities. This resistance is paralleled by sparse engagement with the topic of CSR in French and German universities. In France publications on CSR in English are said to be far and few between (Fairbrass, 2008), and in Germany CSR is not widely taught in business schools (Antal et al., 2009). Amongst authors who have studied German and French CSR there is wide consensus around the explanation for why these two countries are characterized as lagging behind the rest of the world in the area of CSR. Moreover, the explanatory factors for each of the countries are very similar.

German and French resistance towards the idea of CSR are determined by the institutional contexts of those two countries, at both the formal and ideational levels. At the formal institutional level, both countries are characterized by having strong states which dominate in social welfare provisioning. In France, intermediary organizations only play a weak role in the mixed economy. That leaves little room for business involvement and even less space for the idea of businesses taking the lead in social affairs (Blasco and Zølner, 2010, Antal and Sobczak, 2007). Similarly, in Germany business-society relations are already extensively covered by legal requirements and tripartite procedures (Antal et al., 2009). This formalization of the relationship between the German public and commercial sectors dampened any stimulation which might have encouraged businesses to engage in informal philanthropic CSR activities (Hiss, 2009).

The barriers against CSR in the formal set-ups of the French and German mixed economies are further enhanced by multiple points of resistance on the ideational institutional levels. One point relates to the relationship between the public sector and the commercial sector. In both countries, the state enjoys a high level of legitimacy. Research into French attitudes to the role of the state found the centralized power of the French state to be taken for granted as well as approved of (Charkham, 1995). Furthermore, the state is trusted as the exclusive domain for overseeing the interests and well-being of wider society. In contrast, the legitimacy level of the commercial sector in France is low. An attitude of mistrust in the commercial sector is deeply entrenched in French society and is said to be emanating from Catholic perceptions of businesses, which historically deemed businesses un-evangelical (Blasco and Zølner, 2010). This combination of trust in the state and mistrust in businesses means that the French public are naturally inclined to be suspicious of companies that want to engage in domains that are traditionally seen as the state's (Antal and Sobczak, 2007). Perhaps not surprisingly, most French employers are therefore reported to be uninterested in engaging in philanthropic forms of CSR (Blasco and Zølner, 2010). This situation is similar in Germany, where traditional Catholic contempt for trade and commerce is also reported to remain influential (Palazzo, 2002).

Other ideational points of resistance towards CSR in France and Germany emanate from perceptions of ethics and morality, and to related ideas about appropriate behaviour in the public versus the private sphere. In France, a distinction is made between ethics and morality, where morality is understood as that which relates to universal principles, and ethics is considered an individual matter (Blasco and Zølner, 2010). The question of whether or not businesses should engage in social affairs is very much seen as an ethical consideration, that is, a matter for each individual business to decide on their own terms. Stating one's ethical principles in public is seen as bad form, as that is akin to moralizing (Blasco and Zølner, 2010). This 'logic of appropriateness' (March and Olsen, 1989) regarding ethics and the public domain also applies to Germany. German firms have been found reluctant to address normative question publicly (Palazzo, 2002). This has been explained by the fact that, as in France, morality is seen in Germany as something which belongs only to the private sphere. The public domain is reserved for politics and business, and in this sphere business leaders should display only professionalism (Palazzo, 2002).

These national attitudes to ethics, morality and the public sphere help explain why it has been difficult for the idea of corporate social responsibility to be considered a concept which warrants public debate and academic engagement in Germany and France. It is also now clearer why it is particularly difficult for the philanthropic approach to CSR to flourish in the French and German cultural context. Should a company engage in philanthropic activities such as donating money to a charitable cause or becoming involved with a community project, it would not be considered appropriate that this company mentioned its activities anywhere in the public domain, such as in its annual report, on its website, in the media or in advertising. Not only does ethical activity not belong to the public sphere, it is also ingrained in Catholic culture that one does not make known one's 'good deeds' (Antal and Sobczak, 2007). This restraint on public communication has ruled out the potential for using CSR for publicity and hereby harnessing some of the 'business benefits' of CSR, which are considered perfectly legitimate in other cultural contexts, especially the Anglo-Saxon (Antal and Sobczak, 2007). Without such publicity opportunities, philanthropic CSR is arguably a less attractive option for French and German companies than it is for its counterparts elsewhere.

Despite the many institutional barriers against philanthropic CSR in France and Germany, examples of corporate philanthropy do exist in both countries' history. Authors studying CSR in Germany and France conceded that historically CSR played a prominent role in both countries. In Germany, entrepreneurs such as Siemens or Abbe are said to have been admired 'just as much for their economic success as for their public spirit' (Hiss, 2009: 435). Only their activities were of course not known at that time as 'corporate social responsibility'. From this perspective, it is the more recently emerged *concept* of CSR which has been met with scepticism in contemporary Germany. German CSR practices, however, can be dated back to the nineteenth century (Antal et al., 2009) where they are expressed in practices similar to those found amongst English and Scandinavian contemporaries. But just as in Scandinavia, such practices were crowded out as the state increasingly took over as social provider throughout the twentieth century.

As in Germany, some authors consider the origin of French CSR to be the nineteenth century, and more precisely 1891 when the Pope decreed a new social doctrine ('Rerum Novarum') expressing indignation and concern over social inequalities and poverty amongst the working classes (Blasco and Zølner, 2010). According to Blasco and Zølner (2010), the influence of this Catholic doctrine has remained strong throughout the centuries and explains why some marginal degree of philanthropic CSR has existed in France up until today. Although France is a secular state, some business leaders remain inspired by Catholic thinking, particularly regarding how to reconcile one's role as a business leader and a Catholic (Blasco and Zølner, 2010). However, just as in Germany, the inclusion of these marginal activities into a public realm widely known under the umbrella term 'corporate social responsibility' is only a very recent development (Antal and Sobczak, 2007).

When contrasting the uneasy relationship with philanthropic CSR in contemporary France and Germany with the strong English philanthropic tradition described earlier in this chapter, it is the importance of institutions – formal and ideational – which stands out as the factor which significantly influences the development of and approach to CSR in different countries. In England, the comparatively smaller role of the state in welfare provisioning has left more room throughout history for an unbroken tradition of corporate philanthropy. In contrast, the dominating welfare role of the French and German states have crowded out nineteenth-century philanthropic business activities, just as this composition of the mixed economy has rendered CSR an idea which is not considered relevant to the contemporary French or German context. Another contrast is the high levels of legitimacy enjoyed by the French and German states, which is matched by low legitimacy levels of the commercial sector. In England this picture is the reverse (Blasco 2010). And finally, English companies do not experience the same moral dilemmas as their French and German counterparts regarding the appropriateness of engaging in philanthropic activities, using CSR for publicity or debating business ethics more generally in the public arena. The similarities between the German and French experiences of CSR, however, suggest the way in which CSR has come to expression (or not) in each of those two countries are less down to unique national characteristics. Instead, German and French approaches to CSR – and perhaps in particular their resistance towards CSR – seem to have more to do with some of those shared institutional characteristics which have also placed them in the same Conservative welfare state regime (Esping-Andersen, 1990).

Conclusion

The investigation into philanthropic CSR has demonstrated that many commentators and CSR practitioners see a connection between nineteenth-century philanthropy and contemporary CSR. However, the cross-national comparison of England, Denmark, Sweden, Norway, Germany and France also uncovered that CSR stakeholders' views of philanthropic CSR vary cross-nationally. This is because perceptions of philanthropic CSR are very much informed by CSR stakeholders' national institutional welfare setting. Whereas in England, philanthropic CSR is experienced as an unbroken tradition still in existence today, in the remaining countries of the investigation philanthropic CSR as well as philanthropy in general is considered inappropriate and unfitting for any type of contemporary welfare state which favours an expanded and involved public sector. On the most general level the assertion can therefore be made that the likelihood of finding examples of philanthropic CSR in a specific country will depend on the composition of that country's mixed economy of welfare.

Chapter 5
CSR as Social Policy:
CSR in the Public Sector

Introduction

The focus in this chapter is the strand of corporate social responsibility which originated in the public sector and which has been developed by actors within that sector, that is, mainly central governments. This part of the history of CSR originates in the 1980s and 1990s. The analysis will uncover an aspect of CSR which sees CSR applied as a social policy tool. The chapter will also throw light on the connections between CSR and issues around social exclusion and inclusion, unemployment and employment relations. The countries under investigation are: Denmark, England, Germany and France. Sweden and Norway are not dealt with in this chapter as their national CSR agendas did not take shape until the emergence of CSR as a global issue, which will be dealt with in Chapter 6.

Denmark: CSR as a New Social Policy

Whereas in the literature on English CSR and amongst English CSR respondents it is a commonly held perception that CSR is 'nothing new' and can be traced back to various points in history, the development of CSR in Denmark is interpreted and presented in an altogether different way in the academic literature and amongst the Danish CSR respondents. There is a very widely shared consensus around the questions of when, how and why CSR originated in Denmark. The strong degree of resemblance between different people's and different authors' versions of events creates the impression that in Denmark, the history of Danish CSR is a collectively constructed national narrative. In theoretical terms, the national narrative about the history of CSR in Denmark has by now become part of what social constructivists would term the shared 'social stock of knowledge' (Berger and Luckman, 1991 (1966)). Moreover, the experienced objectivity of this narrative is continually reinforced through the 'sedimentation process' that sees new literature on CSR and new Danish CSR stakeholders take for granted and replicate the existing interpretation of events.

When the history of Danish CSR is told, its origin is repeatedly assigned, with great exactitude, to the date of 10 January 1994 (e.g. Rosdahl, 2001, Søndergård, 2002, Hardis, 2003). This was the date when the then Social Democratic cabinet Minister for Social Affairs, Karen Jespersen, launched her ministry's campaign designed to promote the idea of corporate social responsibility. The campaign was initiated in a debate article titled 'It Concerns Us All' published in one of the main Danish broadsheet newspapers (Jespersen, 10 January 1994). It was followed up by a press conference and the establishment of a 'National Network' of business leaders. The National Network were to work as direct advisors to the Minister and as CSR pioneers who were to inspire and set examples to other businesses throughout Denmark. All of these events are frequently cited in the literature as well as by Danish respondents as important milestones in the development of CSR in Denmark (Rosdahl, 2001, Søndergård, 2002, Hardis, 2003, Lund, 2003). A very apparent contrast between CSR in England and CSR in Denmark is in other words already evident. Whereas CSR is considered something which originated and developed within the commercial sector in England, CSR in Denmark has, at least since the 1990s, very much been driven by the government and from within the public sector (Lund, 2003).

Apart from agreeing about the origin of Danish CSR, the literature and Danish CSR stakeholders remain just as committed to the collective narrative when it comes to the background events leading up to the Danish government's launch of CSR in the mid-1990s. Danish CSR is explained as a reaction to the social problems of what Matten and Moon refer to as 'record levels of unemployment and dependency on the government' (Matten and Moon, 2004: 22). Hardis refers the same social problem in terms of an 'increasing amount of the "hard to place", marginalized and long-term unemployed social clients' (Hardis, 2003: 200). Søndergård (2002) elaborates further by linking the Danish government's interest in CSR with the welfare state crisis of the 1980s and the resulting experience that the welfare state had since then been under increasing pressure. Søndergård considers two types of pressures as having influenced the government's involvement in CSR. Firstly, the financial crisis and mass unemployment of the 1980s had led to new forms of social exclusion. Those individuals, who had persistently stayed out of employment throughout the decades, despite the increasingly all-encompassing active labour market measures, were by now considered near-unemployable. In the Danish policy discourse, these individuals had entered their own social category labelled 'people with reduced employment ability' (Søndergård, 2002). This part of Søndergård's analysis is backed up by many of the Danish CSR stakeholders interviewed for this book's case study, some of whom refer to a 'lost generation' of unemployed people. Respondents also recount a growing sense, particularly amongst policymakers, that successive governments had failed this generation by overestimating the effectiveness of active labour market measures on this particular social group.

The second pressure identified by Søndergård is the increasingly felt presence of globalization, which had led successive governments to pursue a policy aiming to enhance the competitiveness of the Danish economy by improving the educational levels and skill sets of its workforce (rather than giving in to the pressure of reducing wages). However, Søndergård explains how the growing demand on the Danish labour market for increasingly skilled labour also led to the heightened marginalization of people with few skills or with other forms of 'reduced employment ability'. The combined impact of these two developments was to put increasing economic pressure on the Danish welfare state's public sector as a generous provider for those out of work. Moreover, the social problem also became a labour market problem in the 1990s as the economy improved and Danish employers started experiencing difficulties with labour shortage. It was this context which motivated the government to promote the concept of 'the inclusive labour market'. Aimed at employers, the message behind the inclusive labour market agenda is that the Danish labour market must not merely focus on highly educated and skilled labourers but should be able to accommodate a broader spectrum of individuals with varying educational, personal and social skills (Søndergård, 2002). It is widely agreed both in the literature and also amongst the Danish CSR respondents that corporate social responsibility in Denmark is part and parcel of the inclusive labour market policy agenda (e.g. Holt, 1999, Søndergård, 2002, Hardis, 2003, Lund, 2003).

The role of CSR within the context of the government's inclusive labour market agenda was explicitly stated in the Ministry of Social Affairs' CSR campaign of 1994. The campaign and its 'It Concerns Us All' slogan were designed to encourage the public, and especially the commercial sector, to rethink the widely held view that the responsibility for social problems in the Danish welfare state must be firmly placed upon the government and the public sector. The government wanted to question this perceived 'traditional' sharing of responsibilities in the mixed economy of welfare (Hardis, 2003, Lund, 2003) and asked businesses to consider taking 'a more active role' (Søndergård, 2002, Hardis, 2003) in addressing the social problems associated with labour market exclusion. The difference between the government's CSR strategy and its other policy initiatives, however, had to do with the government's role. Rather than suggesting that CSR should become a regulatory matter, the government promoted the notion of 'partnerships' between the various sectors in the mixed economy and advocated this as its preferred way for businesses to carry out CSR. Consequently, the partnership concept has been closely associated with the Danish CSR agenda both in the literature and amongst CSR respondents (e.g. Rosdahl, 2001, Søndergård, 2002, Hardis, 2003, Kjaer, 2003, Lund, 2003, Knudsen, 2004).

The Danish government also invested resources into translating the international concept of 'corporate social responsibility', not just into the Danish language but also into the Danish policy context. CSR was conceptualized in a way which reflected the government's particular appropriation of CSR as a policy tool serving the inclusive labour market strategy (Hardis, 2003, Lund, 2003). Consequently, CSR came to be defined as a three-dimensional matter of preventing social exclusion from the labour market; retaining employees in danger of becoming excluded; and integrating already excluded individuals back into the labour market. The effectiveness of this labour market orientated and uniquely Danish conceptualization of CSR is evident as this definition of CSR can be seen reiterated repeatedly both in the literature on Danish CSR and amongst Danish CSR stakeholders.

This collectively agreed interpretation of the development of CSR in Denmark provides some interesting insights into the questions which this chapter is seeking to address. Firstly, CSR is clearly regarded as a relatively new phenomenon in the Danish context, where it has only been in operation since the 1990s. This perception of CSR stands in contrast to the English context, where Chapter 4 uncovered that CSR is constructed as more of a historical continuity. Secondly, in Denmark it is the government who is seen as the main initiator and driver of a national CSR agenda, whereas in England CSR is perceived as having grown organically through the activities of individual businesses operating independently from any government agenda. When it comes to explaining why CSR arose and developed, the literature and the case study's Danish CSR respondents have offered a coherent and plausible explanation which connects Danish CSR closely with the development of the Danish welfare state.

It is possible to reframe the Danish historical narrative theoretically, in terms of some of the core historical institutionalist arguments regarding policy development. It has been argued earlier that CSR can be conceptualized as an 'institutionally independent idea' in the sense that CSR is not part of any national paradigmatic institutional structures, in Denmark or elsewhere (for an elaboration on the book's theoretical framework see Chapter 2). In the history of Danish CSR, as recounted in the literature and by respondents, it is now possible to identify CSR even more specifically as the kind of idea labelled originally by Kingdon as a 'policy alternative' (Kingdon, 1995) and later appropriated by historical institutionalists such as Hall (1992) and Beland (2005). In the national narrative of the development of CSR in Denmark, CSR came about as a new policy idea designed to address the interlinked policy problems of long-term unemployment, social exclusion and a growing labour shortage. It is significant here that the government had reached a point of recognizing that its dominant policy approach to tackling the unemployment problem, through labour market activation, had not been successful in relation to the particular group of 'hard to place', marginalized individuals with reduced employment abilities. As pointed out by Hall, in his analysis of the shift from Keynesianism to Monetarism in England (1992), the timing of the realization of the shortcomings or failure of existing policies is significant, as policy alternatives are often characterized by having been available to policymakers for some time as vague policy ideas but without being taken seriously as a policy *alternative* until the existing policy path becomes clearly untenable (Hall, 1992).

The historical institutionalist approach is also helpful for reflecting on the various causal factors which can be said to have driven the Danish government to adopt CSR as a policy alternative. According to the historical accounts offered in the literature and by Danish respondents, CSR was a reaction to the social consequences of the economic welfare state crisis of the 1980s. From this perspective CSR could be said to be driven ultimately by structural, economic developments. Yet, Beland (2005) reminds us that policy alternatives, in Kingdon's meaning of the term, do not always emerge as responses to social problems. New policy ideas and policy alternatives are just as likely to emerge prior to problems, and only become effectively attached to a social problem later by policymakers or interest groups keen to promote the idea for other, mainly ideological, reasons (Beland, 2005). To pursue this argument it is worth considering whether the Danish government may have had reasons to turn to the policy idea of CSR apart from the desire to solve certain social and labour market problems.

As already mentioned, the initial governmental campaign launched CSR as part of a debate about the appropriate sharing of responsibilities amongst the sectors in the mixed economy for social problems such as social exclusion. But the government also provided its own suggestion regarding the ideal sharing of responsibilities when it argued that the government should not be left alone to solve social problems. Social problems should instead be considered a 'Common Concern' and shared across the whole of the mixed economy. In practice the government advocated the 'partnership' approach, where actors from two or more different sectors in the mixed economy collaborate in order to address various social problems. Once the analytical emphasis is put on these policy goals of the Danish government its CSR policy starts resembling more of an ideological than a problem-solving agenda. On this ideological agenda, the government is adapting CSR as a policy tool not merely for solving certain social problems of the day but more so for the purpose of fostering a shift in the public's ideological perspective on the mixed economy. In theoretical terms it can be said that the government's agenda was targeted at changing prevailing institutional mixed economy sectoral paradigms regarding the appropriate responsibility of the various mixed economy sectors. In the new ideological perspective, the responsibility for social problems is shifted from the public sector and out to other parts of the mixed economy. It might also be suggested that the long-term aim of disseminating such an ideological perspective is to legitimize a gradual retrenchment of the government's involvement in social problems or even in welfare matters in general. However, rather than being an outright retrenchment policy in disguise, the Danish CSR agenda of the mid-1990s appears more influenced by New Public Management ('NPM') thinking. This is apparent in the government's active yet non-intervening role as it promoted CSR via the means of campaigning, debating, funding projects for example setting, establishing new institutions, and by appealing to businesses instead of dictating behaviour through regulatory measures. This is in accordance with the NPM ideals for governments to focus on 'steering rather than rowing' (Osborne and Gaebler, 1992). Another indication is the partnership approach to CSR advocated by the Danish government. This is a CSR model which is also often associated with NPM theories, as in the partnerships the public sector mostly provides the framework whilst non-public organizations provide the actual projects and services (Evers, 2003).

This take on the development of CSR in Denmark is given some credibility by the account of one particularly significant Danish respondent. The quote below is an extract from the interview with Hanne, a policymaker for the Danish government who works in the department which has the lead on CSR. Hanne is in the middle of her narrative of the history of CSR in Denmark, which is significantly informed by her own long-standing professional involvement with the Danish CSR policy agenda. Hanne has already pointed to the influencing factors of the economic welfare state crisis of the 1980s and its social problem of the long-term unemployed, which persisted into the 1990s even as the economy improved. Here she carries on:

> The other main explanation [for the development of CSR in Denmark] can be found in the debate, which was very prevalent at the time, about the limitations of the public sector in terms of its abilities to solve all problems and especially its ability to solve all problems alone. There was talk of the 'legitimacy crisis of the public sector', and its crisis of efficiency. That was about its economic limitations and so on. So people [in government] started to look for new approaches to understanding how to solve some of the heavy social problems, amongst other things and not least the issue of social exclusion.

Although Hanne has pointed to the structural economic situation as influential for the development of CSR in Denmark, Hanne clearly also regards CSR as part of a political and ideological agenda. From such a perspective the social problems, which CSR was promoted as the solution to, are not so much the driving factors as they are part of the political practice known in historical institutionalism as 'framing'. The notion of framing is based on the argument, reiterated by many historical institutionalists, that social problems are not exogenous to politics but are instead socially constructed – or framed – as social problems in order to legitimize a particular new policy idea or a policy alternative (Beland, 2005, Taylor-Gooby, 2005, Starke, 2006). Goul-Andersen (2002), for example, points out how governments in many welfare states have legitimized reforms of public pensions by framing the policies as responses to an 'ageing crisis' (Andersen, 2002). This is very similar to the manner in which the Danish government legitimized CSR as a matter of responding to a long-standing unemployment and social exclusion 'crisis'. The effectiveness of this framing strategy is evident in the way in which several Danish respondents can be seen expressing the perception that the unemployment situation of the 1980s and 1990s was also a crisis situation which not only needed a policy response but which warranted a policy innovation to properly deal with the circumstances. Moreover, the Danish government also framed the unemployment crisis as a *collective* social problem, thereby paving the way for its ideological, New Public Management-inspired agenda of changing prevailing mixed economy sectoral paradigms and thereby shifting the overall balance in the mixed economy.

Apart from the influence from the political discourse of NPM it is also possible at this point to identify the CSR discourse which appears to have influenced the Danish policymakers the most in the 1990s. As outlined in Chapter 3, the partnership approach to CSR and the related NPM perspective on the role of the government in relation to CSR (and the mixed economy of welfare in general) are directly associated with the social democratic CSR discourse. But the influence of the social democratic CSR discourse is also recognizable in the perception – or framing – of CSR as a solution to the welfare state crisis. In this discourse CSR is one way of ameliorating the perceived overload of the public sector if governments can persuade businesses to contribute to solving social problems. Finally, the idea that social problems are a 'common concern' or a collective responsibility also has undertones of the contractarian foundations of the social democratic CSR discourse, in which all members of society, individuals as well as organizations, the government as well as the rest of the mixed economy, are social stakeholders with social responsibilities.

In the historical narratives found in the literature and told by respondents another interesting insight into the important drivers of the historical development emerges. This is related to agency. It has already been argued that the main actor in the development of CSR in Denmark since the 1990s has been the Danish government. However, it is noticeable that the vast majority of the historical accounts considered for this analysis have put a significant emphasis on the individual agency of the then minister for social affairs, Karen Jespersen. Her personal contribution to the development is repeatedly referred to as part of the reason why the CSR campaign was taken seriously by other parts of the government, by the main players in the Danish commercial sector and by the public in general. This lends support to the theoretical argument made in Chapter 2, that what was termed 'influencing individuals' can be as important for bringing about policy change as the more structural factors usually drawn on in historical institutionalism to explain change. It is clear, especially from the way in which the respondents describe Karen Jespersen's efforts, that Karen Jespsersen can be considered what Kingdon terms a 'policy entrepreneur' (Kingdon, 1995), as she made the most of the 'moment of political opportunity' where the timing was right for a new policy idea to be introduced, as a policy alternative, into the exiting institutional settings (Kingdon, 1995). Karen Jespersen also fits the profile of Hansen and King's notion of a 'powerful actor' (Hansen and King, 2001), who as a cabinet minister had the institutional power to translate CSR into a significant governmental policy, and who had perhaps also a personal interest in promoting the policy idea of CSR, for example to heighten her own political profile (Hansen and King, 2001). Further evidence of Karen Jespersen's powerful institutional position and her personal will to use this power in a maverick way is given by several respondents as they recount how she famously and publicly insulted unions and business associations when she set up the National Network of business leaders. The fact that the National Network reported directly to the minister was a break from the Danish institutional tradition in which unions and business associations would, as social partners, expect to be consulted and included in such a new institutional establishment. However, many respondents can be seen deducing that Karen Jespersen, as an experienced politician, had calculated that these social partners, and the unions in particular, would be resistant to the idea of business leaders being so closely involved in the policy process. She therefore deliberately chose to bypass these obstacles or, in historical institutionalist terms, these 'veto players' (Immergut, 1992, Bonoli, 2001).

The extent to which Karen Jespersen and the Ministry of Social Affairs succeeded in establishing a new policy path with the launch of the Danish CSR policy agenda in 1994 becomes evident as the development is followed up until the present day. A significant event in the history of Danish CSR was the change of government from Social Democratic to Liberal in 2001. Respondents recount how the new, right-leaning government at first attempted to dismantle the CSR policy agenda in various ways. Most noticeable was the conceptual re-launch of CSR, from having been translated directly from English into Danish as 'the social responsibility of businesses' to being now renamed 'the social *engagement* of businesses'. It was made clear that the aim of this re-conceptualization was to signal that the new government considered CSR a strictly voluntary and discretionary matter for businesses and it did not, like the previous government, regard CSR as an outright social obligation or responsibility. To use the terminology of the different CSR discourses presented in Chapter 3, the re-conceptualization was an attempt to shift the official definition of CSR away from the existing contractarian perspective inspired by the social democratic CSR discourse and towards the more libertarian liberal CSR discourse. Another strongly felt change was the initiative to take the central administrative lead on CSR away from the Ministry of Social Affairs and to give it instead to the newly established Ministry for Employment. This was a way of signalling that the new government was putting its emphasis on CSR's usefulness for solving labour market issues whilst it was less inclined to pursue CSR as a policy for solving social problems. Other immediate changes mentioned by respondents include the discontinuation of funding for some of the government-sponsored CSR projects and a general decline in the government's enthusiasm for, involvement in and explicit appearance on the CSR agenda. However, despite these attempts, respondents report how the Liberal government was soon made to back down somewhat on its initial strategy. It transpired that Karen Jespersen and the previous government had established a powerful and resilient institution in the National Network of business leaders. Having spent seven years as very publicly visible 'CSR champions' and as enthusiastic example setters, these business leaders did not receive the new government's stance on CSR positively. Instead they made it clear that they believed that CSR is the future; that they wanted to continue working on this basis, and preferably with the government. Many respondents report how this protest from some of the most high profile business leaders in Denmark made the government highly uncomfortable, especially as it, as a Liberal government, wanted to be seen as the guardian of business interests. The overall result, according to several respondents, has been that the Danish government's CSR agenda, since its initiation in 1994, has come across to most CSR stakeholders as a consistent continuation of the path more so than of changed directions. This story of the staying power of a policy agenda once cemented in policy institutions confirms the argument made frequently in historical institutionalism regarding the resilience of institutions once established, and the difficulty of reversing the path dependent dynamics of already existing policies (Pierson, 1994). The story also confirms Cox' argument that governments intentions to change policy direction can encounter obstacles at the ideational institutional level, where the path dependency of ideas such as CSR can prove just as resilient as formally established institutions (Cox, 2004).

The definition of CSR as a labour market issue in Denmark is still apparent in the ways that CSR is practiced by Danish businesses today. One such approach is the work placements for unemployed people, which will be the focus of attention in part III of the book. Mentoring, which is often part of work placement programs, is another measure for unemployed people considered a way in which Danish companies exercise CSR. Another aspect of labour market related CSR in Denmark concerns the already employed. This way of practicing CSR is very frequently mentioned by Danish respondents. Employee CSR can take the form of occupational benefits such as the provisioning of child care on the theme of equal opportunities, and encouraging a healthy life style for employees by providing gyms, subsidizing health club memberships or providing healthy food. But employee CSR can also relate to the theme of preventing social exclusion. CSR measures with this latter focus in mind can see employers provide counseling and other forms of help for employees suffering from problem with substance abuse, mental health or stress-related conditions. A final example of a labour market measure is the so-called 'flexjob'. This measure is frequently referred to by Danish respondents as a form of CSR. Flexjob is a measure designed to overcome either unemployment or threat of unemployment. The flexjob arrangement sees companies receiving government subsidies in return for employing people or retaining employees that have been deemed unable to work in what is referred to as 'the ordinary labour market'. The eligibility for a flexjob is related to health problems, whether physical or psychological.

The Danish government's CSR agenda has evolved so that it now includes a broader set of social issues and a wider range of CSR practices. This development reflects the general widening of the CSR agenda outside the Danish context – an aspect which will be dealt with in Chapter 6.

England: CSR as the Revival of a Lost Tradition

One of the most noticeable contrasts between Danish and English perceptions of how CSR arose and has developed is found in the existence in Denmark of a coherent and internally consistent 'national narrative' about CSR in which the government plays the leading role, whereas in England there exists a slightly more diverse and variable set of historical analyses. As demonstrated in Chapter 4, one of the most commonly evoked themes in the English literature and amongst English respondents is the sense that CSR, as it is known today, is a continuation of a long-standing historical tradition which can be traced back to at least the nineteenth century. Within this long-term historical interpretation, certain forces within the commercial sector are the main drivers of CSR. The English government plays only a minor role, if any. Indeed, a vast amount of the literature on English CSR does not include considerations of the role of the government, and especially not as a driver of the English CSR agenda (as also argued by Moon, 2004). Similarly, most English respondents do not make any references to any specific governmental inputs when they consider the historical development of CSR. This, however, does not reflect a situation in which the English government is altogether uninvolved in CSR. As the following analysis will show, the English government has in recent years become increasingly visible on the CSR agenda, although perhaps less so as the main driver of the development than as an important participant.

Moon (2004) is one of the few authors writing about CSR within the English context who has focused on the government's role in relation to CSR. Like other historical analyses, Moon also traces CSR back to the philanthropic activities of nineteenth century industrialists, and his account of the further development of CSR in England also sees CSR as a form of social provisioning being phased out by the gradual expansion of the welfare state. However, Moon sees the decades between 1970 and 2000 as a period characterized by dramatic changes in the social role of British business, with the growth of CSR being one example of this development (Moon, 2004). The cause of this major change was, in Moon's analysis, the welfares state crisis of the 1970s and 1980s. Moon sees as particularly relevant to the development of CSR what he considers the accompanying 'crisis of governance'. Since this crisis, successive English governments, whether Conservative or Labour, have followed broadly the same strategy of narrowing the public sector's responsibility for the direct delivery of social goods whilst encouraging instead market provision. At the same time successive governments have also sought to reduce public expectations of the responsibility of governments by continuously arguing for the social responsibilities of the family and individuals (Moon, 2004). To rephrase Moon's analysis in historical institutionalist terms, English governments have, in addition to the changes on the formal institutional level of the mixed economy of welfare, also pursued a reinforcing strategy on the ideational institutional level. Moon sees these general political strategies as significant to the development of CSR in England because the withdrawal of the public sector has created a space and a need for replacement social provisioning, whether from the non-profit sector, from commercial sector providers or from a model such as CSR.

But Moon also documents a more direct role played by English governments as drivers of the growth of CSR. Moon goes back to the 1980s as he relates how the then Conservative government reacted to urban riots, inner-city decay and spiralling unemployment by encouraging British business leaders to engage with and share in solving these social problems. The Secretary of State for the Environment, Michael Heseltine, is considered a particularly important actor in this context as he organized inner-city tours for business leaders, and addressed in speeches the 'sense of responsibility' amongst powerful businesses and the need for the private sector 'to play a role again, the way it did more conspicuously a century ago' (cited in Moon, 2004: 8). More specifically, businesses were encouraged to provide training and work experience opportunities for the unemployed and to participate in urban regeneration projects – referred to as 'Community Action Programmes' – in partnership with the government. The government offered subsidies for job creation projects and founded organizations in the non-profit sector working specifically to stimulate public–private partnerships. One of these organizations, Business in the Community, has since then grown to become the single largest business association for CSR (Moon, 2004).

It is interesting to note certain similarities between Moon's analysis of the growth of CSR in England in the last three decades and the Danish 'national narrative' about the origin and growth of Danish CSR since the 1990s. In both cases, CSR is seen to have arisen in the context of the welfare state crisis of the 1970s and 1980s. Once again it becomes apparent that the historical development of CSR is intrinsically linked with the development of the mixed economy of welfare. CSR is also viewed as part of the ideological agenda aiming to transfer governmental responsibility for welfare provisioning to other parts of the mixed economy. The Danish and English governments were in other words both promoting CSR from a New Public Management perspective just as both framed their arguments within the social democratic CSR discourse. Another similarity can be seen in the two governments' active role in advancing the idea of business' social responsibilities, manifested in the championing of the idea by high profile cabinet ministers, such as Michael Hesseltine in the English case. On the more specific policy level, the argument that the commercial sector has social responsibilities was also evoked by both Danish and English governments in order to enlist businesses to help the government solve the issue of unemployment and its related social problems. Finally, the model of implementation promoted by the two governments revolves around similar ideas of partnerships between the commercial sector and the public sector.

There are also some notable differences, however. The English government of the 1980s does not seem to have used the exact term 'corporate social responsibility' when it encouraged English businesses to become more involved in solving social problems. In contrast, the Danish government composed its appeal to businesses in 1994 as an explicit CSR agenda. Furthermore, in Denmark, the suggestion that businesses should get involved in solving social problems was articulated as a novel idea; a break with a tradition which had hitherto seen the welfare *state* – that is, the public sector – take almost all responsibility for the social welfare of its citizens. In England, politicians used the opposite framing tactics, presenting instead the idea of businesses taking responsibility for social problems as a revival of a lost noble tradition which had erroneously become disassociated with the present in contemporary perceptions of how responsibility should be distributed within the mixed economy of welfare. By evoking the image of a better bygone era, English politicians also reinforced the Conservative ideological perspective that the evolution of the welfare state had not been an altogether positive development.

In the English policy context, CSR was in other words not treated as a novel policy idea or as a policy alternative in the same way that it was in Denmark. But it was treated as a policy solution to persistent social problems.

As Moon traces the government's role in relation to the development of CSR in England further into the 1990s, Moon emphasizes the striking continuity between the Conservative and the succeeding Labour government's stance on CSR. From its first year in power in 1997, the New Labour government made clear its intentions of boosting public–private partnerships, especially in the area of education (Moon, 2004, Farnsworth, 2004). CSR has since then become an explicit governmental policy agenda. This has been most visible in the appointment in 2000 of a Minister for CSR and the related assignation of CSR as a specific policy area to the Department of Trade and Industry the same year (since then renamed to, most recently, Department for Business Innovation and Skills).

Considering the many similarities between the ways in which the Danish and the English governments have adopted the idea of CSR, it is not surprising that there are also similarities between the kinds of CSR measures associated with the social policy strand of CSR's historical development. The most evident similarity is the use of the partnership approach to tackling social problems. Yet within this shared approach there are also notable differences. For at start, whereas in Denmark the type of social problems to which CSR gets applied all centre around issues of exclusion from the labour market, the partnership approach is applied to a much wider range of social problems in England. Exclusion from the labour market is just one issue. Others include homelessness, area deprivation and social exclusion in education. Education is an area that is particularly strongly promoted and supported by the government. Consequently, partnerships between businesses and schools are also one of the most widely exercised types of CSR partnerships, as evidenced in the reported overwhelming popularity of this type of CSR amongst Business in the Community members. As a result, social policy commentators have noticed a considerable increase in the involvement of businesses in the education sector (Farnsworth, 2006a). Another difference relates to the balance of involvement between different actors in the partnership. These differences will be discussed in more detail in Chapter 8, where it will become apparent that once the focus moves to the practical implementation of the similar idea of partnerships, deep rooted national institutional differences emerge which influence the ways in which the partnerships are designed.

When English respondents consider the role of the government in relation to CSR not many go back as far as the Conservative government's initiatives in the 1980s described by Moon. Instead most see the establishment of CSR as a governmental policy area in 2000 as the beginning of governmental involvement in CSR in England. By that time the English CSR agenda had evolved so that it covered a broader set of social issues other than partnerships between the sectors in the English mixed economy. As was the case in Denmark, this development reflects the general widening of the CSR agenda outside the English context – an aspect which will be covered in Chapter 6.

Germany and France: Emphasizing Social Responsibility for the Employed

In Chapter 4 it transpired that the philanthropic strand of CSR has not been widely embraced in Germany or France, largely due to the existence of strong institutional barriers against the idea of philanthropy itself. It was also reported that CSR in general has arrived late to these countries with until recently little engagement from businesses, government and academia. Part of the explanation for this situation can be found in the tendency amongst French and German scholars, as well as business people and government representatives, to consider the idea and concept of CSR an Anglo-Saxon invention, whose associated (philanthropic) activities are therefore also only appropriate in institutional contexts such as Britain and the US. But there is also another important reason for the late arrival of an explicitly stated national CSR agenda in conservative welfare states such as France and Germany (for an elaboration on the idea of welfare state regimes see Chapter 2). Many commentators agree that there was for a long time a consensus amongst government representatives and business people in both Germany and France that the idea of 'corporate social responsibility' was superfluous in these countries because German and French businesses were already exercising sufficient social responsibility. This perception was based on the still widely held understanding that a company's social responsibility relates first and foremost to its role as an employer (Maignan and Ferrell, 2001, Hiss, 2009). The rejection of philanthropic business activities is not, in other words, a rejection of the idea that firms have social responsibilities.

In both Germany and France there is an expectation that the social responsibilities of a firm are directed towards its employees. Studies have shown that French and German consumers regard the social responsibilities of companies as a matter of providing occupation, giving employees considerable benefits, ensuring a pleasant working environment and cultivating positive social interactions in the work place (Maignan and Ferrell, 2003). And it has been pointed out by various commentators that the 'social' element of CSR tends to be understood by both French and German speaking CSR stakeholders as relating to a company's employees or its 'internal community' of stakeholders rather than to an external community, such as is the tendency in England and other Anglo-Saxon countries (Antal and Sobczak, 2007).

It is because of the German and French understanding of CSR as concerning employee relationships that there has been a tendency to consider CSR irrelevant to these countries. This is on the basis that employee relationships are already extensively safeguarded by a combination of legal requirements, tripartite social partner structures and societal norms (Antal et al., 2009). Both Germany and France are strongly regulated in the field of labour relations when compared with other countries, and with Anglo-Saxon countries in particular. German and French firms have a high level of involvement of labour representatives in negotiations over working conditions. Employers also take a comparatively high level of responsibility for areas such as vocational training of their workers compared with other countries. It is this corporatist institutional set-up which has for a long time led potential German and French CSR stakeholder to take the view that CSR – interpreted as voluntary initiatives taken by employers to improve their relationship with their stakeholders – is unnecessary in an institutional context such as the German and French. The view is that many of those initiatives that are considered CSR in other countries are already in Germany and France a legal requirement or else covered by the institutional norms (Antal et al., 2009). An example of this attitude to CSR emerges in the German submission to the EU Commission's compilation document of national CSR policies. Here, the German government states in its introduction that:

> In terms of social commitment and social and health protection by business which extends beyond statutory requirements it should be noted that there is already a relatively dense regulatory system in Germany which leaves little scope for further activity. (EU-COM, 2007: 18)

CSR researchers interested in cross-national differences have theorized the employee-centred CSR orientation found in countries such as Germany and France. Matten and Moon (2008) first developed the thesis that one should not so much consider CSR as being absent in countries such as France and Germany, but instead one can consider CSR as existing implicitly. The perception that CSR is absent in traditional European countries only appears when those countries are compared with a country such as the US. Here CSR is more visible because it is explicitly debated and addressed in academia and by the business community. And when a company chooses to engage with CSR in the US, its activities tend to be explicitly labelled and referred to as CSR activities. In countries such as France and Germany, Matten and Moon argue, corporate social responsibility exists albeit more implicitly. CSR is a responsibility which is assigned by 'the entirety of a country's formal and informal institutions' and it is expressed simply through the compliance with values, norms and legal requirements (Matten and Moon, 2008). Matten and Moon explains the cross-national difference in approaches to CSR by linking their distinctions between 'explicit' and 'implicit' CSR to Hall and Soskice's variety of capitalism theory (Hall and Soskice, 2001) (explained in Chapter 2). Whereas explicit CSR is predominant in liberal market economies such as the US', coordinated market economies such as the German and French are argued to foster mainly implicit CSR (Matten and Moon, 2008). In the US, for example, where labour regulation is at a minimum, CSR is also a voluntary matter for individual businesses. Some firms may choose not to engage with the idea that their responsibilities go beyond the financial and legal. Those who do go beyond the legal minimum are on this basis considered socially responsible. In contrast, firms in coordinated economies are more socially embedded and therefore they are already institutionally programmed to consider themselves social contributors. For a firm, showing consideration for its employees is already a legal as well as a normative minimum, and that is why any such initiatives are unlikely to warrant the label 'CSR'.

Seen from the perspective of the implicit/explicit thesis, CSR was already there in Germany and France, before any explicitly stated national CSR agenda was formed and before German or French companies would refer to their behaviour as a matter of having taken on board the new idea of 'corporate social responsibility'. This also lends strength to the argument that the social policy strand of CSR is a long-standing tradition in Germany and France, only the socially responsible behaviour of employers towards employees has been an institutional requirement (both formally and informally) rather than a voluntary option merely encouraged by the government. This makes the conservative welfare states' CSR experience different from England, where 'explicit CSR' in the form of philanthropic business activities are a strong business tradition. The German and French experience is also different from the Danish CSR history, where CSR was launched as an explicit government agenda and also explicitly linked to social policy issues already in the mid-1990s. There are, however, some parallels between the employee focus in the conservative welfare states of Germany and France and the CSR focus in Denmark. As mentioned earlier in this chapter, an important dimension of Danish CSR consists of employers taking social responsibility for their employees. The official government emphasis might be on vulnerable or at-risk employees rather than on employees in general, however when speaking to CSR stakeholders in Denmark one gets a strong sense of a deeply entrenched consensus that employees in general are one of the most important stakeholder groups for whom employers should take social responsibility. It is this taken-for-granted employee concern, which also in Denmark appears to have existed implicitly prior to the introduction of an explicit CSR agenda, which Denmark shares with Germany and France. Although these countries belong to different welfare regimes, their similarities in this area make sense when seen from the perspective of the varieties of capitalism thesis, where all three countries belong to the coordinated market economy model (Hall and Soskice, 2001).

Matten and Moon's thesis is widely supported in the literature on CSR in Germany, France and other European countries (Antal et al., 2009, Hiss, 2009, Tengblad and Ohlsson, 2009). Their interpretation has been applied extensively to explain cross-national differences, especially between those countries commonly considered CSR behind laggers and CSR front runners. More recently researchers have also used the implicit/explicit CSR thesis to identify certain changes in many of those countries where CSR has traditionally been of the implicit variety, towards more explicit CSR measures (Tengblad and Ohlsson, 2009, Hiss, 2009). Such a change has been observed in Germany in recent years, although this is a very new development, taking place only in the last half of the 2000–2010 decade. It is also characteristic for the case of Germany that the moves towards more explicit CSR measures have taken place predominantly within the social policy stream of CSR. In Germany, there are signs that an explicit social policy strand of CSR has been initiated. In 2009 the Federal Ministry of Labour and Social Affairs set up a National CSR Forum comprising of 44 CSR experts from business, unions, non-governmental organizations and the political sector. The stated aim of this forum was to participate in the development of a German national CSR strategy. In 2010 the German government then launched an official 'Action Plan for CSR' which is explicitly stated as being Germany's national CSR strategy (German-Federal-Government, 2010). The action plan promotes social initiatives that involve businesses and which are modelled on the partnership idea similar to those CSR programmes found in England and Denmark. The objectives of the German CSR programmes are also similar to the English and Danish programmes as they focus on tackling current labour market issues such as unemployment, training and employability, socially responsible restructuring, diversity at work, work place health promotion and work/life balance.

When investigating what has made the German government overcome its initial scepticism towards the very idea of corporate social responsibility to now being fully engaged in promoting CSR, a number of explanations are suggested in the literature. Of those explanations that are related to the social policy CSR measures, one points to the unemployment crisis following from the economic crisis at the beginning of the 2000s. According to Antal et al. (2009) this crisis led the German government to ask the commercial sector for help in tackling the social issues arising from this new situation. The authors report that 'public policymakers called directly on the private sector to protect employment and to create new jobs and apprenticeships' (Antal et al., 2009: 291). Subsequently partnerships were created which were designed to stimulate 'new and innovative solutions' to the social and labour market problems of the time (Antal et al., 2009). Also considered important are changes that were already taking place in the German mixed economy of welfare in recent decades. These changes have seen a redefinition of roles and responsibilities of business and society, particularly in the area of social problems where the public sector has over the years increasingly made use of commercial sector providers (Antal et al., 2009).

There are seemingly many strong comparisons which can be drawn between the above German narrative and the Danish and English narratives about the development of the (explicit) social policy strand of CSR in those countries. The same political and ideological developments appear to have been taking place in Germany as in Denmark and England, seeing politicians increasingly interested in remixing the balance of the mixed economy, particularly towards drawing more on the resources of commercial sector. And as in England and Denmark, the economic troubles which Germany encountered in the beginning of the century appear to have provided politicians with a convenient 'window of opportunity' in which they could promote the already existing idea of CSR, now framed as a viable policy alternative. The framing technique also appears remarkably similar, with CSR as the policy solution to a problem framed as an 'unemployment crisis'. Also similar are the CSR partnership measures and their promotion as 'new and innovative' solutions. A final similarity to be mentioned here is the role which the German government envisages for itself in the realm of CSR. Rather than suggesting regulation or active public sector involvement, the emphasis in the government's action plan is on promoting, encouraging, raising awareness, advising, information gathering and dissemination, coordinating, and providing the legal framework (German-Federal-Government, 2010). This terminology is recognizable as being informed ideologically by New Public Management thinking, with its ideals for governments to focus on 'steering rather than rowing' (Osborne and Gaebler, 1992).

Comparing France and Germany, the German social policy strand of CSR is the one that has undergone the most change in recent years. The German social policy strand of CSR has gone from existing predominantly in implicit form, in the shape of formal and informal institutional requirements for businesses to behave in a socially responsible way mainly towards its employees, to having recently been formalized into explicit measures – based on the partnership model – concerned with labour market issues relating also to the unemployed. France has also seen its national CSR agenda emerge as a more explicit policy concern in recent years. However, this development has predominantly been driven by the CSR strand related to globalization, which shall be dealt with in Chapter 6.

Conclusion

The investigation into the strand of CSR which is being developed by national governments in countries such as Denmark, England and Germany has firstly put into a historical context the relationship between CSR and social issues such as social exclusion and inclusion, unemployment and employment relations. But the investigation has also uncovered some important findings about the potential of the idea of CSR when it is attached to a political agenda. The similarities between the English, Danish, and German origins of the explicit social policy CSR agenda have confirmed what is already known in the literature, that political enthusiasm for New Public Management policy ideas is a trend which is not confined to one or two countries, but which has instead informed the policymaking of welfare politicians in several countries in recent years. The investigation here has demonstrated that the notion of CSR is frequently used as a policy tool by national policymakers wishing to consolidate this ideological development. This aspect of CSR will be explored further in Chapter 8, where Danish and English CSR inclusion projects are analysed in detail.

Chapter 6

CSR, Globalization and Anti-globalization: CSR and the Non-profit Sector

Introduction

The focus in this chapter is the strand of corporate social responsibility which originated in the non-profit sector and which has been advanced primarily by actors within that sector, that is, non-governmental organizations and social movements. This part of the history of CSR gained momentum around the turn of the new millennium. The analysis will explore the connection between CSR and globalization. Particular attention will be paid to the significance of conflict between different types of CSR stakeholders for the progression of an international CSR agenda. The countries under investigation are: England, Denmark, Sweden and Norway, Germany and France.

Globalization and the Emergence of an International CSR Agenda

The third strand of the history of CSR is the most recent input into the combined story of CSR told in this book. It is different from the two historical strands addressed so far in that this development has not been driven primarily by commercial sector actors, nor has it been driven primarily by governments and its public sectors. The historical progression of CSR that will be analysed in this chapter is part of the advance in recent decades of multiple developments that are commonly referred to under the umbrella term of globalization (see Yeates, 1999). A significant share of contemporary CSR agendas in West European countries have been influenced by globalization and more specifically by the tension that exists between, on the one hand, economic globalization and the related growing political power of large multinational corporations, and, on the other hand, anti-globalization social movements and general anti-globalization sentiments amongst citizens and consumers. As such, this strand of the historical development of CSR has been driven first and foremost by NGOs and civil society activists. On this basis one can argue that although these actors' fight against globalization takes place predominantly on the international arena, the 'globalization strand' of CSR's history is driven predominantly from within the non-profit sector. Yet, as will become apparent, other sectors and actors have also played a significant role in this development.

It is widely agreed in the literature and also amongst many of the respondents in this study that the social phenomenon known as globalization has had a significant impact on the development of CSR in recent years (Ruggie, 2002, Knudsen, 2004, Farnsworth, 2004, Crowther and Rayman-Bacchus, 2004, Sadler, 2004, Midttun, 2006). Issues around economic, political, ideological, institutional, technological and cultural globalization and its impact on welfare states are already hotly debated in the welfare state literature, from the predictions of future welfare state convergence around minimum levels of social protection (Ohmae, 1992, Mishra, 1999, Teeple, 2000) to the weakening of nation states relative to the growing power of transnational corporations (Farnsworth, 2004, Bridgen and Meyer, 2005) and local and international loci of governance (Jessop, 2004, Goodwin et al., 2005). Many of these same concerns about the effects of globalization are raised in the CSR literature. Crowther and Rayman-Bacchus (2004), for example, refer to the powerlessness of nation-states against large multinational corporations who are now dictating foreign and domestic policies according to their needs and without concern for their social and environmental surroundings (Crowther and Rayman-Bacchus, 2004). Similarly, Ruggie (2002), considers the 'victims' of globalization to be 'the national social bargains' (Ruggie, 2002: 29) as globalization has led to a 'weakening of rules' intended to promote social objectives such as poverty reduction, human rights, labour standards and the environment (Ruggie, 2002: 30). The view amongst such authors is that these negative experiences of globalization have been crucial to the growth of CSR in recent years as this growth has been underpinned by anti-globalization sentiments. NGOs and other forms of social movements are seen as key agents of change in this context. They have translated the growing anti-globalization sentiments into active counter-movements against economic and politically neo-liberal globalization and for different models of corporate social responsibility.

Amongst the key manifestations of the reaction against globalization mentioned by the CSR stakeholders interviewed for the case study in this book and seen as relevant to the development of CSR are the demonstrations against the World Trade Organization's ministerial conference in Seattle in 1999 and, more generally, the rise of environmentalism over the last couple of decades. The Internet is also mentioned by both academic writers (Crowther and Rayman-Bacchus, 2004) and many respondents as having been an important tool in the hands of anti-globalization activists as this new technology enabled activists to disseminate information about corporate misconducts both fast and to a worldwide audience, thereby also spreading and enhancing anti-globalization and anti-corporate sentiment. Finally, CSR commentators as well as respondents take the view that already existing concerns about the negative social impacts of economic globalization were further strengthened when corporate scandals, such as the collapse of Enron, Anderson and Worldcom in 2002, exposed firstly the extent of corruption, fraud and corporate misbehaviour amongst multinational businesses, and secondly its often detrimental effects on innocent individuals and finally the lack of regulatory protection against such occurrences (Crowther and Rayman-Bacchus, 2004, Sadler, 2004). Christina, who works for an English business association as a national level policy maker, is just one respondent who highlights such events as she argues for the influence of globalization upon the development of CSR:

> But why is CSR suddenly on the map? It's because, probably in the last 10, 12, maybe 15 years, there has been a bit more of a spotlight on business in terms of business impact across the world. People's perception of environmental issues coming to the fore. Labour, social issues coming to the fore around the world, helped by things like globalization, the spread of the Internet, you know, the greater access that people have to information. So the spotlight on what business is doing has increased. [...] And I think it's because of NGO activity. I think it's because there have been some pretty bad business failures. There's been some spectacular things that have happened, where people have thought: 'oooh, isn't big business bad!'. You know, Enron, you know, accounting scandals. That's about lack of transparency and honesty.

Within the broad social movement against globalization, the aspect which is most relevant to the growth of CSR is the anti-globalization movement's objections against the diminished accountability, transparency and, ultimately, regulation of businesses. NGOs and activists began to demand that corporations be held accountable for their impacts on society and not just considered beneficial to society based on their economic contribution. As part of that demand, NGOs began to put pressure on governments, at both national and international levels, for more intervention into and regulation of the affairs of businesses. And increasingly, NGOs used the discourse of corporate social responsibility to frame these demands to businesses and governments (Ruggie, 2002, Sadler, 2004).

In the literature on CSR, it has become an increasingly accepted axiom that the growth of CSR in recent years can be explained as a response from businesses to mounting 'pressures', mainly from civil society but sometimes also from governments (Pryce, 2002, Lund, 2003, Macleod and Lewis, 2004, Midttun, 2006, Shamir, 2008). However, when this interpretation is mentioned in only a cursory manner, often as one line in an introduction, it can simplify the extent to which 'globalization CSR' developed not simply as a one way cause and effect but rather emerged out of the dynamic tension between pressures and counter-pressures. This becomes particularly apparent when speaking to CSR stakeholders working from within this space of tension. Respondents, and especially those working at national and international levels, recount how the continuing pressures from NGOs and other pressure groups for more CSR and more governmental regulation has been continuously met with strong resistance from businesses and with efficient lobbying by their business associations of national and international governments against any interventionist measures. Instead the commercial sector as a whole insisted on the importance of leaving businesses to pursue their economic goals under minimum regulatory restraints, and on the sufficiency of self-regulation by businesses for the purpose of minimizing any adverse social or environmental impacts (Macleod and Lewis, 2004). Meanwhile, international governance organizations responded to the dual pressures from NGOs and business associations mostly by acting as neutral conflict mediators. International governance initiatives such as the OECD guidelines of 2000, the UN global compact of 2000 (UN, 2000), and EU Commission communications of 2002 and 2006 (EU-COM, 2002, EU-COM, 2006) largely reflect these actors' attempts to find an official approach to CSR that could be acceptable to both sides of the debate. Denise, who works for the EU as a policy maker in the area of CSR, provides an interesting insight into how the EU Commission let its official stance on CSR be dependent on the outcome of a 'multi-stakeholder forum' hosted by the Commission in 2001 and in which the Commission acted merely as a facilitator of the proceedings:

> The consensus report is essentially defined by what businesses will accept. Surprising unions to some extent. NGO's particularly had great ambitions for CSR. [They] were looking for, I think, the European Commission to start regulating and getting very involved and go beyond simply this definition of saying [CSR is] voluntary. Business, on the other hand, wouldn't budge much, shall we say. And if it's a consensus report, [laughs]. that's, very much how it gets there. I mean, I think that we feel that business could actually have been a bit more constructive, to be honest with you. And personally I think that it would have been in their own interests to be seen to be a bit more constructive. I'm not sure how strategically intelligent it is to simply be negative. But anyway, they know what they're doing and respond to what their members want, so who am I to judge, to some extent.

It is clear from Denise's quote that although the forum was intended to include the views of multiple different CSR stakeholders, it effectively became a negotiation process between two opposing perspectives on CSR represented by NGOs and business associations. Moreover, the successful effort by businesses to win the argument about whether or not CSR should be regulated has until now had the lasting effect that the EU Commission remains committed to CSR as a voluntary activity, as evident in the Commission's official definition of CSR:

> Corporate social responsibility (CSR) is a concept whereby companies integrate social and environmental concerns in their business operations and in their interaction with their stakeholders on a voluntary basis (EU-COM, 2006: 2)

This EU emphasis on CSR as a voluntary activity has again had a knock-on effect upon national governmental approaches to CSR, as most governments of EU member states have, at least officially, adopted the EU definition of CSR.

The particular types of CSR promoted on the global CSR agenda all reflect the current compromise between the parties in this conflict. Globalization CSR measures include environmental and supply chain management, fair trade and issues around human rights and labour rights. An important tool for NGOs and policy makers alike in promoting such CSR measures has been the concept of 'codes of conduct'. These are basic principles of socially responsible behaviour, which businesses are encouraged to adhere to in the absence of governmental regulation (see for example Raiborn and Payne, 1990, Ruggie, 2002, Whitehouse, 2003, Logsdon and Wood, 2005). The UN Global Compact (UN, 2000), where companies agree, on a voluntary basis, to adhere to certain principles in the areas of human rights, labour, the environment and anti-corruption, is an example of a CSR measure based on the idea of codes of conduct. One could argue that whilst NGOs and civil society activists have had to accept that governmental actors are currently more susceptible to the pressure from businesses not to make CSR a matter of regulation than to the pressure from NGOs to regulate more, NGOs have concentrated their efforts to push for change on the ideational institutional level of values, norms and codes of conduct.

The development of globalization CSR is interesting for more than one reason. In terms of the relationship between CSR and the mixed economy of welfare, the rise of globalization CSR is evidence to the fact that CSR is not only a phenomenon which has been driven purely by actors in the commercial or public sectors. The combined historical trajectory behind CSR as it is known today has also been driven from within the non-profit sector, where the anti-globalization social movement represented by NGOs and other pressure groups, such as consumer associations and ethical investor groups, have successfully exerted pressure on businesses to accept responsibly for their social and environmental surroundings. Yet, a second interesting aspect of the development of globalization CSR is the observation that other parts of the mixed economy of welfare also play a role in this development. Strong forces within the commercial sector have actively resisted demands for CSR from the non-profit sector, and governments have acted as mediators seeking to find a compromise between the opposing viewpoints. Globalization CSR is therefore not so much an outcome of what has in historical institutionalism been referred to as 'formative moments' or 'critical junctures' (Collier and Collier, 1991) followed by path-dependent continuity. This pattern is a more appropriate description of the philanthropic and social policy CSR strands (presented in Chapters 4 and 5). In contrast, globalization CSR is an on-going process arising out of continuing conflict and tension – a source of change often overlooked in the historical institutionalist literature (as argued by Thelen, 1999). In the case of the conflict over globalization CSR, the conflicting parties can be seen as representatives of two different CSR discourses, with NGOs representing the radical CSR discourse for more regulation against businesses representing the reluctantly supportive conservative CSR discourse for minimum government intervention.

England and Denmark: Different Degrees of Institutional Mediation

Globalization CSR has had significant yet different impacts upon the way in which CSR is interpreted and applied within different national institutional contexts. Starting with England, it is evident both in the government's broadened CSR agenda (DTI, 2004) and in the examples of CSR measures given by English CSR practitioners interviewed, that the English CSR context is highly influenced by the newly emerging global perspective on CSR. When respondents were asked their views of how CSR can be practiced they frequently mention measures such as supply chain management, ethical sourcing of raw material, fair trade and environmental issues. The expansion over time of the English CSR context is particularly well summarized by Noel, who has dealt with CSR for several years working for a CSR organization operating in the non-profit sector:

> CSR in our organization's world has only come up in the last three or four years.
> It used to be philanthropy to begin with, then charitable giving, it was people up
> in the City writing out cheques, then it became community involvement, then
> community investment, and now it's become corporate social responsibility and
> we benchmark and we look at the work place, the market place, community and
> the environment. There are four areas that we get corporates to look at: how they
> recruit people; how they retain people; looking at supply chains; looking at how
> they market their products ... it goes on.

Noel's experience of the development of the field of CSR in England captures the wide range of the various interpretations, practical approaches and labels for CSR that has already been associated with the English context throughout our historical analysis. Noel's perspective also gives us a sense of the chronology of the three historical strands of CSR presented in Chapters 4, 5 and 6, from the philanthropic approaches to CSR, followed by the work-related CSR measures and finally expanded to the practices associated with globalization CSR, such as supply chain and environmental management.

In Denmark, however, accounts from respondents are testimonies to a somewhat more problematic experience of the influence from globalization CSR. Only a few respondents acknowledge the existence of those CSR measures associated with globalization CSR. Those who do are mainly respondents who are active in the promotion of CSR on the national rather than the local level. They speak of the difficulty they have had in getting globalization CSR measures onto the Danish CSR agenda. That is because the majority of Danish CSR stakeholders – including the majority of the Danish respondents interviewed for the case study of this book – continue to understand CSR as a concept and a range of practices related to the labour market. Globalization CSR measures are simply not considered part of the CSR concept in the Danish context. Steen is a Danish respondent who has had to deal with this particular problem in his role as policy maker for one of the departments in the Danish central administration that does not have the lead on CSR. Here Steen explains how his department has sought to overcome the issue:

> When we enter the scene we use the [English term] 'CSR' [pronounced in English]. Mostly to show that we are talking about an umbrella term, which covers a wider perspective, where we also include the environment, corruption, ethics and all those things. Child labour. All those themes, which are not just about the inclusive labour market.

Steen's department has, in other words, given up trying to incorporate globalization CSR measures into the existing Danish language concept of CSR. Instead it has had to concede that CSR as a labour market concept and activity continues to dominate within the Danish context. As a result, Danish CSR stakeholders now have to make sense of three different CSR concepts. As explained in Chapter 5, two competing Danish language CSR concepts have existed since the current Danish government introduced its own notion of 'corporate social engagement' to rival its predecessor's concept of 'corporate social responsibility'. Now, following the influence of globalization CSR, the third concept of 'CSR' – pronounced in English – has been introduced as a way of enabling the Danish CSR agenda to follow the international CSR agenda.

The difference between the English and the Danish experience of globalization CSR once again demonstrates the importance of different institutional contexts, in this case as mediators of an external influence such as globalization CSR. In the Danish example, globalization CSR has been strongly mediated by the already well-established and resilient national institutional framework built up around the notion of CSR since the mid-1990s. This institutional framework encompasses both the formal level, including the National Network of business leaders (described in Chapter 5) and the particular Danish implementations of partnership approaches, but also the ideational institutional level, where the notion of CSR has been explicitly and efficiently defined as linked to the labour market. In contrast, the English institutional context has had less of a mediating impact upon globalization CSR, reflecting the absence, before the recent growth spurt of globalization CSR, of an explicit national CSR agenda driven by the government and cemented in governmental institutions explicitly dedicated to 'CSR'.

Norway and Sweden: Embracing CSR as Part of Internationalization

It is interesting to compare the Danish experience of CSR against that of its fellow Scandinavian countries, because it transpires that the Danish difficulty of taking on board the globalization strand of CSR is unique to Denmark rather than a Scandinavian-wide experience. In contrast to Denmark, the national CSR agendas of Norway and Sweden are strongly dominated by the globalization strand of CSR. In Norway, for example, the government department who has the lead on CSR is the Norwegian Ministry of Foreign Affairs. As a result, Norwegian CSR policies are tied in with Norway's foreign policy priorities in the areas of environmental policy, and peace and human rights policies. This signals clearly what Albareda et al. (2008) refer to as the Norwegian government's dominant bias towards 'the international dimension of CSR' (Albareda et al., 2008). Similarly in Sweden, the most high profile state initiative on CSR has been the Swedish Partnership for Global Responsibility, established in 2002 (Regeringskansliet, 2011). The focus of this partnership is on human rights and environmental sustainability and on encouraging Swedish companies operating abroad to comply with international CSR guidelines and principles, such as the UN Global Compact and the OECD guidelines (De Geer et al., 2009). Norway and Sweden have followed very similar paths in arriving at their CSR agendas of today, and these paths in turn differ significantly from the Danish historical trajectory.

There is wide agreement amongst academic commentators that the emergence of national CSR agendas in Norway and Sweden is a development which has only taken place very recently, over the last ten years (Albareda et al., 2008, Tengblad and Ohlsson, 2009). Right up until the early 2000s, the idea of corporate social responsibility had been strongly resisted as a concept which was either superfluous or inappropriate in the context of the extensively developed Swedish and Norwegian welfare states. As reported in Chapter 4, this rejection of CSR can be explained by the Swedish and Norwegian propensity to regard CSR as an Anglo-Saxon concept generally expressed as philanthropic business activities and therefore only appropriate in the Anglo-Saxon context. However, this attitude towards CSR started to change around the time when governments and businesses in Sweden and Norway also started engaging with the increasing internationalization of their national business systems and national government policies. Once the issues around globalization had made their way onto the countries' political agendas, perceptions of how CSR can be understood and applied also changed. The link between CSR, philanthropy and the Anglo-Saxon context became replaced by notions of CSR associated with the globalization strand of CSR, such as human rights and environmental sustainability. It was that change in the perception of CSR which made it conceivable for Swedish and Norwegian CSR stakeholders to consider CSR an issue which they might apply within a Swedish or Norwegian context (De Geer et al., 2009, Tengblad and Ohlsson, 2009, Albareda et al., 2008).

Sweden and Norway have, in other words, not shared Denmark's difficulty in appropriating the globalization strand of CSR onto their national agendas. The key factor which explains this difference in experience amongst the Scandinavian countries is the absence in Sweden and Norway of any parallels to Denmark's explicit, high profile and effective government driven discourse and policy on CSR. In Denmark, the social policy strand of CSR was firmly established *before* the CSR issues associated with the globalization strand of CSR were becoming widespread. Moreover, the dominant Danish social policy CSR strand linked CSR to distinctly national social problems and issues around the national labour market. As has already been demonstrated earlier on in this chapter, the effectiveness with which the distinctly Danish CSR discourse has been instilled in Danish CSR stakeholders since the 1990s has in more recent years acted as a barrier against accommodating a wider and more international understanding of CSR. In contrast, Norway and Sweden did not have any already established approaches to CSR which could be said to be distinctly Norwegian or Swedish. Instead, the very notion of CSR had been successfully rejected by unions and NGOs as irrelevant and inappropriate. This situation has meant that, once the globalization strand of CSR started to gain grounds, Norway and Sweden have been better able to receive these ideas with open minds and fewer preconceptions acting as barriers against this external influence. One could say that, unlike in Denmark, globalization has been the external development which has helped rather than hindered in making CSR a concept which is now seen as relevant, important, and appropriate to the Swedish and Norwegian contexts. The inter-regime differences amongst these Scandinavian, social democratic welfare states provide an illustrative reminder of the argument made frequently by historical institutionalists, that 'timing matters' (Hall, 1992, Hansen and King, 2001, Bonoli, 2003).

Germany and France: Tweaking Globalization CSR towards Employment Issues

In both Germany and France the globalization CSR strand has in very recent years been gaining grounds on the national CSR agendas. To illustrate the change in the French context, Fairbrass (2008) compares the French response to the EU Green Paper on CSR in 2001 (EU-COM, 2001) with the French government's submission to the EU 2007 compendium on national CSR policies (EU-COM, 2007). The earlier document reveals a French approach to CSR which focuses on areas such as training, health and safety, industrial relations and social dialogue, revealing an understanding of CSR which is very much centred on the relationship between employers and employees. In its entry to the 2007 EU Compendium, however, the French government reports of a much wider involvement with CSR, including now areas such as codes of conduct, participation in international CSR agreements such as the UN Global Compact, and, most notably, a new strong emphasis on the area of the environment and overall sustainability (EU-COM, 2007).

When considering the factors which have influenced the French government towards broadening its perception of CSR and enhancing its engagement with the CSR agenda, it transpires that the promotion of CSR by supranational organizations such as the EU, the OECD and the UN have played a very important part (Antal et al., 2009). Of particular importance has been the emergence of international agreements, standards and policies in the last decade, from the UN Global Compact, to the OECD Guidelines and the various EU Communications on CSR (EU-COM, 2006, EU-COM, 2002). Amongst analysts familiar with French political culture it is no coincidence that French CSR stakeholders have been particularly quick to support and join such international initiatives. Commentators agree that there existed already prior to the emergence of CSR a strong French tradition of seeing legislation as the optimal approach to securing most forms of social contracts. This tradition made French CSR stakeholders naturally inclined to interpret CSR, when it appeared on the political scene, as something which should be approached with legislation. This is reflected even in the French conceptual understanding of CSR, which tends to translate 'responsibility' to 'liability' (Fairbrass, 2008). This explains why the French government has been one of strongest campaigners for the importance of legislating in areas of CSR rather than leaving those areas to self-regulation or voluntary initiatives, a stance which was emphasized in the French government's response to the EU Green Paper of 2001 (EU-COM, 2001). Beyond the government there is also an inherent French institutional consensus around the importance of legislation. In 2007, France could claim to be the country where the most companies had signed up for the UN Global Compact (EU-COM, 2007). Given this institutional bias towards laws rather than voluntary agreements, it makes sense that the French government has been particular keen to embrace international CSR initiatives which although they do not exactly constitute enforceable legislation, they are at least formalized expressions of institutional expectations of commitment to internationally agreed standards and codes of practices.

The French favouring of legislating also goes a long way to explain why France is frequently referred to as a pioneer in one area of CSR: that of reporting. Although widely considered a behind lagger in all other areas of CSR, socially responsible reporting is one area where France has for many years been ahead of most other countries, having already introduced mandatory corporate social reporting as early as 1977 and further reinforced it in 2001 (Antal and Sobczak, 2007). Such initiatives have only recently been introduced in other countries, such as England (UK-Gov, 2006) and Denmark (Økonomi-og-erhvervsministeren, 2008). The French approach to CSR reporting has been criticized, however, for being more limited in its scope than it might appear (Antal and Sobczak, 2007). Although the law is ambitious in the areas it outlines as necessary reporting aspects, the law only requires businesses to report to the authorities, not to its shareholders or the wider public. There is also no requirement of external evaluations. These limitations have become the subject of internal criticism in recent years in France and the topic of transparency is currently one of the most important issues in today's CSR debates in France (Antal and Sobczak, 2007).

Whilst France has undoubtedly expanded its perception of CSR in recent years and embraced the global dimension of CSR, it is also important not to overstate this development. It is not the case that the French national CSR agenda is now dominated by globalization issues and has moved away from the traditional focus on employment relations. The deeply rooted belief that CSR is fundamentally about employers looking after their employees remains in France. This can be seen in the ways that CSR activities associated with the globalization strand of CSR are being employed. Where codes of conduct, for example, can be used to safeguard ethical business behaviour in a number of areas, the French government has embraced this policy tool to promote diversity at work (EU-COM, 2007, Fairbrass, 2008). And where labelling initiatives are used in a number of ways around the world to inform consumers about everything from environmental compliance to fair trade standards, the French government has focused its labelling work in the area of equality at work (EU-COM, 2007, Fairbrass, 2008). The more recently emerged CSR activities associated with the globalization strand have, in other words, on the one hand been embraced by the French government and French CSR stakeholders, however they have also been tweaked so as to fit in with what is essentially a French 'continuing central concern for the social dimension of CSR' (Fairbrass, 2008).

There are many similarities between the French and the German trajectories towards including globalization CSR onto their national CSR agendas. Hiss (2009) observes a change in the types of CSR activities which German firms engage in today compared with only a few years ago. Whereas earlier, the predominant CSR focus were on employee-centred and often 'implicit' forms of CSR, in recent years German companies are increasingly likely to be engaged in more 'explicit' types of CSR activities, such as environmental projects, codes of conduct, supply chain management, and initiatives designed to protect and improve workers' rights worldwide (Hiss, 2009). There is, in other words, a process of change taking place in Germany which is seeing the national understanding of CSR being expanded to now also include CSR activities associated with the globalization CSR strand.

On the question of what has driven this change in Germany, commentators point to the emergence of corporate scandals and problems with German businesses which have seen the German public loose trust in German businesses (Antal et al., 2009). In that same context, the globalization CSR agenda has also been moved forward in Germany by increasing pressure on firms and the government from CSR stakeholders such as supra-national organizations, NGOs, social movements and civil society in general. Germany has, in other words, experienced some of those same dynamics which were described earlier in this chapter as being generally characteristic of the globalization CSR strand. The emergence and development of this strand is to a wide extent driven forward by the conflict between on the one hand companies – particularly multinational corporations – and governments, and on the other hand civil society and organizations in the non-profit sector.

As with France, it is also important not to overstate the extent of the recent change in Germany's CSR focus. Commentators tend to agree that Germany remains a country whose CSR engagement is comparatively behind that of other countries, and that is the case with the globalization CSR strand as well (Antal et al., 2009, Hiss, 2009). Antal et al. (2009) point out that although Germany has subscribed formally to the OECD Guidelines, the German government has done much less than other governments to promote these guidelines and to put them into practice (Antal et al., 2009). Similarly, both the EU consultations on CSR and the UN Global Compact have been important in putting CSR on the agenda in Germany, however in both cases engagement from German companies in such initiatives has been very limited compared with other countries. Antal et al. (2009)

also considers areas such as codes of conduct and supply chain management to be very much a marginal aspect of German CSR. And finally, Antal et al. (2009) consider that even in the area of environmental responsibility, Germany has gone from having been a widely acknowledged pioneer in Europe in this area to having in recent years fallen behind other countries. Although German companies were the first to develop corporate environmental reporting and eco-accounting, there have in recent years been little innovation or motivation to change the existing model (Antal et al., 2009). On the whole, Antal et al. (2009) detect amongst German CSR stakeholders a tendency to let international CSR waves 'pass them by'; a lack of interest in being amongst the shapers of the international CSR agenda; and an equivalent lack of motivation for ensuring coordinated feedback from international initiatives and experiences into the German CSR agenda (Antal et al., 2009).

From the above analyses it transpires that in Germany, just as in France, the globalization CSR strand may have emerged in recent years, but globalization CSR activities are not in any way the dominant focus in the general national approach to CSR. The German understanding of CSR remains entrenched in the perception that the social responsibility of companies is first and foremost to its employees and therefore a matter of labour relations. Just one indicator of this state of affairs is the fact that the German ministry which has the lead on CSR is the Ministry of Labour and Social Affairs. Research into CSR in Germany also tends to find little engagement with CSR other than in the area of employment relations. Serban and Kaufmann (2011), for example, conclude in their study of small- and medium-sized German companies that such 'businesses prefer to concentrate on their employees (training, social activities, extra-work activities etc.) rather than to integrate, monitor and allocate resources for Corporate Social Responsibility' (Serban and Kaufmann, 2011: 180).

The French and German experience of the globalization CSR strand has more in common with the Danish situation than the English, Swedish or Norwegian. In Germany and France as well as in Denmark, the national CSR agendas were until very recently almost entirely occupied by the social policy strand of CSR. There are therefore similarities between the Danish, German and French experiences of having to overcome certain institutional barriers before the already existing national CSR agendas could be expanded to now also include the issues and CSR activities associated with globalization CSR. But the overall national profile of the globalization CSR strand in Germany and France remains today relatively weakly developed, at least when compared to how prominently the globalization CSR agenda features in other countries.

Conclusion

The investigation in this chapter has thrown light on the historical connection between CSR and globalization. One important finding has been the influential role played by the dynamics of conflict, between CSR stakeholders in the non-profit sector and in the commercial sector, for the establishment and advancement of an international CSR agenda. Another important finding has been the significant differences in national experiences of globalization CSR in the countries under investigation. Those cross-national variations have confirmed the argument often made in historical institutionalism against the idea that similar external influences will over time lead to convergence between different countries. Instead, external influences have here been proven to be mediated by national institutions, hereby maintaining cross-national national differences. The demonstration of the different degrees of institutional mediation has also lent support to the fundamental historical institutionalist argument that 'timing matters', because the analysis uncovered that globalization has had by far the greatest impact on the national CSR agenda in countries (such as Sweden and Norway) which did not already have an established and explicit national CSR agenda.

Conclusion to Part II

Part II's historical investigation of CSR has demonstrated that the first important step towards an historical understanding of CSR is to acknowledge that its historical development cannot be seen as one single trajectory. Neither can CSR's history be described as a series of independent national evolutions. Instead, the current CSR agendas of the European welfare states analysed here have all been influenced to a smaller or greater degree by three parallel developments: philanthropic CSR, social policy CSR, and globalization CSR. The emergence and development of each of those three historical CSR strands are all intrinsically linked to the development of the mixed economy of welfare. One of the ways in which this connection is clear is in the demonstrated association of each strand with a different sector of the mixed economy. The longest-running strand of philanthropic CSR emerged and evolved in the commercial sector; the employment of CSR as a policy tool for addressing social issues has taken place in the public sector; and the idea of using of CSR as a reaction to globalization has mainly been advanced in the non-profit sector.

Current approaches to CSR in England, Denmark, Sweden, Norway, Germany and France reflect at least one and sometimes all three of the historical CSR strands. But each strand does not always come to expression to the same degree in different national contexts. This again depends on the particular country's mixed economy of welfare. For example, because the English mixed economy has a relatively larger commercial sector than any of the other countries in this analysis, the philanthropic CSR strand continues to occupy a significant space in the current English CSR context. In contrast, philanthropic CSR in Denmark, Sweden, Norway, Germany and France is minimal. This is seen by CSR stakeholders and authors alike as a direct result of historical developments, which saw philanthropic CSR being made extinct in the twentieth century by a growing public sector. The public sectors continue to be relatively more expansive today in social democratic and conservative welfare states than they are in the liberal welfare state of England.

At the level of CSR practices, the analysis has also brought to light cross-national differences in the scope for applying CSR to various social issues. In relation to the application of CSR to social exclusion it emerged that whereas in England, associating CSR with social exclusion is just one out of many ways in which CSR can be practiced, in Denmark, most CSR measures are conceptualized in a way which relates them directly and explicitly to various dimensions of social exclusion. France and Germany are somewhere in between those two polar positions, having made a slightly less overt link between CSR and social exclusion, but maintaining a primary and dominating focus on the social responsibility of employers towards their employees.

From a theoretical point of view the historical analysis has established that each of the historical CSR strands have been motivated at the ideational level by different CSR discourses. Whereas the philanthropic strand is mainly influenced by the liberal CSR discourse, the social policy strand is informed by the social democratic CSR discourse, and the globalization strand is driven forward by the dynamics resulting from the conflict between the radical CSR discourse and the reluctantly supportive conservative CSR discourse. On a more general level, the CSR histories presented in Part II are testaments to how contemporary interpretations and applications of similar social phenomena vary according to national historical and institutional contexts.

PART III
Case Study:
Views from CSR Practitioners
in England and Denmark

Introduction to Part III

The following two chapters concentrate on the findings from a case study exploring how CSR is interpreted and applied in the two welfare states of England and Denmark. The case study compares the experiences of CSR practitioners in Denmark and England, with a focus firstly on their knowledge and views of the social impacts of CSR (Chapter 7) and secondly on their perceptions on the wider relationship between CSR and the welfare state (Chapter 8). It is in Chapter 8 that the question will be addressed more directly regarding the extent to which CSR can be seen as an attempt to roll-back the state and roll-out the commercial sector. Chapter 7 considers the question of whether CSR social inclusion projects can be argued to provide new and innovative solutions to the persistent social problem of social exclusion.

The interviewed CSR practitioners were selected from three levels of governance: the international, the national 'central' level and the national 'local' level. On the international and national levels the interviewees were selected on the basis of their capacity as 'key informants' (Gilchrist, 1992), that is as people who play a key role in developing and applying corporate social responsibility on either their national CSR agendas or on the international level. This included people working with CSR in industry, within a policy environment, within the non-profit sector as well as CSR experts from CSR think tanks or consultancies. A particularly high priority was given to obtaining a balance of respondents representing different kinds of interests in corporate social responsibility and based within different sectors of the mixed economy of welfare.

On the local level the focus was on projects where CSR is employed explicitly to overcome social exclusion and to promote social inclusion. In both England and Denmark, CSR projects chosen for the case study were similar on the basis that they offer work placements and other labour market preparation activities for people considered socially excluded, either because they are homeless (in the English projects) or because they are recent immigrants with insufficient knowledge of the spoken language in their country of residency (in the Danish projects). These groups are targeted by CSR social inclusion projects based on the similar view that the target group face severe labour market barriers. They are therefore most likely to find themselves excluded from the labour market for extensive periods of time or even permanently. They have also proven to be especially difficult to reach through 'mainstream' labour market activation means (e.g. Perkins, 2008). In England, the work placement projects include confidence building courses and social support (mentoring). In Denmark, the work placements projects included language coaching in the work place and social support (mentoring). The English and Danish projects used for the case study were very similar in their design and stated aims. The kinds of people interviewed on the local level were local government representatives, local CSR coordinating interest organizations and a number of participating locally based employers, who have put into practice job placement CSR programmes for the socially excluded. The idea behind interviewing these people was to gain insights into the experiences of people involved with social inclusion CSR projects and in particular of their views of the social impacts of these CSR programmes.

A choice was made not to interview people who are generally known as 'clients' on the social inclusion CSR projects, i.e. those homeless people or immigrants for whom the programs are designed. This choice is justified on the basis that the aim of the case study was never to *evaluate* the effectiveness and results of CSR. The case study does not undertake to uncover the specific technicalities, positive or negative, of the local social inclusion CSR projects. Nor does it seek to evaluate the benefits and drawbacks of the social inclusion CSR projects as they are experienced by the relevant clients. The aim is rather to gain an insight into the experience of people who are explicitly involved with CSR in their working lives – people who are consciously engaged in either promoting CSR, furthering the development of CSR or in implementing CSR measures within their own organization. The focus is on how this particular sample of people makes sense of CSR – from its universal and/or specific links to the English and Danish welfare states, to its ability to bring about social change and to its perceived social impacts. That is different from evaluating the 'actual' social impacts, as they are experienced by the client groups. Engaging with the client groups of CSR projects would be interesting and valuable but it would also be an altogether different type of research project.

The interviews were carried out in 2005. The local projects are still in place in both countries today. In order to comply with ethical research guidelines, the original names of interviewees have been changed to code names. Specific locations and organization names have also been changed where these could lead to the identification of the person interviewed.

Chapter 7

Is There a 'Social Case' for Corporate Social Responsibility? Views on the Social Impacts of CSR

Introduction

The concern in this chapter is the question of the social impacts of corporate social responsibility. Current research into the impact of CSR is dominated by a preoccupation with the advantages and disadvantages of CSR to businesses. This branch of the CSR literature is centred around a discussion of 'the business case' for CSR (Dean, 2001). The aim of this chapter is to approach the subject of the benefit of CSR from an alternative direction, asking instead whether it is possible to construct a 'social case' for CSR. Could it be claimed, in other words, that CSR constitutes a positive contribution to society? This question was put to CSR practitioners in England and Denmark by asking them their opinions on the effects which CSR might have on society, positive and/or negative. As previously emphasized, the aim of this approach was not to measure the 'actual' social impacts of CSR. Rather, the objective was to ascertain from people working with CSR how they believe that CSR is impacting upon society.

The chapter begins by discussing the issues raised by respondents regarding the idea of measuring the social impacts of CSR. The succeeding section then presents the themes which emerged from respondents' accounts of the positive social effects of CSR. This is followed by respondents' encounters with, opinions of, and reflections on the negative social impacts of CSR. The chapter concludes with a discussion of the overall impression gathered from respondents regarding whether CSR is mostly a benefit or a disadvantage to society, particularly in relation to the area of social exclusion but also more widely in relation to the welfare state.

Measuring the Social Impacts of Corporate Social Responsibility

When asking the CSR practitioners interviewed for this book about their views on the social contribution of corporate social responsibility, a significant group did not immediately give their answer to this question. Instead these interviewees responded by raising a number of concerns around the issue of measuring the social impacts of CSR. Firstly, some respondents questioned the idea that it is possible to know the effects of CSR on society because it is so difficult to put a measure on the social impacts of CSR. Lene, who works for the English governmental department that has the lead on CSR, elaborates on this complexity:

> I think [CSR] is quite difficult to measure, really. I mean, CSR as a whole is too big and broad. And are you doing it at the level of the country as a whole, or the local impact, or the impact of a particular individual company? And some of them [individual companies] do evaluate obviously what they're doing. [...] You could say that this and that particular local initiative is doing good [...]. I guess it's something which is quite difficult to measure unless you are very clear on the definition of what it is you are measuring.

Lene makes the important point that the difficulty of measuring the social contribution of CSR goes back to the issues around the elusive meaning of the concept of CSR. Because CSR can be defined in multiple ways (as shown in Chapter 3), measuring the social effects of CSR is meaningless unless the measurement exercise positions itself explicitly within the spectrum of CSR definitions. And similarly, because CSR can take the form of various types of activities (as shown in Part II), measuring the social impacts of CSR involves customizing the measuring approach to each type of CSR practice.

Yet even in national contexts where CSR is defined more precisely and applied explicitly to particular social issues, the assessment of CSR's social impacts is not necessarily uncomplicated. This is the situation in Denmark, where respondents are broadly aligned around the perception that CSR should contribute towards overcoming unemployment (as seen in Part II). As pointed out by Brenda, a Danish CSR researcher, what counts as evidence of the social impact of CSR remains uncertain and sometimes controversial:

> There are things [about CSR] which we could measure quite easily, but we just can't be sure that they are caused by CSR. Things like having a high level of employment and not many people on benefits [in Denmark]. But that could be caused by so many things ...

The problem highlighted by Brenda is reiterated by many respondents, and not only in the Danish context. There will always be methodological issues around assessing the exact contribution of CSR towards a social outcome, particularly in quantitative terms and on a large, national scale, when several factors can be argued to have caused the desired outcomes. Certainly, giving CSR the credit for a lowered national unemployment rate is a somewhat questionable leap.

Apart from the methodological challenges of measuring social impacts, the issue perceived as the biggest problem by respondents is the current lack of resources going into measuring or at least exploring the social aspect of CSR. Those respondents addressing the measuring issue unite in describing a situation where information about the social impacts of CSR is non-existent, particularly at national and international levels. Denise, who works with CSR in her role as policymaker for the European Commission, acknowledges this situation as she reflects on the question of social impacts:

> Well, I think the fact that you ask me the question is very significant in itself. Do we have, really, any evidence of the effects of CSR? [...] Well ... [laughs] ... good question. In this Directorate General we are certainly looking for evidence, trying to collect studies and surveys and experiences from across the EU [...]. But we haven't, from this Directorate General, looked at or considered seriously measuring the effects, the combined effects of CSR. That's the problem... it's not just one company – what happens when 1,000 companies do something? And social cohesion? To be really honest ... in policy documents we say that CSR has the knack to promote social cohesion. But I'm not quite sure on what evidence we're saying that.

Denise's assessment of the lack of 'evidence' about the social impacts of CSR at the international EU level is supported by several national level respondents, who also point to a shortage of information nationally. Moreover, many of these respondents are critical about the evidence, measures and indicators which do exist, pointing to shortcomings such as lack of generalizability and comparability.

What comes to light as respondents discuss the issues around measurement is an essential gap, not only in measuring activities but also in the foundations for assessing CSR's social impacts. What is absent is an explicit and internationally coordinated framework clearly outlining the social aims of CSR. Both Denise's and Lene's comments reflect that neither are certain about what they expect – nor about what they are supposed to expect – from CSR in terms of its contribution to society. The social expectations of CSR seem undefined and tentative, from Lene's vague notion of companies and projects 'doing good' to Denise's admission of the unsupported official claims of the social benefits of CSR. These findings are a confirmation of the state of affairs observed in the introduction to this book, where McWilliams et al. (2006) were quoted for finding that existing research on CSR has neglected the aspect of 'the social returns of CSR' (McWilliams et al., 2006: 9).

Asking a group of diverse CSR practitioners to reflect on the social aspects of CSR is an important first step towards filling the knowledge gap which has just been described. In the remainder of this chapter, the focus will be on interviewees' views of the positive and negative social effects of CSR. Their answers will provide an insight into what CSR practitioners are aiming to do with CSR and what social function they believe CSR should fulfil, particularly in relation to unemployment and social exclusion. Focusing on just one type of CSR practice is a useful approach since there is a diversity of ways in which CSR can be practiced but no differentiated measures for each CSR type. Nor is there any existing attempts to amalgamate different CSR efforts at local, national or even international levels.

Likewise, engaging with CSR at the local project level is practical in the absence of aggregated national or international information.

Positive Perspectives: CSR as a Contribution to Welfare

The Success Stories of Labour Market Integration

When considering ways in which corporate social responsibility has contributed positively to society, the reference point for most respondents is their experiences of unemployment related CSR projects. Respondents' accounts of the positive social impacts of CSR are influenced by what they perceive as the successful outcomes of these projects. A widespread perception amongst respondents is that unemployment CSR projects are beneficial to the welfare of the individuals on placements. This can be seen in the general tendency amongst respondents, particularly at the local level, to answer the question about the social benefits of CSR by recounting 'success stories' about individuals who they have witnessed going through the CSR programme. One such story is told by Ulla, who works for a local Danish recruitment agency where she sometimes assists CSR project managers in finding work placements for unemployed people. Here she tells the story of a former work placement participant:

> And one of those employed permanently today [...], [he] comes out here and looks after our green areas. [...] He participated in [the pilot of a local unemployment project]. It's really fun to meet him. [...]. First of all, his language ... just his language has changed dramatically. And he was one of those who didn't speak Danish very well at all even though he had been living in Denmark for many years, you know. But now he's employed [...] and he is extremely happy and ... and I think that that is fun.

The significant aspect of Ulla's story is her perception that getting into employment has led to happiness for the individual in question. The assumption that work and individual happiness, or at least personal welfare, is closely related is widespread amongst respondents. Seen in this light, CSR constitutes a positive contribution to society in helping individuals attain personal satisfaction through employment. Fatima, an English local business respondent who oversees work placements in her organization, is very representative in reflecting this sentiment:

> I feel that people that have been homeless, often they have lost their way completely, and they don't really know what avenue they want to go down. And until they try these different jobs, they don't know themselves. And so it's not that they're a failure it's just that they're completely lost and they don't know which avenue to take so it's just giving them that chance.

The general feeling, particularly amongst those respondents involved in providing work placements, is that work placements are a way of helping individuals, who have 'lost their way'. Work placement providers like Fatima assume that the individuals on placements would like to get into employment but have been unable to. Many respondents, both in England and Denmark, use metaphors similar to Fatima's ideas of 'ways' and 'avenues' to describe the life course of individuals and the socially undesirable situation of unemployment. Unemployment is widely described in normative terms such as the wrong 'road' or 'track', whereas getting into employment is described as a way of getting back onto the 'right road' or 'right track'. In between these two polar opposites, work placements are commonly interpreted as the 'second chance', which offers unemployed people an opportunity to correct their mistakes.

Respondents do not see work placements purely as social service delivery for particular individuals. Many respondents make a direct link between getting individuals into work and contributing towards the overall welfare of society. Grethe, who works locally for an English business where she oversees work placements, makes this connection:

> [CSR] has got to be good for society as a whole because you are encouraging people to get back into something which they may have just fallen from for a period of time, but actually want to get back into. [...] But if you've got somebody that you supported, you can then get them back into the work place and then [they can] be self-sufficient and start getting back into the local environment themselves, whether it is by paying their taxes, that they are then ploughing back into the rest of society in general.

Grethe's analysis combines the idea that CSR helps individuals back to a more satisfactory way of living with the view that society benefits as a whole when individuals are made self-sufficient.

An underlying ethos is emerging is from the way that respondents speak about the benefits of CSR unemployment projects to the individuals on the projects. The interviewees appear to take for granted that the route to employment also constitutes the route to social inclusion. This ethos is stated very explicitly by some of the respondents at the national level, for example by Hanne from the Danish government department that has the lead on CSR. Here she explains the purpose of CSR in relation to unemployment and social exclusion:

> I guess it is very important to state that in the Danish tradition the whole way of thinking about CSR has always, right from the beginning, been connected to the moral perception that in our society, with our protestant work ethics, we form our identity widely through work. That makes the work place perhaps the most important socializing space for most of us. And especially for those who have perhaps been marginalized a bit in other social contexts. So we feel that the

work place as a space of integration and as a factor for the social integration of individuals is by far the most important [thing].

Similar views are put forward in England. Here Noel from the head office of the non-profit organization that runs the CSR work placements for homeless people throughout England explains the idea behind the unemployment CSR projects in England:

> I always say, on a CSR level, that you are addressing a key social issue. And I think that what is so unique about what we do [is that] we provide a unique and innovative approach to tackling homelessness. Enabling companies to have a direct impact on homeless people's lives, but at the same time they're addressing a social inclusion agenda.

Hanne and Noel's quotes show that the ideological thinking behind the CSR work placement projects are strongly informed by the discourse where social exclusion is seen as best overcome by integrating socially excluded people into society via the labour market. This is the discourse which Levitas (2005) coined the social integrationist discourse ('SID') (see Chapter 3). And it is clear from the views of the respondents at the local level that their opinions on the social benefits of CSR are also significantly influenced by this SID discourse. Situating CSR within the SID discourse thereby provides the analysis with the first clue to the social purpose of CSR in relation to social exclusion.

Lightening the Welfare Burden

Another way in which respondents answer the question of how corporate social responsibility has contributed positively to society is by referring to the quantity of people that have gone from unemployment to employment as a result of going on a work placement. Simon, who works for a non-profit organization as the project manager of the local CSR project for homeless people in England, describes this approach as follows:

> Oh, [CSR's] impact on society? I think the advantages, speaking from my background of working with homelessness, is the fact that since September last year [2004] we put 30 people through a two day training course and eight of those have gone on into work, of which I would say at least three of them wouldn't have without it. And the other five needed this to get them across the line. So those were eight people who are now no longer signing on, no longer taking benefits. You know, they are giving back to society after having taken from [it] for a while. So that's an advantage of corporate social responsibility.

Simon's perspective mirrors that of most of his fellow respondents in taking for granted that the conversion of unemployed people into workers is a gain for society. In Denmark, Svend, the project leader for the local unemployment CSR project, reasons in very similar ways to Simon when considering the positive social effects of CSR. Svend quotes his success rate as getting 71 per cent (or 17) of 24 unemployed people into employment in 2004 and 85 per cent (or 51) of 60 people into employment in the first half of 2005. In the quote below Svend extrapolates these results onto the national level:

> I think [CSR] has created some movement in society's unemployment. Because there will always be a group of unemployed people [...] So I believe that if you could keep these people going, and also those who are a bit heavy. They may lose their job once in a while, but the more ... the faster they get going! That means they are not just sitting around at home. They must move on to the next thing. And perhaps live with being day-labourers for a year or so....if they don't have qualifications to do more. And then hope that one can appeal to them that they must learn more skills. But I say: movement in the labour market, that is the most important thing. That no one is allowed to become long-term unemployed, long-term ill, and all that.

Svend's and Simon's ways of thinking about the positive effects of CSR are very much built into the unemployment CSR programs. Both in England and in Denmark, the main funders of the unemployment projects – the English and Danish public sectors – set targets and reward project leaders based on how many unemployed people they get into employment. Simon and Svend's comments also hint at a certain perception of unemployed people as being not so much victims of structurally caused social exclusion as they are the products of their own individual failings. Svend paints an image of unemployed people as 'just sitting around at home' unwilling to engage with the idea of 'learning more skills'. The reason that such people are long-term unemployed is, according to Svend's perception, that they lack initiative. Furthermore, their mental attitude puts them in a special category of socially excluded people, as 'those that are a bit heavy'. What Svend means by that is apparent in his frequent use of the weight metaphor throughout his interview: long-term unemployed people, such as those immigrants on Svend's work placements, are harder work for the social services striving to get them back into work and thereby they are also more of a burden to the rest of society than other unemployed people, not just financially but also administratively. Simon's reference to long-term unemployed people as 'having taken from [society] for a while' evokes a similar understanding of long-term unemployed people as being a strain on society. Simon and Svend's perceptions of the unemployed people on work placements are widespread amongst both English and Danish respondents both at national and local levels. To take just one example from the national level, Gillian, who works for a Danish national business association, states explicitly her view that unemployed people are a burden on society as she gives her views on the positive social impacts of CSR:

> We've got more people working. That is a positive effect, you could say. Because
> the idea is that the welfare burden has to get smaller.

In Gillian's reasoning CSR has the positive social effect, in relation to the welfare
state, of increasing the overall welfare of society because CSR helps reduce
the collective welfare burden of unemployment. Overall, the representation of
unemployed people by these respondents is reminiscent of the discourse identified
by Levitas as the moral underclass discourse ('MUD') (Levitas, 2005), where
unemployed people are understood as welfare dependants and as a macro-economic
liability. A few respondents come close to expressing explicitly a MUD-inspired
view of socially excluded people. Fatima, the English local business respondent
quoted earlier, is one:

> This is my personal view. I feel that all these people in the community – the
> homeless, people who don't work – [the government] should make them ...
> or maybe not make them, but encourage them to get back into work. 'Cause
> there's an awful lot of people out there that don't want to work. And I think that
> everyone has a responsibility to earn their keep. And I think that the government
> needs to do more as far as that, instead of just giving money, benefits. Because
> the people that are able to work, they should be [working]. [The government]
> should do more projects to encourage [the unemployed] to work.

It is characteristic, however, that respondents like Fatima expressly emphasize
that their perceptions of the unemployed as people 'that don't want to work' are
personal rather than necessarily representative of the CSR project as a whole. On
balance, respondents do not appear to subscribe strongly to the MUD discourse.
SID is by far the most influential discourse in respondents' conceptualization of
why the CSR work placement projects are beneficial, to the clients as well as
to society. The majority of respondents emphasize the benefits of 'encouraging'
unemployed people to seek employment and 'appealing' to their motivation for
training and education, rather than on forcing individuals into work and using
work placements as a form of penalization. The apparent coexistence of both SID
and MUD discourses does not reveal a contradictory approach to social exclusion
amongst respondents but rather confirms the ideal typical status of Levitas's
discourses and the ways in which such ideal types will inevitably blend together
'in reality' (Levitas, 2005: 27).

Changing Attitudes to Social Exclusion with CSR

The two types of positive contributions to society attributed to CSR so far have
been related to the socially excluded individuals on CSR programmes. The third
social benefit of CSR often mentioned by respondents relates to those people who
are generally considered the socially included in the social exclusion literature,
namely those already in employment. A number of respondents have experienced

that they and their other involved colleagues have had their attitudes changed towards socially excluded individuals. These respondents have reached a greater understanding of the situation of homeless people and/or immigrants as a result of being involved with CSR. This transformation in attitude is considered yet another of CSR's positive social outcomes. This sentiment emerges particularly strongly amongst local level respondents working in the commercial sector. Michelle, a local English business respondent, reflects on the positive aspects of CSR in this way:

> I think our own people just get so much out of it. It really opened employees' eyes, I would say, and changed perceptions of what a homeless person is, you know. [...] I used to work in Bath and could walk down the streets in Bath and see people sat there begging. And you do, sort of, ashamedly tend to walk on by, turn a blind eye to it. And when we meet people, you know, you realize that they're there because they could probably not go anywhere else. So, it's been a real, beneficial thing to do for both their side and our side, certainly.

A similar view is put forward by Ulla from the Danish local recruitment agency. In Ulla's case, the change in attitude is related to immigrants:

> I knew absolutely nothing about immigrants or strangers or anything, really. I had no idea about how they were received on the Danish labour market. Or, really, apart from what you make up yourself or read or hear or believe, but that is not really grounded in reality.

Later in the interview, when asked about the impact of CSR on society, Ulla goes on to include this learning process as a positive social aspect of CSR:

> Well, one: hopefully more people will get work. That in itself is positive. And two: just the fact that there will be more knowledge and a better understanding of things. It's about learning about those people who may be finding things a bit difficult. That I feel is quite important. Knowledge and attention in itself.

The social benefit of transformed attitudes towards socially excluded people is also important to those respondents who consider CSR more generally. This is often respondents working in the public sector who have experience of working with unemployment and social exclusion. They see CSR as contributing towards breaking down some of the barriers to labour market entry for socially excluded individuals. From this perspective CSR is seen as having potential long-term social benefits. Alan, an English local respondent working for the council, describes this benefit of CSR as he considers the achievement of the local English CSR project. Here he refers to those people who have gained employment as a result of being on a work placement:

These are people who previously perhaps the business community wouldn't have looked at twice. So in that sense I think there's some very interesting ... mm-mm ... social inclusion work going on. [...] OK, I mean, as we are at the moment, trickle by trickle, drop by drop, we're seeing some profit-making businesses delivering schemes that in themselves won't address social exclusion, but certainly can be part of the patchwork of reducing social exclusion and homelessness.

Overall, there is wide agreement that personal engagement with social problems and with individuals considered a social problem leads to a more sympathetic attitude towards such people. This finding is consistent with existing research on the effects of volunteering in general, outside the realm of CSR. Buchanan et al. (2004), for example, report a change in attitude towards homeless people and homelessness amongst a group of students required to volunteer in social work with homeless people as part of their course. The change identified related to a greater belief that homelessness arises from social causes rather than through the failings of individuals. Likewise, Brooks (2007) observes in an experiment where participants were required to volunteer for Amnesty International that the volunteering led to changed perceptions amongst volunteers towards asylum seekers and a more critical attitude toward media representations of this group. Cloke et al. (2007) testify to similar attitude changes towards homeless people amongst volunteers in homeless services. They explain that the transformative power of volunteering lies in the enhanced probability that volunteers will begin to identify with those individuals previously perceived as the 'other' (Cloke et al., 2007: 1094). In respect to the effects on the employee volunteers of working with CSR, the positive outcome of their changed attitudes to socially excluded people is not exceptional. What is unique, however, is the already reported finding that CSR programs are recruiting volunteers from a previously untapped source of volunteers (de Gilder et al., 2005). Compared with the socio-demographic profile of what is consistently found to be the 'typical' volunteer – women, people who are married with children, well educated, and often religious – de Gilder finds that employee volunteering through CSR initiatives is a way of reaching people outside this social category. Volunteering is widely perceived, in the literature on volunteering, to be a form of activity which promotes social cohesion (Smith, 1997, Dekker and van den Broek, 1998, Rajulton et al., 2007). From this perspective, CSR constitutes a social benefit because the CSR programs involving employee volunteering will not only contribute to social cohesion – CSR has also expanded the social stock of volunteers.

A Unique and Innovative Approach to Tackling Social Exclusion

So far in the analysis, respondents' immediate responses to the question of the positive social impacts of CSR point to the relatively measurable effects of CSR as having reduced unemployment and thereby also overcome social exclusion for some individuals; and having changed perceptions of social exclusion within parts of the labour market, thereby beginning to break down some of the barriers to labour market inclusion. However, there is also recognition amongst respondents, and particularly by those respondents working in the public sector within the areas of unemployment and social exclusion, that such claims about the positive social impacts of CSR should not be overstated. Sue, who has years of experience of working with unemployment and works in a local public sector organization, puts the results of the local English CSR project into perspective:

> We [Sue's organization] have targets about the number of people we move into work. And I have to say that the contribution from [the local CSR projects] is a very small part of our target. You know, I think we've got to get something like 16,000 people a year into work and the project maybe in a year will get 10, 20. And I'm not knocking the project, because that is ten or 20 people that we may not have been able to help. But [...] it's not huge in terms of performance.

Sue's comparison between the overall local unemployment target and the results of the local CSR project gives an idea of the modest size of CSR's contribution in terms of lowering unemployment. As such Sue's insight confirms the reservations held by other respondents, quoted at the beginning of this chapter, against looking to unemployment statistics as a way of measuring CSR's social performance. Sue's numbers show that arguments about CSR's positive contribution to society in relation to social exclusion cannot solely rely on CSR's quantitative achievements. Yet Sue remains positive about CSR's social contribution as she points out that the CSR project has reached 'people that we may not have been able to help'. This particular statement represents a perception of CSR which is widely held by respondents and which sees in CSR certain unique qualities that render CSR a positive influence on society regardless of its modest measurable results. CSR is widely seen as offering a new and better solution to tackling social exclusion, particularly in relation to excluded groups considered 'hard to reach', such as homeless people or parts of the immigrant population (Perkins, 2008). This belief about the uniqueness of CSR has already been indicated in earlier quotes when for example Noel, the national level project manager of the English CSR project, was quoted earlier stating that 'we provide a unique and innovative approach to tackling homelessness'. And Simon, Noel's local project manager, was quoted earlier assessing that at least three of his clients would not have managed to get work without the CSR project. These claims are generally backed up by respondents working in the public sector such as Sue and also Alan, who works in England for the local council. Here he reflects on the results of the local CSR project where eight of 30 homeless people achieved employment:

I wouldn't expect necessarily that sort of hit level for the general population
that had been unemployed for some time, let alone the homeless population. So
obviously they are doing something right.

In Denmark, the same sentiment can be found regarding the uniqueness of the
CSR projects. Svend, the Danish local project manager, reflects on his results of
getting 17 of 24 immigrant unemployed people into work:

I think that it is a good result when you consider how badly many of them spoke
Danish [before they went on the CSR program]

Danish respondents express even more explicitly than their English counterparts
not only a view of the uniqueness of the CSR projects, but also a widely held
negative view of labour market activation measures run by the public sector.
Several respondents refer to evidence that such measures 'don't work' and that
commercial sector activation projects are more successful. Moira, who works
locally for a CSR non-profit organization, is particularly vocal in her rejection of
public sector activation programmes:

I believe, speaking very generally, that public sector activation projects are
created by the Devil. They are not all bad, but it is the wrong way to go about
it in my opinion. […]. It is hard to motivate people in public sector activation
projects. It is easier to motivate them when the projects are based in a private
company because they are closer to the labour market. There is actually a much
bigger chance that they will get a job. […] And I have worked as a project
manager of a public sector run activation project myself. […]. It is hard. […].
[The unemployed] don't get to experience a business with a management and
that kind of thing. They'll be dealing with social workers and project leaders and
activation … people. People who have never worked in a business. […]. [In a
business] there is a completely different dynamic. There is competition. And you
need that too. A bit of drive, right?

Moira's beliefs about the advantages of activating unemployed people in
the commercial sector rather than in public sector projects indicate a certain
perspective not only of CSR but of the mixed economy of welfare more broadly.
This perspective is reminiscent of New Public Management ('NPM') thinking
(Osborne and Gaebler, 1992, Lane, 2000, Christensen and Laegreid, 2001). Moira
sees the commercial sector as a better option than the public sector in relation to
addressing social issues because the commercial sector is perceived as possessing
certain qualities unique to this sector, such as dynamism, drive, and competition.
By implication, these characteristics are lacking in the public sector. Moira is also
critical of public sector employees on the basis of her assumption that 'they have
never worked in a business'. Elsewhere Moira elaborates on this view, explaining
that people running activation projects in the public sector are not in a good position

to prepare unemployed people for working life because they themselves have no commercial sector education, experience or knowledge of areas such as business finance, product development, sales, marketing and HR. It appears that Moira equates the commercial sector with the 'real' labour market, rendering the public sector one step removed from this sphere. Overall, Moira and many respondents like her both in England and Denmark seem to subscribe to this view that CSR unemployment projects are superior to existing labour market activation measures because they are modelled around the principles of the commercial sector rather than the public sector. It is evident that respondents' ideas of how CSR contributes to society are very influenced by the NPM perspective on the mixed economy of welfare. Another statement influenced by NPM thinking comes from Hanne, who works for the Danish government:

> I am not saying CSR has meant that we've now got this many less excluded people. But I can say that the discussion and the readiness and the attention which there is around this [CSR] make it easier to develop and use and sell some tools which can contribute towards tackling exclusion. Deep down, the utmost important factor is still production and economic policy and all that. I don't suffer from a misperception about how we are tackling social exclusion by discussing social responsibility. During the period where we discussed CSR very intensely in Denmark I cannot say how many thousand people we got employed just as a result of that discussion. But I *can* say that the Government used its economic policy and created jobs for 160,000 people. And you just can't compete with that. So I'm not trying to say that. But I think that it is important to create the foundation for those efforts. [...] I believe that [CSR] is important because [...] I do believe that it has had an impact on the way that we think. The state. The welfare society. The public sector. Ourselves, etc. [CSR] constantly reminds us that it is not a natural given that we have to let the government solve everything.

Hanne emphasizes that the value of CSR for the Danish government comes from CSR not being a direct interventionist policy. Instead CSR is an idea which the government can promote and thereby use for influencing or 'steering' rather than 'rowing'. Considering CSR in the light of the statements of Hanne, Moira and the other respondents, the social benefit of CSR, it would seem, lies not simply in reducing unemployment and in being a vehicle for enhancing social inclusion. CSR is a means through which to promote a particular conceptualization of the mixed economy of welfare in which the public sector should not be solely responsible for addressing social problems. Instead, both individuals and companies should take more responsibility than they currently do and, by implication, start behaving as social or corporate citizens. This social outlook suggests that when it comes to respondents' understanding of the broader social value of CSR, respondents are largely influenced by what was identified earlier as the social democratic CSR discourse (see Chapter 3). This discourse is premised upon notions of a social contract and of the reciprocity of rights and responsibility applying to all agents of society, whether individuals or organizations. That respondents should mainly be informed by the social democratic discourse on CSR and also by the social integrationist discourse on social exclusion gives credence to the suggestion made earlier in the book that these two discourses are compatible (see Chapter 3). In the light of the combined SID and social democratic CSR discourse, both of which are generally promoted by social democratic or 'New Labour' parties, the importance of the employee volunteering aspect of CSR also acquires a new significance. In the broader political discourse where SID and the social democratic CSR discourse is located, volunteering has for a long time been promoted in England as an integral part of an 'active citizenship' agenda aiming to get more people to engage with social and political issues, including social problems (Blunkett, 2003, Mayo and Rooke, 2006). The profile of this agenda has been significantly heightened recently, since the 2010 government change to the current Conservative/Liberal-Democrat coalition. For the Conservatives in particular, volunteering is one of the cornerstones of their 'Big Society' policy programme (UK-Gov, 2010). Similarly in Denmark, labour market policies as well as broader public conceptions of employment and unemployment have for decades been framed in the terminology of 'activation' and 'the active labour market' (Cox, 1998a, van Oorschot and Abrahamson, 2003, Halvorsen and Jensen, 2004).

Once CSR is situated within the context of the broader discursive contexts of SID, the social democratic CSR discourse, NPM and the active citizenship agenda, CSR becomes more than merely an interesting approach to tackling social exclusion and unemployment. Within the historical institutionalist framework, Hanne's interpretation in particular suggests that CSR is also influential on the level of ideas. In Hanne's words, CSR has been useful for 'selling' certain new policy 'tools'. This conceptualization evokes Hall's terminology and his multi-tiered framework (outlined in Chapter 2) in which the decisions of policymakers to apply certain policy tools are informed by overarching policy goals at the ideational institutional level (Hall, 1993). When applying CSR to this framework, CSR becomes an idea appropriated by policymakers for the purpose of setting new 'goals' in relation to the mixed economy of welfare. Accordingly, involving the commercial sector in labour market activation practices becomes the tool employed to reach this goal and to potentially instigate a paradigm shift at the level of what is termed here 'mixed economy sectoral paradigms'. (This employment of CSR as a vehicle for institutional change will be discussed in more detail in Chapter 8).

Critical Perspectives on the Social Aspects of CSR

This section now turns to what respondents have said about the negative social impacts of corporate social responsibility. Moreover, whereas the previous section on positive contributions gave a picture of strong similarities in respondents' thoughts on CSR, this section will draw out some of the differences in the ways in which respondents in England and Denmark think about CSR.

The 'Failure Stories' behind Labour Market Integration

Earlier in this chapter, when asked to consider the positive social contribution of CSR, respondents used as examples what they saw as the 'success stories' of individuals who had achieved employment by participating in a CSR unemployment project. However, when asking respondents to consider the negative social aspects of CSR it emerges that the success stories are only part of the picture. Most of the respondents working with work placements have experienced situations where the CSR project did not deliver the intended welfare to individuals. This is when a work placement does not lead to employment, either because a participant does not complete the programme, is not offered a vacancy or cannot take up employment for other reasons. These participants are in other words the individuals who make up the other side of the project statistics quoted earlier by the local project managers in England and Denmark. In those situations, respondents witnessed CSR projects turning into a negative experience for those very individuals whom they are meant to benefit. Participants are left feeling disappointed and rejected. Such 'failure stories' are the kinds of experiences which many respondents draw on as they reflect on the negative social aspects of CSR.

In England, several respondents blame the unsuccessful outcomes on institutional constraints existing within the welfare and economic system. Peter, a local public sector employee whose organization offers work placements, is one respondent who expresses his frustration with these constraints:

> I think that certainly the work placements are very positive, but it's the ultimate success that we don't have too much of. You know, getting somebody permanently back into work. Because there's so much red tape attached around ... when somebody comes off the street in terms of their benefit. And if they are going to work [the local authorities] stop their benefits, they can't afford the houses that they live in ... and it's just the frustration! You feel that you've gone so far, but it almost doesn't pay because ... there are barriers! People eventually [say]: 'I can't actually afford to go to work, because if I go to work they'll cut that benefit and I can't afford the house'. And you just feel a little bit frustrated sometimes in that your efforts are not ultimately leading to where you want to be.

Another English respondent, local CSR project manager Simon, was quoted earlier for having a success rate of getting eight out of 30 people into work through his CSR project. Here Simon explains that amongst those people who do not end up in employment following program completion, some actively turn down job opportunities:

It would be at such a small salary that you are better off staying on benefits, to be honest. [...] The majority of people I work with are on Income Support rather than Job Seeker's Allowance. So Income Support, you know, they build that up over time, the Disability Living Allowance and all those other sorts of things. So they might be taking home about 78 pounds a week as well as having all their rent paid. It's quite difficult [...] to match that. Because the rent would be incredibly high staying where they are, equivalent to what they'd be taking home.

The connection Simon makes between the complications of the benefit system and the low pay of the kinds of jobs that work placements typically lead to explains why it is difficult to achieve better social inclusion results with CSR alone. Simon's analysis supports the critique raised against the social integrationist approach to social exclusion which points out that paid work does not necessarily take an individual out of poverty if the work is marginal, low paid and insecure (Labonte, 2004, Bailey, 2006). Moreover, once these critical institutional problems of the work placement programmes come to light, the CSR projects become subject to the same types of criticisms widely directed against active labour market policies. If the work placements only raise the prospect of employment in low paid, short-term and precarious jobs they cannot be seen as genuine attempts at including the socially excluded. Instead, they are akin to the more penalizing 'workfare' approach to the socially excluded, which many commentators feel characterizes the labour market activation agenda. According to this criticism, the emphasis in labour market activation programmes is on making benefits conditional upon working whilst not addressing structural inequalities within the labour market. The activation agenda fails to recognize how labour market inequalities contribute to reproducing and reinforcing wider social inequalities outside the labour market (Rodgers, 1995, Peck, 2001, Aust and Arriba, 2005, Smith et al., 2008).

In Denmark, there are also critical voices amongst respondents relating to the gap between the ideal of the CSR projects and the reality of social exclusion. There is a significant difference in the fact that respondents do not make any references to the poverty trap mentioned by English respondents. This reflects the significance of welfare institutional difference when it comes to carrying out similar ideals and seeking to achieve similar objectives. It is well known that financially the Danish welfare system is more generous than the English system, just as the Danish labour market is characterized by having a higher minimum wage and more employment protection than the English labour market. This could go some way in explaining why the measured success rate of the Danish local CSR project, where 71 per cent and 85 per cent achieved employment, is significantly higher than the English local project's 27 per cent. Yet, these numbers still leaves the Danish projects with 29 per cent and 15 per cent 'failure rates'. Svend, the project manager of the local Danish CSR projects, refers to this statistic again when he considers the negative social aspects of CSR. Here he reflects on how this 'failure rate' could be minimized:

Well a negative effect is that one is pressurizing people even when everyone can see that [...] it is pointless. We get some people ... they are dressed in black from head to toe, are big and fat and ill, have had seven children and no work experience. They have grown up in a hut and eat with their hands sitting on the floor. They have lived in Denmark for 15 years and have learnt nothing and still don't speak Danish. In their own culture they would be considered elderly [and wouldn't have to work]. Why demand that they should work? I would say, once you have accepted people into the country you can't demand that they work. [...] It's pointless. They will never get a job. We might as well accept it [...] and just let them be.

It is telling that a respondent like Svend, who is overall very enthusiastic about CSR and who supports the social integrationist thinking behind the CSR unemployment projects, should also provide such a damning critique of CSR. Svend describes a reality where social integration is taken too far. Even in an institutional context such as Denmark where socially excluded individuals do not face getting caught in the poverty trap as a result of forced labour market activation measures, there are still issues to be raised around the conditional and penalizing nature of the active labour market. The job prospect offered in the Danish work placement programmes may be adequate in terms of pay, but many respondents still point out that the types of jobs on offer are still of the kind that most (Danish) people are reluctant to occupy, such as cleaning and catering. This makes the Danish work placement projects equally similar to workfare on the basis of the definition proposed by Peck, that 'workfare is not about creating jobs for people that don't have them: it is about creating workers for jobs that nobody wants' (Peck, 2001: 6). Although it is questionable whether Svend's criteria for 'the too hard to reach' would find support amongst social policy academics, Svend does echo those critical voices in the literature on social inclusion and the active labour market which point out that recent policymaking is so focused on making individuals take responsibility for becoming socially included by taking up work that the issue of their social rights is being overlooked (Cox, 1998b, Lewis, 2003, Dwyer, 2004). Overall, the critique of the CSR work placement programmes and their likeness with workfare programmes is once again testimony to how blurred the lines are between the social integrationist approach to social exclusion and the moral underclass discourse about the socially excluded.

The Limits of Innovation

Apart from relating unsuccessful outcomes in CSR work placements to wider structural divisions in society, respondents also relate 'failure stories' to flaws in the designs of the CSR programmes. Many respondents, both in England and in Denmark, feel that some failures could be avoided had there not been a lack of expertise amongst employers in knowing how to deal with problem situations related to the work placement participants. Thomas, who works for a Danish CSR consultancy specializing in evaluating projects like the CSR work placements, comments on this problem:

> Organizations should get trained in how to receive new colleagues who aren't necessarily like all the other staff and who might have some specific needs [...].
> I have heard companies say: 'we feel lost, because when problems arise we lack the right tools to handle it'.

Respondents like Thomas regret the lack of expertise amongst work placement providers because ultimately it leads to a negative experience for the participants. Furthermore, having experienced the challenge of dealing with people with severe social problems, these respondents also question CSR at a more fundamental level. Rune, a local level Danish business respondent, is just one example of a respondent raising the issue of the appropriateness of leaving employers to tackle social problems:

> How many problems apart from unemployment can we deal with as a business? [...] If we take on groups that are too heavy we won't get them employed. And then they suffer defeat ...

Rune points to the lose-lose situation for both employers and work placement participants when individuals fail to complete their placements: businesses waste their resources and the participants experience defeat. These experiences, which are reiterated by many respondents in England, put into perspective the New Public Management inspired arguments made earlier in this chapter that CSR constitutes a unique, innovative contribution to tackling social exclusion which is superior to measures offered by the public sector. Existing research examining such claims has emphasized that such assertions are often based on very little or contradicting evidence (Farnsworth, 2006b, Davies, 2008). Whilst the shortcomings highlighted by respondents in relation to CSR unemployment projects do not directly disprove the claims of innovation and uniqueness, they are a reminder that those superior characteristics attributed to the commercial sector, such as competition and dynamism, are not always sufficient – or indeed the most important – when it comes to dealing with socially excluded individuals.

The Welfare Burden of CSR?

When asking respondents to consider the negative social impacts of corporate social responsibility in relation to society, one of the themes emerging very strongly from the analysis is the theme of exploitation. Respondents raise a number of concerns about exploitation in relation to CSR, but one concern stands out as it is brought up repeatedly by Danish respondents. This concern relates specifically to 'flexjobs'. This labour market arrangement is unique to the Danish context (explained in Chapter 5). Several respondents in Denmark explain that it has recently come to the attention of politicians and the general public that a number of Danish employers are exploiting the flexjob arrangement. Companies are being suspected of employing people who are not or should not be eligible for flexjobs. In this way they get fully 'able' employees as well as government subsidies.

The exploitation of CSR for the purpose of gaining public money is seen as a negative social impact of CSR by respondents because it spoils the positive reputation of CSR in the public arena. Some respondents feel that this would also affect the momentum amongst 'genuine' CSR practitioners. Overall, it is felt that this could induce a downward spiral affecting the future proliferation of CSR. Union respondents also express concerns about the threat of CSR to employees on the 'ordinary labour market' if companies start to seek out new recruits that come with government subsidies. But there is also a further observation to add to this negative social aspect of CSR. Earlier in this chapter it was reported that respondents consider it a positive social effect that CSR can contribute to minimizing the strain that unemployed people put on public funds (the 'welfare burden'). In relation to this argument it is something of a paradox that Danish companies appear to be exploiting CSR for the purpose of gaining access to these same public funds. If socially excluded people are considered morally flawed for taking unemployment benefits when they should be and are considered fully capable of working, by the same token are the companies taking government subsidies on behalf of fully capable workers not equally morally flawed? In the quote below Hanne from the Danish government department which has the lead on CSR considers what she terms the flipside of the government's financial support to CSR arrangements:

> I think there is a flipside to this which is that the public subsidies have the effect of institutionalizing social responsibility. We [the government] feel [subsidies] help by quantifying [CSR]. But you could point out that it wasn't like that before [...]. Only ten years ago you could still find some Petersen [employed] doing the odd job here and there. A bit of sweeping. 'He is not that capable'. But he still got paid. And it might be that those kinds of jobs are no longer realistic in the context of globalization, enhanced competition etc etc. But beforehand, social responsibility was taken by just accepting people who can do less.

Hanne's interpretation of Danish CSR as institutionalized is interesting because the terminology can be taken to imply a certain degree of indolence amongst Danish companies when it comes to CSR. Companies are not inclined to take social responsibility independently – they expect public subsidies. Again, there is a striking and paradoxical parallel to MUD's often drawn on notions of welfare dependency and lack of incentive amongst people on social benefits (Murray, 1994).

The other aspect of Hanne's quote relates to the issue of social exclusion rather than to companies. Hanne raises a concern regarding the extent to which CSR measures such as 'flexjobs' have made the Danish labour market less inclusive than it was before such measures existed. This concern is shared by several other Danish respondents who express the same unease about a development where boundaries have been drawn up between people who are 100 per cent able to live up to the demands of the labour market and those who cannot. In Hanne's scenario – which is replicated by many other respondents – those individuals who fall beneath the 100 per cent threshold can only be accepted into the labour market if subsidized by the government in schemes such as flexjobs. In the past, employers were more flexible and tolerant and would accommodate workers according to their individual skill sets and abilities. As such, the public subsidies have created stronger contrasts between the excluded and the included, between those inside and those outside the labour market. This concern is also well known in the literature on the Danish approach to CSR. Søndergård (2002), for example, points out the internal contradiction between the Danish government's demand for higher educational standards on the labour market (as a way of coping with enhanced international competition) and the demand for employers to be inclusive towards individuals with lower skill sets (Søndergård, 2002). These voices of concern coming from Denmark are also interesting in relation to Levitas's favoured social exclusion discourse, RED, which sees redistribution from the government as key to tackling social exclusion (Levitas, 2005). The negative outcome of the Danish government's subsidies to vulnerable people on the labour market is an example of a situation where redistribution has led to greater rather than less inequality, and to the arrival of new areas of social exclusion rather than to the eradication of existing exclusion.

Rolling Back the State?

The final negative social impact of CSR raised by respondents relates more broadly to the effects of CSR upon the mixed economy of welfare. A few respondents raise concerns about a lack of debate about how far CSR supporters are intending to take CSR when they promote CSR as a vehicle for increasing the commercial sector's involvement in social issues. One such respondent is Holger, who works for a Danish national research institute:

> There is an old discussion [...] which we try to get going once in a while. That is: are there limits to corporate social responsibility? Because what kind of responsibility is that? And what will it mean if you hand over responsibility to businesses? You could look to the US and see how things are going there and we don't like that idea!

From Holger's perspective, CSR ought not to become a vehicle for rolling back the state and creating a less universal welfare state akin to the residual American model, and Holger supposes that most Danes would not 'like that idea' either.

In England, Alan from the local council elaborates upon a future scenario where CSR has been employed as a means to minimizing the public sector's responsibility for social problems:

> I think the disadvantage [of CSR] to me [...] is that we don't have any more a clear ideological understanding about which bodies are responsible for addressing social exclusion. And my sense is that [...] it is essentially Government's responsibility. [...] If [social exclusion] is increasingly met by businesses and not by Government, then you're actually shifting not just responsibility away from Government, but that responsibility that is accountable – or vaguely accountable – to an organization that is essentially accountable to itself. It's a profit-making company. As long as it doesn't breach the various bits of law that concern trading or monopolies. Then it's a very fragile thing. [...] If there was a shift, then I think it would be easy for Government to roll itself back a little further and rely on profit-making businesses to do what is essentially Government's responsibility.

Alan goes on to state that the danger of handing over public sector responsibility to the commercial sector is that it would be a one way shift. Once social issues are the responsibility of the commercial sector, individual businesses might decide to stop their CSR efforts in the longer term, and then Alan doubts that it is possible for the general public to influence businesses to carry on their social efforts. Unlike politics, where voting and demonstrations can have an impact, the electorate does not have a direct influence over businesses. On this basis Alan sees the social benefits of CSR as being compromised by the danger of letting the CSR agenda become a tool for replacing the public sector with the commercial sector.

The concerns expressed by these respondents show that the enthusiasm expressed by other respondents, about the New Public Management inspired principles of enhancing the role of sectors other than the public sector in solving social problems, are not universally shared amongst the respondents. The issues they raise here will be discussed further in Chapter 8.

Conclusion: Navigating the Positive and Critical Voices

This chapter opened with the question of whether it is possible to construct a 'social case' for CSR, a social case that can complement the already extensively championed 'business case' for CSR. In the context of a distinct lack of data and research into the social impact of CSR (a situation which was confirmed by the CSR practitioners interviewed for this book), the investigation focused instead on the claims that CSR practitioners make about the advantages (as well as disadvantages) of CSR to society. The positive aspects highlighted by respondents included the integration of socially excluded individuals (via the labour market) after being on CSR work placements; lowering the 'welfare burden' of unemployment; and changing attitudes towards social exclusion amongst the 'socially included' on the labour market. In considering how CSR achieves these positive social effects, respondents credit CSR for its unique and innovative approach to tackling social problems. This approach builds on a less involved role for the public sector and more involvement by the commercial sector. But the positive perspectives are also tempered with some more critical viewpoints. Respondents were regretful of the negative impacts on work placement participants when work placements do not lead to employment. Such negative experiences had led respondents to question the suitability of work placements for the very individuals they target, and also the suitability of the commercial sector to deal with vulnerable individuals. Some respondents were also led to doubt the broader social policy ideal of integrating all socially excluded people into the labour market. With the jobs on offer through the work placements being mainly low pay, precarious, and in sectors where the general population refuse to work, the CSR work placements could be argued to resemble less an innovative approach to social exclusion than just another version of workfare. Finally, a few respondents voiced concerns about the extent to which CSR is part of a broader political agenda where the public sector is being replaced by the commercial sector in core welfare areas. This issue will be the basis of the discussion in Chapter 8.

From a theoretical point of view it is interesting to note that there appears to be widespread agreement about the positive social impacts of CSR across the two national institutional contexts of England and Denmark. Moreover, the arguments are framed within the same broader social discourses. Both in England and Denmark, the CSR work placement projects are clearly made sense of through the 'social integrationist' discourse, just as the social democratic CSR discourse emerges as influential in both countries. When it comes to the question of the negative social impacts, however, experiences differ amongst English and Danish respondents. It is unique to the English context, for example, that wages in certain parts of the labour market are so low that many low paid jobs offer no financially viable alternative to staying on social benefits. At the same time, it is unique to the Danish context that public subsidies to certain CSR arrangements are so generous that employers are suspected of exploiting the arrangement, claiming subsidies where eligibility is questionable. The public subsidies have also had the adverse effects of making employers less flexible towards vulnerable individuals or people with lower skill sets, hereby pushing people that used to be accommodated by the labour market into the realm of social exclusion. These differences suggest that the similarities identified in this chapter may operate mainly on the ideational level of discourse. Because when it comes to the practical application of CSR, significant differences arise from the different institutional contexts. This disparity between ideas and implementation is something that shall be examined in more detail in Chapter 8. For now the observation can be made that national settings are significant to the experience of CSR, or, to phrase it theoretically, that institutions influence they ways in which CSR can affect society.

Chapter 8

CSR and the Changing Welfare State: Does CSR Constitute a Roll-back of the State?

Introduction

This chapter tackles the question of whether corporate social responsibility is a vehicle for rolling back the state and rolling out the commercial sector. Addressing this question is first and foremost an empirical concern. But it is also a means to contributing to contemporary debates in comparative social policy regarding welfare state change and continuity. In this chapter there is a particular emphasis on relating the empirical findings from the case studies to the theoretical framework of the book, and to contributing to current welfare state debates.

The investigation of welfare state change will focus more precisely on occurrences of welfare state 'retrenchment'. A broad perspective on this notion is taken here. This means that retrenchment will be considered in relation to both the formal institutions and the ideational paradigmatic structures of the English and Danish welfare states.

Looking for expressions of retrenchment in England and Denmark also provides an opportunity to add to the long-standing discussion in comparative social policy regarding the extent to which welfare states are developing towards a converged welfare state model or whether divergence continues to outweigh convergence.

It is important to emphasize that this book's in-depth exploration of CSR in England and Denmark cannot be regarded as a way of directly 'measuring' whether the emergence and development of CSR has led to retrenchment in England and Denmark. But it *is* possible to draw on the insights from CSR stakeholders and on the understanding of the local CSR unemployment programmes to establish whether these particular manifestations of CSR do in any ways *indicate* that institutional changes are taking place. It is also possible to discuss the degree to which CSR has itself contributed to any changes detected.

The first part of this chapter focuses on the degree to which indications of welfare state change or continuity can be found in the local CSR unemployment projects. In order to take into account the various institutional levels on which change can take place, this part of the analysis is structured around Hall's framework for investigating change (outlined in Chapter 2). Starting with Hall's notion of 'first degree' change, the analysis begins at the institutional level of 'settings', which is paralleled here to the level of funding in the mixed economy of welfare. From here the analysis moves to Hall's second degree of change at the institutional level of 'instruments', which is paralleled here to the levels of provisioning and formal regulation. Finally the chapter goes on to consider change at Hall's third degree level of paradigmatic change. In the context of this chapter, the level of paradigmatic change includes the various paradigmatic layers of ideational regulation outlined in Chapter 2. The assessment of whether change can be said to be taking place in England and/or Denmark is measured against the largely theoretically informed perceptions about the current make-up of the English and Danish institutions presented in Chapter 2. A summary of the findings on the various institutional levels is presented in Figure 8.1 at the end of this section, on page 148.

The second part of this chapter goes on to discuss the past, present and future of corporate social responsibility. As part of this discussion the question of what drives the development will also be addressed.

Change, Continuity, Convergence and Divergence in the CSR Unemployment Projects

'Settings': Path-dependent Divergence at the Level of Funding

When asking respondents about the funding arrangements in the local CSR unemployment projects, two different pictures become immediately apparent. In Denmark the CSR work placements are heavily subsidized by the public sector, whereas in England, the programmes are designed to function without public sector funding. Respondents emphasize that these funding arrangements do not just relate to the specific CSR projects studied for this book but to CSR unemployment programmes in general. A key difference is how work placement clients are paid during the time they are on placement. Whilst in England they are paid a salary by the work placement provider, in Denmark they continue to receive social security benefits. In Denmark public subsidies are also available to employers to pay for the training of business employees to become mentors for work placement clients. Danish employers hereby participate in CSR without incurring direct monetary expenses in relation to the individuals they take on work placements. Pelle, who works for a Danish non-profit CSR organization at the national level, acknowledges that this arrangement reflects a contextually specific relationship between the commercial sector and the public sector in Denmark:

> [Employers] don't do an awful lot of social responsibility work if they don't get subsidized. Well, that's how we are brought up here in Denmark. So the voluntary [aspect of CSR] doesn't really apply to the economic side of things.

Pelle's comment about the particularly Danish way of practicing CSR reflects a situation in which Danish CSR stakeholders take for granted that employers should to a large extent be financially compensated by the public sector for engaging in CSR. There is, in other words, an institutionally grounded expectation amongst Danish employers that responsibility for the funding side of CSR belongs to the public sector. This state of affairs only begins to appear less than self-evident once contrasted with the approach to CSR in England. In the quote below Oscar, who also works for a Danish non-profit CSR organization at the national level and who has substantial knowledge of how CSR is interpreted and applied in different countries, offers his analysis of the differences between the English and Danish attitudes to the funding aspect of CSR:

> Well, we have completely different social models. The [English CSR projects] I know of function completely without public subsidies. [When I speak to Danish companies] they say they are doing [CSR] on a voluntary basis, but there is never one which has not received public subsidies. [...] And that is not the case in England, not to the same extent. Plus they say, in [some of the English CSR projects I speak to], that they would also rather do without [funding from the public sector] so that [CSR] can function on market conditions. Whereas we don't quite have that same attitude here [in Denmark]. [...] If [businesses] are to [take social responsibility] they expect the state to pay for it. [Businesses] don't want to lose money on it. And [businesses] probably don't want to [lose money] either in England, but then they choose to only run projects that can function on market conditions. Our Minister of Employment didn't think that would work in Denmark. And I think he's got that one right [laughs].

We see from Pelle's and Oscar's observations and analyses that although the notion of 'corporate social responsibility' implies commercial sector responsibility, once applied within the national institutional setting of Denmark, CSR is adapted to the path-dependent expectations of Danish social actors regarding how the funding responsibility for addressing social issues should be divided between the public and commercial sectors in a social democratic welfare state regime such as Denmark (Esping-Andersen, 1990). (For an elaboration on welfare state regimes see Chapter 2). At the level of funding in the CSR projects there are, in other words, strong indications of regime-dependent continuity in Denmark rather than of welfare state retrenchment.

In contrast to Denmark, it is a widely held understanding, both amongst the Danish and English respondents, that in England CSR is the responsibility of the commercial sector also at the level of funding. Oscar highlighted this difference, and his assertion is here confirmed by Peter, who works with CSR at the English local level for a public sector employer:

> Private organizations are crucial to [CSR]. Because public organizations, whilst we can provide the sort of time and the resources, we can't provide the money. And you need the private organizations, who can sort of, you know, hand over cash.

Peter goes on to explain how any costs incurred as part of running the CSR programmes, such as hosting events for training, fund raising or awards ceremonies, are as a matter of course met by commercial sector businesses. Speaking to other English respondents it also emerges that the types of CSR projects that are targeted at socially excluded groups or areas are typically sponsored heavily at the national level by large national businesses. It is questionable, however, whether such commercial sector self-reliance should be considered an indication of welfare state change. It might be feasible to talk of retrenchment if the applied measure is one of Pierson's conceptualizations of retrenchment as 'cost-containment' (Pierson, 2001b). But this requires establishing that the CSR work placement programmes are reducing or 'containing' the costs for the English public sector in relation to homeless unemployed people and in relation to addressing the issues around their social exclusion. As already discussed in Chapter 7, evidence of such a direct causal relationship between CSR and social inclusion does not currently exist, and it would also be a challenge to substantiate any such claims. In Chapter 7 respondents also implied that the contribution of CSR towards converting unemployed people into employed people is more or less insignificant when measured in quantitative terms and compared with the public sector's overall quantitative unemployment targets. Therefore, rather than seeing the English CSR projects as a form of welfare state retrenchment at the level of funding, the view here is that the minimal funding involvement of the English public sector combined with the commercial sector's economic self-reliance in the area of CSR is the outcome of already existing and institutionally dependent preferences regarding the division of funding responsibilities in the mixed economy of welfare. In the same way as businesses in Denmark take for granted that, in general, it is the responsibility of the public sector to meet the costs of activities relating to addressing social problems, the liberal welfare paradigm to which England belongs (Esping-Andersen, 1990) prescribes an arm's length relationship between the public sector and the commercial sector. What is more, this kind of relationship is just as much a priority for the public sector as it is for the commercial sector. This explains the scenario described above by Oscar where English businesses involved in CSR have stated that 'they would rather do without' funding from the public sector. This finding supports the conclusions of another comparative study into the participation of English and Danish firms in active labour market measures, which found that 'Danish employers have expectations about the legitimate scope of government that their British peers do not share' (Martin, 2004: 43).

At the level of funding the CSR unemployment programmes point strongly towards path-dependent institutional continuities in both England and Denmark. Moreover, these path-dependencies point in different directions and they thereby uphold the perception of England and Denmark as belonging to 'different social models' in Oscar's words, or to divergent rather than convergent types of welfare state institutions.

'Instruments' 1: Different Retrenchment Patterns at the Level of Provisioning

At the level of provisioning, the most immediately apparent uniqueness of the CSR unemployment programmes is the involvement of the commercial sector in the provisioning for socially excluded individuals. In Chapter 7 it was brought to light that most respondents consider the local CSR projects a unique and innovative approach to tackling social exclusion. The question now is whether on this basis the CSR projects can be considered a change in terms of welfare provisioning in England and Denmark and more specifically, whether they are a form of welfare state retrenchment. From a broad retrenchment perspective, the very involvement of the commercial sector in welfare provisioning seems to comply with one of Pierson's other retrenchment indicators, which specifies institutional retrenchment as involving 'major transfers of responsibility to the private sector' (Pierson, 1996: 157). From this perspective both England and Denmark appear to be converged in similar models for overcoming social exclusion and unemployment. Many researchers have argued for such convergence in analyses that place England and Denmark in the same, active labour market or 'workfare' regime (Torfing, 1999, Lødemel and Trickey, 2001, Lindsay and Mailand, 2004). However, as pointed out by Martin (2004) in her comparison of the involvement of British and Danish employers in active labour market programmes (in which she includes CSR unemployment programmes), whilst similarities and indications of convergence may be the most immediately apparent, important cross-national differences come to the surface once one takes a closer look at the details around the implementation of the active labour market programmes (Martin, 2004). This argument is also relevant to the CSR projects and case studies of this book.

The cross-national difference that stands out the most at the level of provisioning is the key supplementary roles held in the CSR projects by either non-profit sector organizations, in England, or the public sector, in Denmark. This difference largely reflects different national approaches to the idea of 'partnership'. As seen already in Chapter 5, when the English and Danish governments adapted CSR as a policy tool for addressing social exclusion they also promoted the concept of partnership working as the means of implementing CSR. However, beyond the rhetorical level, where enthusiasm is shared for the general idea of partnerships, English and Danish approaches to the implementation of partnership vary greatly. This becomes apparent when English and Danish CSR stakeholders elaborate on how they understand the partnership notion in the context of CSR. In England, Lene from the government department that has the lead on CSR represents the prevalent English interpretation of the partnership idea as she highlights her government's interlinked promotion of CSR and partnerships:

> Partnership approaches are very much favoured. Government departments are also encouraged very much to work with the voluntary and community sector in terms of helping to support them to reach some of these goals. To use the voluntary and community service providers.

In Lene's account, the non-profit sector appears taken for granted as essential to the partnership approach. This understanding stands in contrast with the Danish understanding of the partnership concept. Hanne from the Danish government department that has the lead on CSR summarizes this Danish outlook:

> The partnership perspective was very central to us from the beginning [of the government roll-out of CSR]. And that of course is because in Denmark, nothing happens, at least not within [the realm of social exclusion and unemployment] without the public sector. So when the businesses enter the stage, they won't be entering it alone. They will always be entering the scene in collaboration with some form of public institution, almost always the local council.

Whereas it is clear that the partnership approach is seen as key to CSR in both England and Denmark, it is equally evident that what respondents understand by this concept once it is applied in practice vary greatly, particularly in the different degrees of importance assigned to either the non-profit sector (in England) or the public sector (in Denmark).

The English interpretation of partnerships as involving a close relationship with the non-profit sector continues to be apparent when examining the provisioning roles of the various mixed economy sectors in the local CSR projects. Here respondents from the English CSR project all report how the program depends on the initiative, lead and continued input from the project leader. This project leader is based within a CSR organization in the non-profit sector. It is the job of project leaders to recruit businesses to provide work placements, and also to recruit clients to go on the work placement. Project leaders organize training and other events, and they continue to be the main point of contact between the various partners in the project. The extent to which this central role of non-profit organizations is seen as built into the partnership idea in England is evident amongst all English respondents. In the quote below Peter, whose employer is a partner in the local English CSR project, explains what this means for his engagement with CSR issues:

> We're now a member of [non-profit CSR organization X]. So the drive from the top of the organization was: 'if you're going to get involved with the community, we'd like you to go through our partner, [non-profit CSR organization X], in the sense that we are paying for membership of that organization, use them as an intermediary, to support you with your business activities'. So, that was the general message. So, of course, a lot of the work outside this particular project I've done with [non-profit CSR organization X] and this was a project that they told me about. I was already well known on other campaigns.

Peter implies that his work with 'the community' goes back further than CSR and the partnership approach, but that he is now being instructed 'from above', by management, not to engage with CSR activities without using a non-profit organization as an intermediary. Peter's account therefore implies that the partnership approach is a change from the past in England and that there is a sense in which provisioning responsibilities are being transferred, in line with Pierson's retrenchment criteria (1996). However, the transfer is perhaps less significant in relation to the commercial sector than it is in relation to the non-profit sector. This indication is supported by observations made in other mixed economy analyses. Carmel and Harlock (2007), for example, have found a general increase in the use of non-profit sector organizations to deliver public services in the English context. Moreover, this development is associated with the promotion of partnerships since the 1990s and is found to have intensified in the last decade (Carmel and Harlock, 2007). The CSR projects – or, what can now be termed the 'CSR partnerships' – can in other words be seen as indications of retrenchment taking place at the level of provisioning in the English context in the sense that the public sector is transferring provisioning responsibilities to the commercial sector but even more so to the non-profit sector.

When shifting the focus to the details around the Danish way of implementing the partnership idea, one gets a different sense of change than in England. Earlier on in this chapter Hanne from the Danish central administration interpreted the partnership approach as a cooperation between the commercial sector and the public sector. This interpretation is echoed amongst all Danish respondents. And when speaking to respondents involved in the CSR partnerships, it soon becomes clear that the local government plays a key role in the partnership. Moreover, the exact nature of that role is remarkably similar to the functions fulfilled by the non-profit sector organizations in the English CSR context. This includes the recruitment of businesses to provide work placements and clients to go on work placements, and being the main point of contact between placement participants and placement providers. In addition, public sector service to businesses has been enhanced in the newly created 'company consultant' roles, which sees local council employees specializing in providing support for businesses engaged with CSR. On the national level, business respondent testify to the widespread perception that this is how partnerships operate. These respondents report that they consider the local council their first port of call in instances when they or anyone else within their organization wish to implement any new CSR initiatives.

The indications of retrenchment, when understood as public sector transfers of responsibilities, are arguably smaller in Denmark than they are in England at the level of provisioning. In the Danish CSR context, rather than having identified a significant removal of responsibility from the public to the commercial sector or the non-profit sector what has emerged is an 'internal' reassignment of responsibilities within the public sector, with the public sector's involvement in social exclusion measures noticeably enhanced at the local level (see also Martin, 2004).

Considering these cross-national differences arising from the different interpretations and implementations of the partnership idea, there are no strong indications of convergence between England and Denmark at the level of provisioning. On the contrary, whereas in the English CSR context public sector engagement in social exclusion issues is transferred to the commercial and the non-profit sector, in the Danish context there is a relatively smaller relocation of responsibilities as the transfer to the commercial sector is outweighed by the increased provisioning efforts at the local public sector level. What unites the English and Danish CSR partnerships, however, is a sense in which the immediate impression of the notion of CSR as a significant transfer of public sector responsibilities to the commercial sector is somewhat reduced when taking into account the more significant practical provisioning roles played by other sectors, whether the non-profit sector or the local public sector.

'Instruments' 2: Changing Responsibilities at the Level of Formal Regulation

Whereas stronger indications of cross-national divergence than of convergence were found at the levels of funding and provisioning, the picture is different at the level of formal regulation. Here the institutional differences begin to disappear and instead some strong similarities emerge between the English and Danish CSR contexts. The first of these relate to the very strong emphasis in both countries on CSR as a voluntary business activity rather than a legislative requirement. This emphasis on voluntarism has already been encountered several times throughout this book, from the centrality of this particular aspect of CSR in the liberal CSR discourse and its acceptance within the social democratic CSR discourse (Chapter 3); to the tension over this issue in the globalization strand of CSR's historical development in England and Denmark (Chapter 6); and to the inclusion of the voluntary dimension in the official CSR definitions of the EU commission (Chapter 6). The consequence of the voluntarism principle in relation to the level of formal regulation is the widespread perception amongst CSR stakeholders in both countries that CSR is an area that remains outside the government's regulatory remit. It is instead considered a matter of 'self-regulation' for the commercial sector. This outlook is further consolidated by the current emphasis on self-regulation prevailing in the international domain. It seems reasonable on that basis to talk about retrenchment taking place in both England and Denmark at the level of formal regulation in the area of CSR and hereby also in the area of social exclusion and any other welfare area which CSR engages with.

The practical realities of self-regulation in relation to the commercial sector are not specified by many respondents beyond implying a minimum of governmental legislation. Berit, who is one of the respondents from the EU commission, is one of the few exceptions. In the quote below she firstly offers her interpretation of the self-regulation principle in relation to CSR:

> The whole concept of corporate social responsibility is based on self-regulation. Instead of having legislation mandating a given behaviour, there is a kind of unwritten contract between companies, businesses and society, saying: 'there is a given problem or issue to solve. Instead of you the government telling us how to do it we commit to finding a solution and do something.

Berit justifies the self-regulation approach from within the social democratic CSR discourse as she points to an unwritten social contract between business and society. It is this social contract which can sustain a self-regulatory environment, just as Berit also later in the interview emphasizes the importance of trust between business and society. Berit does concede, however, that the self-regulatory ideal cannot be expected to work perfectly on the basis of the commitment to the social contract alone. In the quote below she explains how she envisages that the commercial sector can implement its self-regulatory regime in a way which makes it workable in practice:

> Solving the issue of free riders [is] the challenge for this kind of self-regulation. It [cannot] only [be] a commitment, it has to be implemented. How can a given economic sector control all its actors? Because why should a few [businesses] do something [CSR] whilst the others are free-riders? It won't help. So that raises certain questions [about] how to put in place governance systems in a given sector, in a trade association, in an industry association, so that they will do the policing themselves. [...] The industry association [could] say: 'We have a new product for the whole sector, so we will do something [CSR], we will reduce the CO_2 emissions. If you don't, as a member of this organization, do something you will be excluded and you will be blacklisted'. You need to have a kind of sanction. [...] There is an interest of the good companies to police the others to avoid that everything goes bad and then [they] still [end up with] legislation.

Berit's argument that CSR should be regulated by the commercial sector itself is reiterated by the majority of respondents in both England and Denmark. However, Berit is exceptional in not merely arguing against governmental intervention but also suggesting that the commercial sector needs to implement the self-regulation idea in practical and operational ways.

Beyond the commercial sector's own role in sustaining a system of self-regulation, many respondents in both England and Denmark frequently speak of an enhanced responsibility now placed upon actors from the informal sector such as the media, consumers and investors. In Denmark, one respondent argues that the media has an important role in 'keeping an eye on' the public subsidy arrangements in order to ensure that the potential abuse by businesses (which was discussed in Chapter 7) is kept at a minimum. Investors and consumers are also often highlighted as actors that now play an increasingly important role in the absence of formal regulation of CSR. Christina, who works for an English national business association, is an example of a respondent who refers to the regulatory importance of actors in the informal and non-profit sectors in relation to CSR:

> From our perspective, what we have found is that, sure, as with everything there are some bad businesses. But there is enough of a system, we feel, like, you

know, peer pressure, NGO pressure, the media, all this kind of thing, to ensure that some of those difficulties are rectified.

Christina's argument that there is 'enough of a system' reflects her preference for relying on regulatory inputs from the wider mixed economy rather than on governmental legislation. What unites those respondents who refer to regulatory alternatives to legislating on CSR is the recognition of the need for different forms of sanctioning actions, whether in the shape of formal governance systems such as Berit's suggestion or as the ad hoc reactionary behaviour favoured by Christina.

The pronounced emphasis on self-regulation amongst respondents is to a wide extent a reflection of how contentious and widely debated this issue has been amongst CSR stakeholders not only in England, Denmark and the EU but also in the wider global domain. There is a danger, however, in interpreting the frequently and explicitly stated priority of self-regulation as an indication that the public sector has retreated entirely from the realm of CSR in England and Denmark. This is far from the case. In fact, it transpires from the interviews with respondents that both the English and Danish governments are highly active in the area of CSR as is the EU. Only the activities are almost entirely non-legislative. Denise, who works for the EU commission, outlines below the many ways in which EU Commission is involved with CSR:

> There is a role for us [EU Commission] in plenty of soft stuff. Let's get hold of the best European experiences, let's make them available to everybody, let's promote understanding, research, awareness raising of this concept. There's a lot of group things being done in all kinds of different sectors across the EU, let's try and capture those and replicate them. There are almost endless possibilities for what can be done very usefully in that regard. But [without] introducing standards or rules.

Denise's examples of governmental activity in the area of CSR are reiterated by many other respondents. Promotion of the idea of CSR through means such as knowledge gathering, research, and dissemination of 'best cases' is also a big priority for the governments of England and Denmark. In Denmark, for example, respondents recount how the government has developed an internet based 'knowledge database' on CSR containing 'the good examples'. Related to the idea of promoting through awareness raising are also efforts in the area of education. Both in England and Denmark government respondents report how they have set up different forms of educational schemes to train business managers in understanding and applying CSR.

When elaborating on the government's role in relation to CSR it is noticeable that different respondents often draw on the same terms to describe the many ways in which governments can be active without regulating. Lene from the English government is just one example of a respondent expressing her view of the government's role in what appears to be a prewritten language of non-legislation:

> We see CSR as what business itself is doing over and above say the legal
> minimum and our role there is to encourage and facilitate it. [...] Government
> itself needs to do what it can to create the right enabling environment framework.
> [...] It has a role in trying to set the right policy framework and as necessary
> offering incentives such as tax relief for particular activities.

The key terms in Lene's statement which are used repeatedly by other
respondents include 'facilitating', 'encouraging', 'enabling', 'framework
setting', and 'incentives'. Respondents generally see 'framework setting' as
relating to minimum legislative standards such as minimum wages. Respondents
also acknowledge that when public funding is involved in CSR, the public sector
regulates the rules around this funding. Less formal legislative frameworks also
mentioned by respondent are the EU National Action Plans for Social Inclusion
(Socialministeriet, 2006, DWP, 2008). When business respondents refer to the
government's role as 'facilitating' and 'enabling' they mean mostly ensuring
that there are as few barriers to CSR engagement as possible. But the notion of
facilitating is also sometimes used in a government context to mean bringing
together opposing CSR stakeholders in order to 'facilitate' dialogue, as the
EU Commission did when they hosted the EU stakeholder forum meetings
(mentioned in Chapter 6). 'Encouraging' is partly part of the educational and
awareness raising efforts, but it also means influencing the CSR agenda towards
the government's own interests and priorities. Hanne from the Danish government
is just one example of a respondent who emphasizes this governmental priority:

> The government has a role to play [in relation to CSR] and they can, as part of
> their interest in securing employment and fighting social exclusion, benefit from
> participating in this debate [on CSR] and influence it.

Examples given of governments exercising influence in the area of CSR include
in the Danish context the initial CSR campaigns run by the government in the
mid-1990s, (covered in Chapter 5), and subsequent governmental campaigns on
themes such as long-term absence from the work place and employee health. In the
EU context various EU Commissioners have used different summits to appeal to
businesses (EU-COM, 2001). Finally, when respondents speak of 'incentives' they
usually mean financial enticements such as Lene's suggestion of tax relief and in
the Danish context the various subsidies for unemployment projects and training
schemes. Some respondents refer to such incentives as public sector 'tools' for
encouraging the uptake of CSR.

There is, in other words, a considerable array of ways in which the public sector
is involved with CSR on the formal regulatory level. Yet the involvement cannot
be considered a form of 'formal regulation' as it is not based around legislation.
This is important in the context of CSR because it means that these public sector
initiatives are accepted as legitimate by CSR stakeholders who do not see them
as governmental intervention. In that sense the area of CSR can still be regarded

as an area of self-regulation. However, the impression of commercial sector autonomy implied by the notion of self-regulation should by now be considerably moderated. As much as the CSR stakeholders interviewed for this book may argue that CSR is currently strictly a commercial sector domain and a discretionary business activity, and as much as this view is reiterated in the business literature, governments play significant roles in influencing the CSR agenda, as also argued by Martin and Swank (2004).

From a theoretical perspective, the above finding has also exposed a fundamental weakness in the mixed economy of welfare analytical framework as it is currently being applied. By predominantly defining 'regulation' as formal governmental rule, the MEOW framework misses not only regulation at the ideational level, as already argued in Chapter 2, but also the various non-legislative yet not entirely ideational governance systems operating in all sectors of the mixed economy. It has now been shown that the notion of self-regulation in relation to CSR can have potential practical non-legislative yet regulatory implications for not only the commercial sector, but also the informal, non-profit and public sectors. In the case of the public sector it has emerged that in England, Denmark and the EU, governments are employing a range of 'governance tools' – what Denise referred to as 'soft stuff' – in order to influence or 'regulate' the CSR agendas in the direction of their own interests. Moreover, beyond the realm of CSR the governance notion is becoming increasingly salient within comparative social policy (for an overview see Treib et al., 2007) and so there is arguably a need for the MEOW framework to be updated to reflect this development. The proposal here is that, rather than distinguishing between 'funding', 'provisioning', and 'regulation', the latter category is replaced by the notion of 'governance'.

In relation to the theoretical investigation of retrenchment and convergence, remarkably similar developments have emerged to have taken place at the level of governance in England and Denmark. These developments could be cast in the light of retrenchment away from public sector formal regulation. Yet, when examining in more detail the implications of the self-regulation idea in relation to CSR it begins to emerge that changes are taking place at the formal regulatory level in England and Denmark which cannot simply be reduced to the assessment that responsibility is being shifted away from the public sector. Instead, it is rather a matter of regulatory responsibilities being redefined for different sectors in the mixed economy. In order to understand fully whether such changes constitute retrenchment it is necessary to explore the underlying ideas behind the redefined roles and responsibilities at Hall's level of 'overarching goals'. This will be the subject for discussion in the next section.

'Goals': CSR Partnerships as Indicators of Paradigm Shifts?

After having considered the formal arrangements of the CSR partnerships in terms of their funding, provisioning and governance arrangements (what Hall terms 'settings' and 'instruments') it is now time to turn to the ideational institutional level. Can the CSR partnerships be said to give any indications that paradigmatic changes – that is, changes in overarching 'goals' – are taking place in England and/ or Denmark? As outlined in Chapter 2, the ideational institutional level consists of the further three levels of policy paradigms, mixed economy sectoral paradigms, and welfare state paradigms.

Policy Paradigm   Starting at the policy level, England and Denmark are regarded here as belonging to the same policy paradigm in relation to their policy goals for employment and their policy approaches to unemployment (as already stated in Chapter 2). Both England and Denmark have since the 1980s pursued what is known in policy terms as an 'active labour market policy' (ALMP), which has seen successive governments changing unemployment benefit systems from 'passive' to 'active' (Cox, 1998a) in the sense that the receipt of public benefits has become increasingly conditional upon active job seeking and often also participation in various labour market 'activation' programmes. This perception of a common ALMP policy paradigm is extensively supported in the literature (Torfing, 1999, Lødemel and Trickey, 2001, Taylor-Gooby, 2001, van Oorschot and Abrahamson, 2003, Lindsay and Mailand, 2004, Aust and Arriba, 2005), where its social impacts have also been debated. One aspect already discussed in more detail in this book is the shift in English and Danish policy approaches to issues around social exclusion, which now focus increasingly on paid work rather than on material redistribution as the route to social inclusion (MacGregor, 2003, Levitas, 2005, Beland, 2007).

Questions around whether the English and Danish convergence around ALMP constitutes retrenchment – for example as a form of 're-commodification' (Pierson, 2001a) – or even a shift away from either of those countries' welfare state regimes are also widely debated in the literature (Torfing, 1999, Cox, 2004, Halvorsen and Jensen, 2004). However, that debate is not central to this chapter. The main question here regards the extent to which the emergence of CSR and its application to the policy area of unemployment and social exclusion indicates a shift away from the overarching 'goals' of ALMP. This question has, to a wide extent, already been answered earlier in the book. In Chapter 5 it was established that the CSR partnerships emerged as part of the 'social policy strand' of CSR's historical development. Within this strand English and Danish governments have since the 1980s and 1990s employed CSR as a social policy tool for linking issues around social exclusion to the labour market. This historical connection shows that CSR is very much embedded in the ALMP paradigm rather than reflecting a shift away from this policy paradigm. Other authors studying ALMP have supported this view when they include CSR labour market measures in their overall considerations of ALMP (Lødemel and Trickey, 2001, Halvorsen and Jensen, 2004, Lindsay and Mailand, 2004, Martin, 2004). Another way of approaching the question could also be to ask if the respondents give any indications that the introduction of commercial sector providers in the implementation of ALMP has lead to any changes in the overarching ideas behind ALMP. This question has also already been considered earlier in the book. In Chapter 7 it emerged that respondents involved in the CSR partnerships regard the partnerships as a way for businesses to simultaneously contribute to solving the social problem of social exclusion and help socially excluded people become included via the labour market. Moreover, the CSR partnerships were predominantly made sense of within the compatible approaches to CSR and social exclusion which are framed within the social democratic and social integrationist discourses. On this basis it can be said that whilst the (still proportionally marginal) involvement of the commercial sector at the provisioning level of ALMP may constitute a novelty in terms of implementation, CSR has not brought about changes to the overarching goals of ALMP. On the contrary, at the policy level CSR appears to have had the opposite effect of reinforcing an already existing policy path. Seen from this perspective CSR is also cementing rather than fragmenting the already existing convergence between England and Denmark within this policy area

Mixed Economy Sectoral Paradigms   At the level of mixed economy sectoral paradigms it has been noted earlier that the Danish mixed economy of welfare relies on public sector provisioning, funding and regulation to a wider extent than the English mixed economy. These mixed economy balances are to a large degree informed by the overarching welfare state paradigms which see actors in the Danish social democratic model more inclined to view the public sector as synonymous with 'the welfare state' whilst regarding other sectors as less legitimate welfare producers. In contrast hereto, actors in the English liberal model are more likely to question the legitimacy of the public sector whilst favouring welfare production by either the commercial, non-profit, or informal sectors (Esping-Andersen, 1990). The question then is whether any of the changes or continuities observed so far in the CSR partnerships can be taken as indications that any of these two divergent mixed economy sectoral paradigms are undergoing change.

The most significant indication of change seen in the CSR partnerships in relation to the mixed economy is the redefinition of roles and responsibilities at the level of governance in both England and Denmark. At this level a shift was observed from regulating with legislation to regulating with alternative governance tools such as facilitating, enabling, encouraging, incentivizing, framework setting, and influencing. This shift reflects an institutional redirection in both countries towards governments adopting the ideas of New Public Management ('NPM'). This change is already widely discussed in the literature, where authors cover implementation issues around performance management, quasi-markets, and the general application of management techniques to public services (Lane, 2000, Dent, 2005, Newman and McKee, 2005, Taylor-Gooby, 2008b). In this book's case studies, however, the main NPM aspect of the CSR partnerships is the general ideational NPM emphasis on steering rather than rowing (Osborne and Gaebler, 1992). The connection between the CSR partnerships and NPM has already been identified at various points in this book, for example in the historical investigation (Chapter 5) and in the exploration of the social impacts of the CSR partnerships (Chapter 7).

Understanding the CSR partnerships as embedded within the overarching ideational goals of NPM also influences the understanding of some of the changes that have been noted beyond the level of governance. At the level of provisioning in particular, the involvement of the commercial sector in the CSR partnerships has been shown to also enhance the scope for further provisioning involvement by the local level public sector in Denmark and the non-profit sector in England. In the Danish case, this development can now be made sense of on the basis of observations already made in the literature on NPM, where it has been argued that the idea of public sector steering rather than rowing inevitably involves 'simultaneous upward and downward flows of power' (Newman, 2001: 38), and therefore often results in various modes of public sector decentralization (Taylor-Gooby, 2008b). In the case of the English enhanced role of the non-profit sector as provider in the CSR partnerships, a similar diversion, rather than retrenchment, of public sector regulatory power can be identified. This becomes apparent when speaking to Alan, who is the local government partner in the English CSR partnership. From his interview it transpires that the central provisioning role played by the non-profit sector organization in the CSR partnerships is in fact predominantly paid for with public sector money. It is not sustained financially by the non-profit organization itself or by commercial sector sponsorship. For example, in the case of the local project leader of the CSR partnerships, who works from within a non-profit sector organization, the local council pays this person's salary and other office overheads directly from a grant made available to local authorities by the national government. This revelation means that what was identified earlier in this chapter as a transfer of provisioning responsibility from the public to the non-profit sector can now be described more accurately as a form of public sector outsourcing. From this perspective the English government is decentralizing its regulatory steering 'by the back door'. The government may have transferred the provisioning or 'rowing' responsibility to the non-profit sector, but by remaining involved as the main funder of the service it also maintains its regulatory influence over the partnerships. In the quote below Alan explains the background to this arrangement:

> Most of the organizations, which we fund to use that grant, are – in fact all of them – are voluntary or private or housing association sector agencies. We don't ... we have occasionally used a grant to fund [local council] services, but we took a decision two years ago [2003], that we would mainstream those services, by which I mean fund them from the big pot of local authority money, in order to commission specialist services.

Alan's explanation further reveals that the arrangement in the CSR partnership is representative of a larger development in which local authorities are 'mainstreaming' their services by commissioning non-profit organizations to provide services on their behalf. This development is recognized in the wider mixed economy literature, where Carmel and Harlock (2007) further argue that the partnership approach is a way for the English government not only to increasingly use the non-profit sector as a service provider but also to hereby carve out for itself the whole of the sector as its own new 'governable terrain' (Carmel and Harlock, 2007).

At the mixed economy sectoral level it can, in other words, be observed that similar changes are taking place in the relationship between the public, commercial and non-profit sectors in England and Denmark. The two countries converge around a new commitment to NPM ideas. As such it is reasonable to talk of retrenchment, although not predominantly in terms of public sector cost-containment or transfer of responsibility. Instead Pierson's notion of 'recalibration' can be applied here (Pierson, 2001a) on the basis that both governments are 'rationalizing' their provisioning involvements in social problems and 'updating' their regulatory approaches to adapt to new societal demands and norms. In both countries, these new societal expectations are related to an increased questioning of the legitimacy of the public sector. In England it has already been observed by other commentators that the English government has sought to enhance the legitimacy of ALMP programs such as the CSR partnerships by making its own role as inconspicuous as possible and instead transferring provisioning responsibilities to non-public sector intermediaries (Martin, 2004). The same has been said of partnerships in England in general (Pemberton and Lloyd, 2008). It was already apparent in the historical investigation that some Danish respondents linked the introduction of CSR as a policy alternative to the legitimacy crisis of the public sector. It emerges on that basis that at the ideational level England and Denmark converge around the same shared experience regarding the contested role of the public sector. It must not be forgotten, however, that the legitimacy of the public sector, although challenged, still remains comparatively stronger in Denmark than in England. That explains why the Danish government has not followed the same model as its English counterpart in transferring provisioning responsibility to the non-profit sector. This perception is supported when Danish respondents explain why the non-profit sector is not widely considered or included in Danish conceptualizations and implementations of the partnership concept. One such example is Brenda, who researches CSR for a Danish national research organization:

> The state is the sun, right, and everything orbits around that. And the likelihood that two of the other small planets – that is, businesses and non-profit organizations – that they should get together without being influenced by the giant [sun/state] is not particularly natural.

The CSR partnerships have in other words indicated that both England and Denmark are in a process of transformation at the mixed economy sectoral level. Moreover, they are moving in similar directions towards the ideas of New Public

Management. Yet path-dependent differences in attitudes towards the public sector are still sustaining a degree of divergence in terms of the implementation of the NPM ideas. Another way of putting it is that whilst there are overlaps in the two countries' new approaches to steering, differences remain in the practical details around the rowing. Finally, there are strong indications that when CSR is applied to the area of social exclusion it is a means through which governments are seeking to consolidate the NPM paradigm. In that sense CSR is in itself an additional contribution towards these changes rather than merely an indication of change.

Welfare State Paradigms   The last ideational level to be considered here is the level of welfare state paradigms. Here England and Denmark belong to the liberal and social democratic regimes, respectively (Esping-Andersen, 1990). Are any of the changes and continuities discussed so far signs of England and Denmark moving away from these two different paradigms and perhaps moving towards converging welfare state paradigms? So far in the analysis the CSR partnerships in both countries have emerged as incorporated into the already existing and cross-nationally shared policy paradigm involving active labour market policy goals. Moreover, these goals are implemented in path-dependent and diverging manners when it comes to their funding arrangements. At those two levels the CSR partnerships are therefore not associated with any paradigm shifts, nor any institutional retrenchment. On the other hand, the emergence of CSR has seen the commercial sector become involved as a provider in relation to social exclusion. The roles and responsibilities of the different mixed economy sectors have been redefined even more widely at the level of governance. And finally, it has been established that these changes are supported at the ideational level where the notion of CSR is being embedded within the mixed economy sectoral paradigm and policy goals of New Public Management. The difficult question now is determining whether this mix of changes and continuities can be interpreted as indications of change at the overarching level of welfare state paradigms.

This question can be approached from two directions. The combination of changes at the provisioning, governance and ideational levels can be taken as evidence that England and Denmark are changing and now converging around what researchers have labelled the 'new welfare settlement' (Lewis, 2007, Taylor-Gooby, 2008a). This recently emerged paradigm is the outcome of a collective move away from the passively providing welfare state towards 'social investment' welfare strategies. This new form of social policy sees government seeking to integrate social and economic goals by enhancing self-activity, responsibility and mobilization into paid work among citizens (Taylor-Gooby, 2008a: 4). It could be argued that England and Denmark are now part of this newly emerged 'social investment' welfare settlement. The evidence includes the active labour market policies and the New Public Management governance approaches in which CSR is embedded, but also the idea of commercial sector social responsibility reflected in the notion of CSR itself (sometimes also referred to as corporate citizenship). Yet the question can also be approached from a different direction. If taking

		Change or continuity?		Retrenchment?		Other change		Conv/ Div
		England	Denmark	England	Denmark	England	Denmark	
Formal Institutional Level	**Settings: Funding**	**Path-dep :** *CSR Projects market-funded*	**Path-dep :** *public sector subsidization*	No				Div.
	Instruments 1: Provisioning	**Change** *Involvement of commercial sector in social problems*		Yes: *as transfer of public sector responsibility to commercial sector. Not large scale*		*Large scale transfer of public sector responsibility to non-profit sector*	*Internal re-assignment of public responsibility from central to local level*	Div.
	Instruments 2: Governance	**Change** *CSR as commercial sector 'self-regulation'*		**Yes:** *New Public Management agenda: retreat of public sector from 'rowing' to 'steering'*				Conv.
Ideational Institutional Level	**Policy Paradigms**	**Path-dep:** *CSR projects immersed in ALMP Paradigm*		No, *not as retreat from already existing ALMP Paradigm*				Conv.
	Mixed Economy Sectoral Paradigms ('MESP')	**Change** *CSR used to further New Public Management agenda*		Yes: *as 're-calibration'; focus away from public to non-profit sector*	Yes: *as 're-calibration': focus away from central to local public sector*	*'Covert' public sector role: sponsors non-profit sector involvement*	*Continued legitimacy of public sector involvement in social issues*	Div.
	Welfare State Paradigm	*Combination of continuity & change at different institutional levels*		**Some**. *Most significant at levels of MESP, governance + provisioning*	**Some**. *Most significant at levels of MESP + governance*			Div.

Figure 8.1   Change, Continuity ('Path-dep'), Convergence ('Conv.') and Divergence ('Div.') in the CSR Unemployment Projects

into account the details around the implementation of the policy goals, and in particular the funding arrangements, it will become clear that what appears similar at the ideational level can have widely different social impacts for the individuals and social groups affected by the new policies and practices. This discrepancy was already suggested in Chapter 7, where it emerged that, compared with the Danish CSR partnerships, the English CSR partnerships are much less likely to overcome experiences of social exclusion and to fundamentally address structural inequalities inside and outside the labour market due to the types of jobs on offer and their minimal income prospects. From this perspective of social impacts, path-dependent differences informed by the diverging welfare state paradigms very much remain significant.

These two different ways of approaching the question of welfare state paradigmatic change, and their tendency often to result in conflicting conclusions regarding welfare state change and continuity, convergence and divergence, are widely recognized in the literature. The dilemma also raises the question of how to draw conclusions regarding paradigm shifts based on Hall's (1993) framework for analysing change when, as is the case in this book's case studies, institutional change is identified on the levels of instruments and goals, yet path-dependency dominates on the level of settings. In Hall's conceptualization of change, paradigmatic 'third degree' change involves not just shifts at the ideational level but implies consecutive changes at first the level of settings (first degree), then also at the level of instruments (second degree), and finally on all three levels including the level of goals (third degree). The question is whether such 'bottom-up' sequencing is the only appropriate way of determining change. If standing by Hall's framework it must be deduced here that whilst various institutional changes have been detected in England and Denmark, these changes do not amount to a shift in these countries' overarching welfare state paradigms. However, if Pierson's (1994) notion of 'time lag' is applied it is not impossible to imagine that retrenchment could still happen at all levels. From this perspective, the current lack of visible retrenchment at the level of funding could be a result of a delay in effect of the retrenchment initiatives at the other levels rather than evidence of path-dependency. Overall, however, the most important conclusion is the observation that whilst this chapter's exploration of the CSR partnerships has uncovered both institutional changes and continuities, the main levels on which CSR constitute a contribution to, rather than merely an indication of, institutional change are the levels of governance and mixed economy sectoral paradigms.

CSR Past, Present and Future

CSR as a Vehicle for Change in the Mixed Economy

In the previous section it was established that when CSR is linked to issues around social exclusion from the labour market in England and Denmark, the idea of CSR is employed as a means of renegotiating the roles and responsibilities of the various sectors in the English and Danish mixed economies of welfare. In particular, CSR exerts the most important influence at the ideational level of mixed economy sectoral paradigms. The question to ask now is where this development is going next. Where are the limits to CSR's promotion of mixed economy change? Is CSR, for example, going to eventually result in an ever increasing roll-back of the public sectors whilst commercial sectors are rolled out more and more comprehensively in England and Denmark? The CSR stakeholders interviewed for this book did not believe that this outcome is the goal of CSR. When asked if they felt that CSR should be a replacement of or a supplement to public sector welfare activities, not one expressed agreement with the former suggestion. Respondents in both England and Denmark and across the spectrum of CSR stakeholders strongly reject the idea that the commercial sector could or should take the full range of responsibilities for providing, funding and regulating welfare services. Such views were particularly fervent in relation to core welfare areas such as health and education. This does not mean, however, that all respondents reject altogether the idea of enhancing commercial sector involvement at some levels in the mixed economy. In England, Christina, who works for a national business association, is flexible in her views of welfare roles and responsibilities:

> It is a difficult one, because countries will [be at] different stages [in terms of how] things are done. For instance, in the UK there's a kind of blurring between whether the public sector delivers public services or whether the private sector does, because that's kind of where we are at the moment. Two centuries ago it was a slightly different blurring, because the public sector wasn't delivering anything and the private sector was. [...] There are some services that one would I think automatically nowadays say: 'it really is for the Government to deliver'. And whether they are actually doing that themselves or whether they are recruiting companies to help them do that doesn't matter, that's just a detail. We are talking about things like basic health care, basic education. [...] [In relation to social exclusion] I think the role of Government is to identify the areas across the country where there might be unemployment issues [and] issues to do with social exclusion [...] because the Government does have the range of the national consciousness and a business doesn't. So that is the kind of thing that Government is best [positioned] to try and understand.

Christina makes the important point also made previously in this book that mixed economy balances not only vary cross-nationally but constantly change over time within countries too (Lewis, 1995, Winther, 1996, Stewart, 2007). She also recognizes that what is currently taken for granted as a public sector responsibility is only an expression of institutionally informed attitudes at a particular point in time and that this can therefore change. When she considers public sector responsibility in relation to social exclusion, she makes a practical rather than normative case against commercial sector take-over. The argument she makes is reiterated by many other respondents. She points out that the commercial sector will never be in a position to fully take over responsibility for social exclusion because its actors consist of autonomous businesses that individually or even collectively can never reach the same national overview and understanding of the situation as the interconnected governmental agencies in the public sector.

In Denmark, Moira, who works for a CSR organization based in the non-profit sector, also elaborates on her rejection of the idea of replacement:

> I think it [CSR] should be a supplement. Because I don't think firms should be taking over the responsibility of the state. But I do think that the limits of the role of the state should be up for discussion all the time. It ought to be a collective, ongoing social debate. That [debate] has been dead for too many years.

Moira makes the point, which was also made by other Danish respondents earlier (in Chapter 7), that in the Danish welfare context, CSR has been welcomed by many as an opportunity to initiate a broader social debate about the welfare state. CSR is in that regard a means for encouraging welfare state citizens to reflect on the current mixed economy balance rather than take for granted the all-encompassing role of the public sector. From the differences between Christina's and Moira's statements it emerges that, whereas in England, CSR stakeholders are already institutionally accustomed to consider the mixed economy as an issue which is under constant review, in Denmark, the idea of CSR constitutes more of a clash with the existing preconceptions of the mixed economy. On this basis CSR also offers for Danish CSR stakeholders a comparatively more 'revolutionary' potential in terms of deviating from what is considered – by people like Moira – a far too cemented mixed economy institutional path (Martin, 2004). Apart from these cross-national differences in the English and Danish 'institutional starting positions', the conclusion can be reached that English and Danish CSR stakeholders share the belief that there are limits to the mixed economy changes which CSR is employed to instigate.

Beyond respondents' specific views of CSR in relation to the mixed economy, what is also interesting here is how respondents envisage the future of CSR in general. When respondents were asked this question their responses elicited a remarkably identical future scenario. Firstly, the vast majority of respondents believe that CSR will continue to grow. This is perhaps not surprising considering their predispositions as CSR stakeholders towards supporting and believing in the idea of CSR. As such this group of respondents are a self-selecting group. The more interesting result is the broad consensus amongst respondents across the different institutional contexts regarding the way in which they see CSR developing. Starting at the international level, Denise from the European commission here outlines her view of the future:

> I think that those that have in the past dismissed CSR simply as a management fad, they might be correct in terms of terminology. You know, ten years from

now it is possible they won't be using the term 'CSR'. But I definitely don't believe that knowledge about and understanding of the social and environmental impacts of business and how they deal with those is going to suddenly disappear from what companies are required to know. I doubt that. I think it will be completely opposite. [...] If you pick up, at random, five copies of the Financial Times from this year and take five copies of the Financial Times in 1995 and see how many strictly business-related stories are related to environment, poverty, transparency, corruption. [...] You open the FT or even the Economist these days [...], ok the Economist won't use the term CSR, but I mean, I don't care what anyone calls it, those issues are becoming mainstream.

Denise's belief that the ideas and issues around CSR will become increasingly mainstream whilst the concept of CSR might die out is very much echoed by Pamela, who works as a CSR director for a large English business:

I think [CSR] is getting increasing support. And the business case is slowly becoming established, in my view. I think that will lead to a continuation of this mainstreaming, embedding it. And probably then, you could say that it might, if it becomes a natural part of doing business, that all managers just inherently do it. I mean, I look at the sort of people that are being recruited to [my] organization at the moment. Particularly graduates. I mean, they just understand [CSR] instinctively. They don't need a label of CSR. In fact, it is almost unhelpful. So looking a long way into the future, I can see the end of CSR as a separate discipline, and hopefully that it's more natural, you know, a natural and completely embedded part of business.

And finally, to take a Danish example, Pamela's prediction that CSR as an idea will become 'embedded', 'inherent', and 'natural' is once again evoked by Bolette, who works for the Danish government in the department that does not have the lead on CSR:

I don't believe any more that [CSR] will die out. I did a few years ago. But now I think it will become a concept which will become more and more cemented, or natural. Like Human Resources, for example. That's also a concept which you can't really prove [makes] economic [sense], but it has become cemented anyway. No [business] does not have an HR focus. I think that over time, [CSR] will be just like the environmental area. That is now something so natural for most businesses. And every firm has its own interpretation of what it means and what their task is.

These future scenarios of Denise, Pamela and Bolette are very much representative of the majority of the remaining respondents. Many reiterate the belief that the term 'corporate social responsibility' will disappear whilst the idea of CSR will continue.

From a theoretical point of view the frequent use of terminology such as 'mainstream', 'embedded', 'inherent', 'natural', and 'cemented' is particularly interesting. These terms indicate that respondents envisage a future institutionalization of CSR. CSR is being predicted to become transformed from its current state as a free-floating idea to become embedded in the ideational institutional structures of not just England and Denmark but in nations throughout the world. Once embedded, it can be further predicted that CSR will no longer remain a potential agent for institutional change. Instead CSR will become an ingrained norm and value and from here CSR is more likely to contribute towards perpetuating path-dependent continuity than instigating institutional change. From this perspective, the future institutionalization of CSR predicted by respondents is far from insignificant.

The respondents' future scenario is significant for the English and Danish mixed economies but not only in terms of the balances between the different sectors. The vision of CSR as a future institutionally embedded value is also relevant to paradigmatic ideas about the appropriate behaviour of actors *within* mixed economy sectors. If CSR is predicted to become mainstream for businesses and to disappear as a separate concept, this prediction would also appear to imply that firms will in the future become more socially embedded as actors in the mixed economy. This impression is confirmed when discussing issues around business motivations for CSR with respondents. Whereas many reiterate the range of business cases already well known in the business literature (Smith and Hasnas, 1999, Dean, 2001, Joseph and Parkinson, 2002, Knudsen, 2004), the vast majority of respondents go on to concede that, ultimately, CSR is driven by the values and sometimes ethical convictions of those individuals within organizations who believe in the idea rather than the economic reward of CSR. Steen and Bolette, who work together in a Danish government department that does not have the lead on CSR, represent just some of the respondents expressing this view:

> Steen: We have been given a good indication that many [organizations] do [CSR] not because they believe they will reap economic rewards, but simply because they have some values. Especially small and medium sized business. It is our experience that [CSR] is about values. 'We can't count it in money terms. We just do it because it is right'. We have been given that answer many times. And one shouldn't ignore that.

> Bolette: One shouldn't ignore that businesses are like people. We have this hypothesis about us being rational. But when it comes down to it we are not always that rational.

The argument against businesses as rational entities puts the partnership between CSR and New Public Management in an interesting new light, because whilst the latter is premised upon ingraining commercial principles in the public sector, CSR now emerges as aimed at instituting firms with social or even moral agency. But more importantly, when looking beyond the CSR partnerships it would seem that the idea of CSR can be considered more than a policy tool for shifting mixed economy balances and challenging institutionally cemented ideas about their appropriate composition. It must be remembered that CSR is not only applied as social policy within national realms of social exclusion. As was shown in Part II, CSR is also applied as various other practices throughout the mixed economy. Likewise, the idea of CSR is not only being employed to instigate changes at the national level but also in supranational and global domains. From this perspective it becomes clear that CSR is considered by most CSR stakeholders to be more than a vehicle employed by policymakers to achieve mixed economy changes and to further promote the policy goals of New Public Management. Beyond the policy context, CSR constitutes a broader ideational challenge from actors across the mixed economy of existing mixed economy sectoral paradigms regarding the appropriate behaviour of actors within sectors and particularly of organizations in the commercial sector. CSR challenges those widely held perceptions about mixed economy sectors as being driven by distinct 'logics' and about the actors within different sectors as being predetermined by distinct forms of agency, which were discussed in Chapter 2 and which are also often reiterated in the mixed economy literature (Le Grand, 1991, Goodin, 2003, Drakeford, 2007). Whilst a paradigm shift at this level remains part of the future rather the present scenario, it is interesting to note this potential of CSR. Going forward one might imagine England and Denmark beginning to converge around more similar 'varieties of capitalism' (Hall and Soskice, 2001) in which firms in both countries will become gradually more socially embedded than they are at present.

Drivers of Past and Future Developments

CSR has now been considered not only in relation to the present but also in relation to the past and the future. Taking into account the historical analysis (Part II) and the future predictions made by the respondents, this section now turns to explore what insights can be gained from these analyses regarding the drivers and mechanisms of institutional change and continuity. In the historical analysis it was observed firstly that changes in socioeconomic structures were frequently highlighted both in the literature and by respondents as significant for the emergence of each of the historical CSR strands. The philanthropic CSR strand emerged in the context of the industrial revolution, the social policy CSR strand was established in relation to the welfare state crisis, and globalization CSR developed in response to economic globalization. Yet it still seems to far a leap to deduct on that basis that the economy alone has driven the development of CSR. As with functionalist economic explanations of welfare state emergence and evolution (Kerr et al., 1960, Wilensky, 1975, Flora and Alber, 1981), theories that see the economy as the main driver of historical developments oversimplify the developments as functions of structural changes. If a straight forward causal relationship between economics and CSR is assumed this does not explain why different strands of CSR arose sometimes in periods of economic growth and sometimes in periods of economic crisis. In the same way, economics does not explain why the welfare state expanded during nineteenth- and twentieth-century economic growth periods yet is considered under threat by the economic growth model of globalization (Ohmae, 1992, Geyer, 1998, Mishra, 1999). And finally, when it comes to the future of CSR, some respondents argue that CSR will depend on economic developments, yet views differ again as to whether CSR is likely to benefit the most from economic contractions or expansions.

Another development driver which is recognizable from the welfare state literature is politics. In the historical investigation of CSR, politics was seen as significant by some authors and respondents, especially in relation to the establishment of the social policy CSR strand. However, as with the economic explanation, political interest cannot explain the development of CSR in and of itself. This was particularly clear when it was found that the same (social policy) CSR strand was initiated by different political parties in England and Denmark. Moreover, beyond the point of formation, changing governments were found to become progressively less able to reverse the paths already created or even to change the development in the direction of their own party-political interests. Institutions were, in other words, found to prevail over political interests. Like economics, some respondents also consider politics decisive for the future development of CSR. These respondents argue that different parties will move the development in different directions when in government, and some also emphasize that centre-left governments are more inclined to be financially supportive of CSR than centre-right governments. But an equal number of respondents argue that politics makes no difference and that CSR has a momentum of its own.

What most respondents highlight and agree about, however, is the overarching importance of individuals for the future survival of CSR. Individuals were also central to the development of the historical CSR strands. Particularly the types of individuals who act independently of and often against their contemporary institutional structures. The pioneering philanthropic Victorian business owners, the maverick policy entrepreneurs of the 1980s and 1990s, and current anti-establishment, anti-globalization voices all have in common that their actions are less dictated by their formal or ideational institutional context and more by their personal beliefs in the idea of CSR. Similarly, respondents continually argue that the future of CSR depends ultimately on people who are seen to have unique qualities as CSR champions. These can operate in various realms; in the commercial sector as business leaders, managers or employees; as policy entrepreneurs working in central government; and also in the non-profit sector.

The type of agency referred to most by respondents as important to the development of CSR is political leadership. This reflects to a large extent the central role given to the Minister for Social Affairs, Karen Jespersen, in the Danish historical narrative about CSR as a policy alternative. But outside the Danish context, EU respondents also make frequent references to the significant role played by the former EU president, Jacque Delors, in being an early champion of the CSR idea. A few English respondents also believe that prime ministerial leadership affects the direction of the English CSR agenda. Another type of agency repeatedly emphasized as important for the future development of CSR is champions within companies. The significance of these types of actors is highlighted especially by business respondents and respondents working for CSR organizations in the non-profit sector in both England and Denmark. Simon, the local project leader in England who works for a non-profit CSR organization, is just one respondent expressing this view:

> You find that it's one individual in the company who is leading on [CSR] and
> so if they don't get the buy-in from the rest of the company and if that one
> individual leaves it just kind of falls by the way-side [...] you do have to have
> individual sort of company champions.

Flemming, who works as a HR director for large, nation-wide Danish business, reiterates Simon's view:

> Individuals are important. [...] [CSR] depends on 'fiery souls', who takes
> personal responsibility for [CSR] on a day to day basis.

Many respondents join Simon and Flemming in highlighting the importance of individuals within businesses. But also emerging is an emphasis on business leaders as particularly crucial for sustaining a business' commitment to CSR. This view is expressed by Pelle, who works for a Danish national CSR organization:

> Based on my knowledge of Danish businesses and their commitment to CSR I
> can see that CSR is very much driven by personal engagement, and particularly
> by an individual in the top management. [...]. I can't actually think of any
> examples, where businesses have sustained their commitment to CSR and where
> that hasn't been driven by an individual who just believes in [CSR]

Respondents in England also speak of the importance of business leaders in sustaining an organization's commitment to CSR, amongst other ways by supporting individual CSR champions further down the hierarchy. Peter, who works locally for an English nationwide public sector employer, shares his own experience:

> In a large organization it does very much rely on the commitment and the
> enthusiasm of particular pockets of people. And I'm not unique, there are
> several people across the organization who recognize the value of [CSR]. But,
> you know, if they move on, there's not necessarily the people or the structure.
> It's not inbuilt sufficiently into our organization at the moment to make sure
> that that's immediately picked up and just carried on. [...] I mean, when I had
> responsibility for my own area that was when [CSR] came from the top and we
> were able to do it. But with the current restructuring we're going through and

the responsibility that's been taken away from me I haven't got the control and therefore I haven't got the direction.

Finally, Moira, who works for a non-profit CSR organization at the local level in Denmark, reflects on experiences such as Peters and once again emphasizes the view that individuals matter in driving CSR and in sowing the seeds for embedding CSR within organizations:

> ... Then [businesses] get a new executive director and then they are back at square one again. That's life, the complex life of a business. [CSR] really does depend incredibly on people and personal involvement, and on who owns the business, and what kind of culture emerges under the leadership of various top managers and so on.

It should be clear by now that an important driver of change is the often overlooked agency of 'influencing individuals' (for an elaborated account of this type of agency see Chapter 2). But it is also clear that economics and politics are by no means irrelevant to the historical development. But rather than any of these two factors being the direct causes of future changes, economic and political changes constitute the 'windows of opportunities' (Kingdon, 1995) in which influencing individuals can optimize their chance of bringing about institutional change, for example by championing an institutionally free-floating idea such as CSR and 'framing' it to fit their own agenda (Cox, 2001, Beland, 2005, Taylor-Gooby, 2005, Slothuus, 2007, Steensland, 2008).

Conclusion

When the notion of corporate social responsibility was first explored in Chapter 3, it was observed that, throughout the different CSR discourses identified, there was a shared sense that contracts of various sorts are currently up for negotiation, whether this is the idea of a contract between business and society, the mixed economy, or an even broader global social contract. It has now been established that, at this point in time, when CSR is linked to issues around social exclusion from the labour market in England and Denmark, the idea of CSR is employed as a means of renegotiating the roles and responsibilities of the various sectors in the English and Danish mixed economies of welfare. To phrase it differently, CSR is currently being applied within the social policy context of social exclusion as a vehicle for achieving institutional change at the ideational level of mixed economy sectoral paradigms. From this chapter's investigation of CSR partnerships in England and Denmark it has emerged that the attempts at instigating institutional change with CSR are as yet not being rolled out on a significant scale at the formal institutional levels. The CSR partnerships represent one of the ways in which the commercial sector is being drafted in by English and Danish governments as a provider in active labour market policy schemes, but the contribution of CSR in this area remains marginal. Moreover, the funding arrangements of the CSR partnerships follow path-dependent patterns regarding the appropriate division of responsibilities between the commercial and public sectors. The formal level on which CSR contributes the most to the efforts of bringing about change is at the governance level, where CSR remains an area officially designated as 'self-regulatory'. This means that the commercial sector is in principle regulating its own involvement with social exclusion issues whilst the public sector is focusing on governing not with formal legislation but instead with more ideational regulatory tools such as 'encouraging', 'facilitating' and 'influencing'. It is now clear that at this institutional level the notion of CSR is being embedded within broader New Public Management policy goals and employed here to reinforce a public sector shift towards governance rather than government (Shamir, 2008). On the whole, CSR currently exerts the most significant institutionally transforming influence over the English and Danish mixed economies at the ideational level of mixed economy sectoral paradigms.

Whilst the idea of renegotiating roles and responsibilities of the various sectors in the mixed economy can to some degree be translated into attempts at instigating welfare state retrenchment, it has emerged throughout the analysis that such retrenchment is not currently taking place on a significant scale in England and Denmark. Where there are some signs of retrenchment, such as in the roll-out of the non-profit sector in England, this development cannot be said to be happening as a result of CSR. As a consequence, institutional divergence also continues to characterize the English and Danish welfare states more so than convergence. In relation to the question of whether more retrenchment can be expected to follow from CSR in the future and whether there is going to be a limit to such retrenchment, the views of the respondents on these matters indicate that whilst CSR stakeholders in England and Denmark are broadly in favour of renegotiating mixed economy roles and responsibilities, none of these same CSR stakeholders support the idea of CSR as a vehicle for total replacement of the public sector by the commercial sector. Instead, CSR stakeholders are more inclined to consider CSR important in relation to more fundamental future changes at the ideational level. The majority of respondents envisage a future scenario in which the currently free-floating idea of CSR has become embedded in the ideational institutional structures of England and Denmark, making CSR thereby redundant as a separate concept. The significance of this ideational institutional ingraining relates not so much to any resultant changes in formal mixed economy balances, but more so to changes to institutionally determined perceptions of the appropriate responsibilities and behaviours of actors in the commercial sector. According to this future scenario it is, in other words, possible to envisage a future in which firms will become increasingly more socially embedded rather than remaining one-dimensionally committed to institutionally prescribed commercial sector paradigms around rationality and profit-seeking.

The investigations of CSR in relation to retrenchment, convergence, and the future development of CSR have enabled theoretical observations regarding change and continuity in the mixed economy. In relation to the theoretical framework of the mixed economy, it has been suggested that the analytical level of formal regulation be updated to reflect current developments, which are increasingly seeing governments govern with various governance tools other than formal legislation, such as is the case in the area of CSR. It has also been observed that Hall's framework for analysing institutional change makes certain assumptions about the sequencing of changes at the various institutional levels, and that such sequencing does not necessarily reflect the way in which change happens in institutions. Finally, the combined knowledge of the history of CSR and respondents' future predictions about CSR have provided rich material for reflecting further on the ongoing comparative social policy debates regarding the drivers of institutional change and continuity. Here, the theoretical arguments made in Chapter 2 have been confirmed. This chapter emphasized the significance of the agency of influencing individuals in relation to institutional change. The histories of CSR in particular have strengthened the view that influencing individuals can instigate institutional change when armed with an institutionally free-floating idea such as CSR and capable of using 'windows of opportunity' presented at times of economic or political upheaval. As the notion of economic upheaval undoubtedly brings to mind the current situation of the global economic crisis, the following chapter, Chapter 9, will reflect on the future of CSR and the welfare state.

Chapter 9
Conclusion:
The Welfare State, CSR and the Future

The Findings and the Future

What does the future hold for corporate social responsibility? In the context of the current economic recession is there room for the idea that businesses and employers have responsibilities beyond their economic and legal obligations? Or is it inevitable that in an economic downturn CSR activities will also be down prioritized? This book will conclude by considering these questions. But before engaging in such future reflections, another question will be addressed in the first half of this chapter, namely that of how this book has established that CSR is relevant to the politics and study of the welfare state. The section below will draw together the findings from the various chapters and it will consider the overall conclusions reached concerning the relationship between CSR and the welfare state.

Why Corporate Social Responsibility is Relevant to Welfare State Politics and Studies

The overarching motivation of this book has been to further our understanding of the relationship between corporate social responsibility and the welfare state. This relationship has now been illuminated from three angles: the conceptual relationship between the notion of corporate social responsibility and social issues; the historical evolution of CSR in the mixed economy of welfare; and finally, through a case study exploring how CSR is interpreted and applied in the two welfare states of England and Denmark.

The chapters of the book have also been connected by an underlying interest in understanding CSR theoretically. Having chosen to adopt the theoretical lens of Historical Institutionalism, the theoretical element of the book has consisted in a two-sided inquiry. The two questions have been: on the one hand, to what extent do historical and institutional (welfare state) contexts influence the ways in which CSR is interpreted, applied and linked to social exclusion? And on the other hand, to what degree do the ideas and practices of CSR influence the institutional structures of welfare states?

Cross-national Differences and Similarities

Throughout the chapters of the book the conclusion was reached repeatedly that the historical and institutional contexts of welfare states are highly influential upon the ways in which CSR is interpreted, applied and linked to social exclusion. In the historical analysis it emerged that in several different types of welfare states (including England, Denmark, Sweden, Norway, Germany and France) today's interpretations and applications of CSR are the products of three parallel developments. 'The' history of CSR is, in other words, a history consisting of three historical strands: philanthropic CSR; social policy CSR; and globalization CSR. Each of these strands have been driven from within a different sector in the mixed economy and have been legitimized in accordance with different CSR discourses. The historical analysis demonstrated that it is welfare institutional settings which to a large degree allows or disallows different variations of CSR to come to expression to differing degrees in different countries. In relation to the philanthropic strand of CSR, for example, it emerged that this expression of CSR is widely considered incompatible with the social democratic and conservative welfare states of Scandinavia, Germany and France. Meanwhile, philanthropic CSR remains an unbroken and strong business tradition in the liberal welfare state of England. It has, in other words, been possible to assert that institutional structures have played a highly significant role in enabling and constraining the development of CSR.

The influence of national institutional structures upon social actors was also brought to light in Part III of the book, which contains the comparative case study of CSR in England and Denmark. Throughout the interviews with English and Danish CSR stakeholders it was apparent that the welfare state context in which they found themselves was highly influential upon their conceptualizations of CSR and on their preconceptions and expectations about how CSR should be applied now and in the future. For example, whereas English and Danish respondents appeared to approach the local CSR unemployment projects from the same practical perspective that the 'partnership idea' is the preferred model of implementation, on closer inspection it transpired that the interpretations of that idea varied between the two nationalities. Where Danish respondents took for granted a high level of involvement by the public sector in such partnerships, English respondents expected and preferred a much lower level of public sector involvement. Despite the use of similar terminology, the practical arrangements of the CSR partnerships hence turned out to follow path-dependent patterns regarding the appropriate division of responsibilities between the commercial and public sectors. Overall, these findings support the general historical institutionalist standpoint in which a development towards cross-national convergence amongst welfare states continues to look unlikely. Instead, national institutions continue to prove themselves resilient and able to mediate the effects of new ideas such as corporate social responsibility.

The Social Impacts of CSR

It was never within this book's remit to determine in a precise and quantitative manner the social impacts of CSR at national levels. However, the book has achieved its aim of initiating the widely neglected discussion about the social impacts of CSR. This objective has been approached firstly by exploring the social effects implied by different conceptions of CSR. The conceptual links made between CSR and social exclusion in Chapter 3 have strengthened the argument that CSR is relevant to welfare politics. And this relevance is only enhanced by the fact that the meaning of CSR is under negotiation. Policy makers and social policy academics alike should have an interest in participating in current debates about the appropriate way of interpreting CSR, because different CSR conceptions imply different approaches to addressing social issues such as social exclusion.

Secondly, the historical perspective on CSR has simultaneously situated the various practices of CSR found in different countries in their historical contexts as well as in the context of their varying intended social impacts. And finally, the question of the social effects of CSR was explored by inviting central English, Danish and EU CSR stakeholders to reflect on, discuss and share their opinions on this particular part of the CSR debate. The findings from these interviews have provided important insights into what CSR practitioners in England, Denmark and the EU are aiming to do with CSR and what social functions they believe CSR should fulfill. For example, in relation to unemployment and social exclusion more specifically, the interviews revealed that on the whole, people working with CSR in this area believe that they are producing a social good by transforming socially excluded individuals to socially included people (via the labour market); by lowering the 'welfare burden' of unemployment; and by changing attitudes towards social exclusion amongst the 'socially included' on the labour market.

All of this knowledge is important groundwork for anyone wanting to ascertain the social impacts of CSR on a wider social level, whether national or international. Moreover, knowledge about the intended social outcomes of CSR can also prove valuable to research wishing to evaluate the social impacts of CSR according to those social groups and individuals who the various CSR measures are aimed at. The social impacts of CSR still remain to be investigated from a wealth of angles. But while the research area of CSR waits for the development of national level and international comparative CSR impact indicators, statistics, surveys or evaluations of CSR activities, exploratory studies remain the best available sources from which to gather indicative information about the social impacts of CSR. At the same time it is also important to bear in mind that even as research into CSR matures, qualitative studies will always be valuable for advancing knowledge within this area on the basis of the ability of this form of inquiry to produce more in-depth, context-sensitive and sometimes also unexpected insights.

Change, Continuity and CSR

The issue of change and continuity is central to the politics of the welfare state. This book has also demonstrated that although CSR may appear to be a notion mainly relevant to the sphere of business, it does also have great political relevance, particularly as CSR is far from neutral on the matter of social change. This has been demonstrated in the book firstly in the conceptual analysis, where it transpired that different CSR conceptions imply different degrees of social change and continuity. From the interviews with CSR stakeholders in England and Denmark it also emerged that different CSR discourses currently inform and motivate different CSR stakeholders towards different forms and degrees of social change. This is just one of the many reasons why policy makers and social policy academics should be interested in participating in current debates about the appropriate way of interpreting and applying CSR.

On the theoretical level, the book's investigation of CSR as a vehicle for change and/or continuity has constituted a contribution to ongoing theoretical debates regarding welfare state retrenchment, convergence and divergence, and the drivers of institutional change and continuity. The book's findings have lent support to the argument made in Chapter 2 regarding the importance of the agency of influencing individuals in relation to institutional change. The histories of CSR in particular strengthened the standpoint that whilst institutions do have an inherent tendency to sustain continuity and thereby uphold existing frameworks, change is possible for example when influencing individuals – whether political, policy or social actors – armed with an 'institutionally free-floating idea', such as CSR, are capable of using to their benefit 'windows of opportunity' presented at times of economic or political upheaval. This has been particularly apparent in the history CSR in Denmark, where the personal investment of the then Minister for Social Affairs, Karen Jespersen, is widely acknowledged to have been instrumental in bringing not just CSR, but a particularly Danish social policy take on CSR, onto the political agenda. With this argument in mind the remainder of this chapter shall now turn to discuss the future of CSR in the light of recent socioeconomic events.

Considerations on the Future of CSR

In the early part of 2009, when an English financial journalist commented on CSR in the context of the recent economic downturn, his article opened with the proclamation: 'Thank goodness, now the recession's here we can forget all that nonsense about corporate social responsibility (CSR) and get back to trying to make some money' (Stern, 2009). In expressing this view of CSR, Stern claimed to represent many of England's top business leaders. And in supposing this connection between CSR and the economy, Stern also represents widespread popular opinion about CSR as a business activity associated with business financial surplus and periods of overall economic prosperity. However, Stern's article elicited strong responses from the English CSR community, where for example the CEO of Business in the Community, Stephen Howard, refuted Stern's assessment and argued that the view represented by Stern is based on a misinformed conceptualization of CSR. CSR, Howard stressed, 'is about how companies run their business, not how much money they give to charity' (Howard, 2009). This dispute is evidence to the fact that the contest over the meaning and application of CSR continues to be relevant today. Whilst the financial press and many business leaders continue to argue against CSR from within the conservative CSR discourse where 'the business of business is business' (Friedman, 1979), government and business-backed CSR organizations also continue to argue for CSR from within pro-CSR discourses – in Howard's case the liberal CSR discourse – in which being in business and engaging with CSR does not constitute a conflict of interest.

The arguments used above to debate the future of CSR in an economic downturn also raises questions more specifically about the future of the philanthropic strand of CSR. When the CSR stakeholders interviewed for this book commented on the notion of philanthropy respondents on the international level expressed the view that this approach to CSR is outdated, that it will over time become an increasingly marginal aspect of CSR and instead be completely replaced by stakeholder-informed conceptualizations of CSR. As the historical investigation demonstrated, philanthropic CSR is already considered a thing of the past in countries such as Germany, France and in Scandinavian. This stood in contrast to the English context, where corporate philanthropy is still widely considered part of the CSR domain. However, in the interviews with English CSR stakeholders it transpired that many national level respondents are working towards moving the English CSR agenda beyond philanthropy and towards stakeholder ideas and business case motivations. Achieving this development is seen as central to the future growth of CSR, because philanthropic CSR is regarded as a form of behaviour that is too easily disposed of when business circumstances change. Research appear to support this perception as the propensity to engage in corporate charitable giving has been linked to profitability (Campbell et al., 2002). What these respondents' perceptions once again expose is not so much that 'economics matters' in relation to CSR as a whole, but more so that 'definitions matter'. As long as it is assumed that CSR is (only) about philanthropy, then it is also easier to argue that CSR will suffer in an economic recession.

If the economy is not the main determining factor for the future of philanthropic CSR, what is then the important influence? The view here is that 'institutions matter'. This involves firstly the formal composition of the mixed economy of welfare. In Chapter 4 the argument was made that the extent of philanthropic CSR within an institutional context is closely linked with the size and centrality of that country's non-profit sector. In England, corporate charitable donations are mainly channelled to charitable causes via organizations in the non-profit sector. Likewise, CSR 'community involvement' activities are now predominantly carried out through non-profit intermediaries, as Chapter 8 uncovered. This means that as long as the current English government continues to champion and boost the non-profit sector, philanthropic CSR is also likely to continue rather than disappear. In that respect there is a degree to which 'politics matters'. Yet, party-political interest appears to make little difference as in England both the previous Labour government and the current Conservative–Liberal Democrat coalition can be seen promoting the expansion of the non-profit sector in areas of welfare provision. Political support for the non-profit sector appears, in other words, to be path-dependent in England for the foreseeable future (Benjamin, 2009).

Ideational institutions also matter. In Chapter 4 it emerged that, in the Scandinavian, German and French contexts, the very notion of philanthropy is considered inconsistent with the broader institutional mixed economies and their 'logic of appropriateness' (March and Olsen, 1989). In England, on the other hand, philanthropy is more widely accepted, not just in relation to businesses but more broadly throughout the mixed economy. In recent years, philanthropic activities by businesses and individuals have increased not just in volume but even more so in the attention this development is getting in policy circles and in the media (Breeze, 2008). There appears, in other words, to be no indications that philanthropic behaviour is becoming institutionally incompatible with the English mixed economy. Whilst philanthropic CSR may be tempered and the non-profit sector may suffer temporarily during the recession (Brindle, 2009), the philanthropic strand of CSR is not on its way out of the English CSR context.

Meanwhile, there are signs that philanthropic CSR is becoming slightly more acceptable in countries beyond the Anglo-Saxon institutional context. In France, activities such as corporate donations, employee volunteering and the establishment of corporate foundations have started to emerge. And the German government has in recent years started to promote the idea of 'civic engagement', meaning volunteerism, as part of its still embryonic national CSR agenda. In Denmark, a few respondents already pointed out that the non-profit sector has been the subject of increasing interest from Danish governments, not least the current centre-right coalition. Research also shows that the non-profit sector is growing in Denmark (Boje et al., 2006), and this might generate a space for philanthropic CSR. This prediction does not, however, extend to anything resembling a suggested future convergence between England, France, Germany and Denmark. Despite its recent growth, the Danish non-profit sector remains significantly smaller than the English and also the smallest in Scandinavia; its activities are centred round sport, culture and leisure rather than welfare production (Boje et al., 2006). Likewise, observers of CSR in France and Germany will also emphasize that philanthropic CSR remains marginal in these countries (Blasco and Zølner, 2010). Moreover, the view here is also that path-dependent attitudes towards the overarching centrality of the public sector to the Scandinavian social democratic welfare state and the central state to the German-French conservative welfare state regime will continue to keep philanthropic CSR at the very margins in these CSR contexts.

When international respondents considered philanthropic approaches to CSR outdated in the international CSR context they predicted at the same time that the future of CSR lies with the globalization strand of CSR. EU respondents believed that the CSR activities of businesses will increasingly become focused on global issues around supply chains, human and labour rights, ethical sourcing and environmental performance. Governments will also increasingly converge around linking their CSR policies to broader agendas on economic and social sustainability. These predictions already appear to have become fulfilled. As was shown in Chapter 6, the globalization strand of CSR is already dominating the national CSR agendas of countries such as Sweden and Norway, where neither philanthropic CSR nor the social policy strand of CSR ever gained foothold. In England, the government has in recent years updated its CSR policy so that it is now more explicitly linked with globalization and sustainability issues, for example by amending its official definition so that it now includes the statement: 'The Government sees CSR as the business contribution to our sustainable development goals' (BERR, 2009). In accordance with this amendment, England's main CSR non-profit intermediary, Business in the Community, has now expanded its main CSR areas to now also include an international dimension. In Denmark, where only a minority of CSR stakeholders used to consider CSR beyond the realm of the labour market, there have in recent years been indications that this is changing. Within government realms, CSR has been moved once again one step further away from the Ministry of Social Affairs, where CSR was initiated in the 1990s, and also away from the Ministry of Employment, from where CSR was led since the change of government in 2001 and during the time of the interviews in 2005. CSR is now led from the Ministry of Economic and Business Affairs, the Danish equivalent to the English governmental lead department on CSR, Department for Business, Enterprise and Regulatory Reform. The Danish government's latest report on CSR reflects a broad, international outlook which takes into account the various ways in which Danish businesses can practice CSR in an international context (Regeringen, 2008). Like the English government, the Danish government has also changed its official definition, which now includes a reference to businesses 'contributing to the solving of societal challenges, of both national and global nature' (Samfundsansvar.dk, 2009). These changes indicate that popular perceptions of CSR now include the global realm. Media investigations into supply chain concerns, for example, now link such issues to the concept of CSR (Witt-Hansen and Rothstein, 2007).

There are no signs that this trend will be diminished in the near future by either economic or political developments. This is partly because globalization CSR is predominantly driven by social movements, and they will continue to make their case for CSR within discourses – primarily the radical CSR discourse – where considerations of financial obligations or financial rewards will never overtake social concerns. If anything, the social movement side of the globalization CSR stream arguably now only has a stronger base on which to argue for the need for CSR, considering the recent uncovering of widespread financial mismanagement, excesses, and even large-scale fraud amongst many of the banks and financial institutions previously seen as the engines of economic globalization. In comparison, those national and international business lobbies who have successfully been 'pushing back' against anti-globalization movement demands for more corporate regulation and control now appear to have had their positions weakened. Governments across the Western world, regardless of their political affiliation, are now looking into ways of enhancing their regulation of the commercial sector in order to curb excessive executive pays, close loopholes in corporate taxation, and to create disincentives for reckless financial risk taking. In the context of CSR, where governmental regulation seemed out of the question at the beginning of the millennium, governments are now more open to considering various forms of regulatory intervention. In the UK, the government already introduced an update of its Companies Act in 2006 so that directors of companies are now required to give some consideration to how their decisions affect the interests of the community, the environment and suppliers (UK-GOV, 2006). Most importantly, companies are required to disclose information about its suppliers, which means that they can no longer claim not to be responsible for bad practices amongst their suppliers in areas such as the environment or labour conditions. The Danish government followed suit in 2009 by passing a law which will require listed companies, state owned companies and institutional investors to report on their work with CSR activities. These are initiatives from liberal or fairly liberal minded governments. The current economic recession, with the accompanying crisis of confidence in the promises of economic globalization, has if anything created a 'window of opportunity' (Kingdon, 1995) for the advancement of globalization CSR framed from within any of the CSR-supportive CSR discourses.

The increasing salience of globalization CSR and the indications that national contexts are converging around this agenda begs the question of what this means for the application of CSR to issues around social exclusion. On the one hand it would appear that countries like England, Denmark, Sweden, Norway, France and Germany are converging towards similar CSR agendas, with the social policy strand of CSR being phased out by the globalization strand of CSR. As such this development seems to support current perceptions in comparative social policy regarding the strong influence of international and especially supranational policies over national social policy agendas (Wilding, 1997, Jessop, 2004, Goodwin et al., 2005). On the other hand, when moving beyond the discursive level of governmental policy papers to consider instead how CSR is currently practiced, it emerges (as demonstrated in Chapter 6) that in France and Germany in particular, the globalization strand of CSR remains marginal compared to the dominant perception that the social responsibility of a firm is firstly and most importantly to its employees, and perhaps then secondly to those outside the labour market. But also English and Danish businesses continue to engage in CSR activities related to social exclusion. In both England and Denmark, the CSR partnerships examined for the case study in this book are still in place. In Denmark, all employers shortlisted for the prestigious national annual 'CSR People Prize', are year after year nominated on the basis of their engagement in the area of social exclusion from the labour market rather than in global issues (VFSA, 2010, Netværksprisen, 2009). In England, partnerships related to social exclusion issues continue to be promoted by the government backed Business in the Community, and many businesses continue to participate in social inclusion initiatives as part of their overall CSR activity.

The sustained popularity of CSR practices related to social exclusion can be interpreted as path-dependent continuations of now institutionally entrenched approaches to CSR. But they can also be seen as indications of a time lag between policy and implementation. The view here is that in relation to the social policy strand of CSR, politics does make a difference. As a form of public policy, this strand of CSR does depend on the lead set by governments, just as at the local levels the partnerships rely on input from the public sector. Economics matters less, because, as Chapter 5 demonstrated, economic developments can be used successfully for different political purposes depending on how policies are framed by policy makers (Kingdon, 1995, Cox, 2001, Beland, 2005). One could therefore imagine governments accepting that businesses can do less in the area of CSR and social exclusion whilst they are focusing on surviving in the downturn. But one could also imagine policy makers using the recession as an opportunity to appeal to businesses' sense of social responsibility, for example when they recruit or lay off staff.

Within all of these contrasting scenarios, what matters greatly for the future of CSR, and particularly in relation to social exclusion, is how institutionally embedded the idea of CSR has really become over the last decade and will become going forward. How socially entrenched is the idea that businesses has a responsibility towards society other than generating wealth through its financial activities? This again goes back to how CSR stakeholders define CSR and also to how CSR stakeholders view the different roles and responsibilities of actors in the mixed economy. The view here is that as long as there is widespread, institutionally ingrained acceptance of the perception that business must focus on making money and can sacrifice social concerns in the process, and as long as such views prevail not just in the commercial sector but also amongst the majority of actors in the mixed economy, CSR will continue to be a free-floating idea and its survival will therefore depend on the successes of its 'ideas champions', whether policy makers, CSR campaigners, or CSR pioneers within the commercial sector.

It is, however, important to stress that regardless of how much longer the idea of CSR continues to clash with existing institutional perceptions of the role of the commercial sector and the appropriate behaviour of its actors, such ideas will always be socially constructed rather than reflections of an unchangeable reality. Ideational institutions can, as social constructions, ultimately be 'unconstructed', under the right circumstances. As a reminder of this, the book will conclude with the words of the social constructivists Berger and Luckman and their apt example of how ideational institutions tend towards continuity yet always contain the possibility of being changed:

> As a businessman I know that it pays to be inconsiderate of others. I may laugh
> at a joke in which this maxim leads to failure, I may be moved by an actor

or a preacher extolling the virtues of consideration and I may concede in a philosophical mood that all social relations should be governed by the Golden Rule. Having laughed, having been moved and having philosophised, I return to the 'serious' world of business, once more recognise the logic of its maxims, and act accordingly. Only when my maxim 'fail to deliver the goods' in the world to which they are intended to apply are they likely to become problematic to me 'in earnest'. (Berger and Luckman, 1991 [1966]: 59)

It is, in other words, possible to imagine that CSR can become a socially embedded idea in the future, one which will at some point be a taken-for-granted part of the normative institutional fabric in the same way as today's welfare state citizens take for granted ideas about the importance of democracy, freedom and human rights. For the development to go in this direction, however, enough people – employers and employees, policy makers and social movements, shareholders and further stakeholders – need to reach the point where it is widely agreed that the current dominating maxim, that profit creation is the primary responsibility of businesses, has 'failed to deliver the goods'. As long as such a consensus remains elusive there will be a place for the continuing championing of CSR by the growing group of stakeholders who do believe in the idea of CSR. And in the future scenario preferred by this author, there is also continued scope for applying CSR to strengthen rather than to weaken the welfare state and to contribute towards the welfare state's overall future sustainability.

List of References

ABRAHAMSON, P. 2003. Different social Europes – Different partnership contexts. *In:* KJAER, L. (ed.) *Local Partnerships in Europe.* Copenhagen: The Copenhagen Centre.

ALBARED, A.L., LOZANO, J.M., TENCATI, A., MIDTTSUN, A. and PERRINI, F. 2008. The changing role of governments in corporate social responsibility: Drivers and responses. *Business Ethics: A European Review*, 17, 347–63.

ALBAREDA, L., TENCATI, A., LOZANO, J.M. and PERRINI, F. 2006. The government's role in promoting corporate responsibility: A comparative analysis of Italy and UK from the relational state perspective. *Corporate Governance*, 6, 386–400.

ALCOCK, P. 2001. The comparative context. *In:* ALCOCK, P. and CRAIG, G. (eds) *International Social Policy.* Basingstoke: Palgrave.

ANDERSEN, J.G. 2002. Change without challenge? Welfare states, social construction of challenge and dynamics of path dependency. *In:* CLASEN, J. (ed.) *What Future for Social Security?* Bristol: Policy Press.

ANTAL, A.B., OPPEN, M. and SOBCZAK, A. 2009. (Re)discovering the social responsibility of business in Germany. *Journal of Busines Ethics*, 89, 285–301.

ANTAL, A.B. and SOBCZAK, A. 2007. Corporate social responsibility in France: A mix of national traditions and international influences. *Business and Society*, 46, 9–32.

ANTONNEN, A. and SIPILÄ, J. 1996. European social care services: Is it possible to identify models? *Journal of European Social Policy*, 6, 87–100.

AUST, A. and ARRIBA, A. 2005. Towards activation? Social assistance reforms and discourses. *In:* TAYLOR-GOOBY, P. (ed.) *Ideas and Welfare State Reform in Western Europe.* Basingstoke: Palgrave Macmillan.

BAILEY, N. 2006. Does work pay? Employment, poverty and exclusion from social relations. *In:* PANTAZIS, C., GORDON, D. and LEVITAS, R. (eds) *Poverty and Social Exclusion in Britain: The Millenium Survey.* Bristol: Policy Press.

BAKAN, J. 2004. *The Corporation.* London: Constable and Robinson.

BALDWIN, P. 1996. Can we define a European welfare state model? *In:* GREVE, B. (ed.) *Comparative Welfare Systems.* London: Macmillan.

BANERJEE, S.B. 2010. Governing the global corporation: A critical perspective. *Business Ethics Quarterly*, 20, 265–74.

BARNARD, C.I. 1938. *The Functions of the Executive.* Cambridge, MA: Harvard University Press.

BAUMAN, Z. 1998. *Work, Consumerism and the New Poor.* Cambridge: Polity Press.

BELAND, D. 2005. Ideas and social policy: An institutionalist perspective. *Social Policy and Administration*, 39, 1–18.

BELAND, D. 2007. The social exclusion discourse: Ideas and policy change. *Policy and Politics*, 35, 123–39.

BENJAMIN, A. 2009. Beyond the limits. *The Guardian*, 18 February.

BERGER, P. and LUCKMAN, T. 1991 (1966). *The Social Construction of Reality: A Treatise in the Sociology of Knowledge.* London: Penguin.

BERGHMAN, J. 1995. Social exclusion in Europe: Policy context and analytical framework. *In:* ROOM, G. (ed.) *Beyond the Threshold: The Measurement and Analysis of Social Exclusion.* Bristol: Policy Press.

BERLE, A. and MEANS, G. 1932. *The Modern Corporation and Private Property.* New York: Macmillan.

BERMAN, S. 2001. Ideas, norms, and culture in political analysis. *Comparative Politics*, 33, 231–50.

BERR. 2009. *What is Corporate Responsibility (CR)?* [Online]. Available at: http://www.berr.gov.uk/whatwedo/sectors/sustainability/corp-responsibility/page45192.html/ [Accessed 18 February 2009].

BEVIR, M. and RHODES, R.A.W. 2004. Interpreting British governance. *British Journal of Politics and International Relations*, 6, 130–36.

BLANK, R. and BURAU, V. 2006. Setting health priorities across nations: More convergence than divergence? *Journal of Public Health Policy*, 27, 265–81.

BLASCO, M. and ZØLNER, M. 2010. Corporate social responsibility in Mexico and France: Exploring the role of normative institutions. *Business and Society*, 49, 216–51.

BLUNKETT, D. 2003. *Active Citizens, Strong Communities: Progressing Civil Renewal.* London: Home Office.

BOJE, T.P., FRIDBERG, T. and IBSEN, B. 2006. *Den frivillige sektor i Danmark: Omfang og betydning.* København: SFI.

BONOLI, G. 2001. Political institutions, veto points, and the process of welfare state adaptation. *In:* PIERSON, P. (ed.) *The New Politics of the Welfare State.* Oxford: Oxford University Press.

BONOLI, G. 2003. Social policy through labour markets: Understanding national differences in the provision of economic security to wage earners. *Comparative Political Studies*, 36, 1007–30.

BOWRING, F. 2000. Social exclusion: Limitations of the debate. *Critical Social Policy*, 20, 307–30.

BRAMMER, S. and MILLINGTON, A. 2004. The development of corporate charitable contributions in the UK: A stakeholder analysis. *Journal of Management Studies*, 41, 1412–34.

BRAMMER, S. and MILLINGTON, A. 2005. Corporate reputation and philanthropy: An empirical analysis. *Journal of Business Ethics*, 61, 29–44.

BRAMMER, S.J. and PAVELIN, S. 2006. Corporate reputation and social performance: The importance of fit. *Journal of Management Studies*, 43, 435–55.

BREEZE, B. 2008. *The Coutts Million Pound Donors Report*. Canterbury: University of Kent, Centre for Philanthropy.

BRIDGEN, P. and MEYER, T. 2005. When do benevolent capitalists change their mind? Explaining the retrenchment of defined-benefit pensions in Britain. *Social Policy and Administration*, 39, 764–85.

BRINDLE, D. 2009. The worst is yet to come. *The Guardian*, 18 February.

BROOKS, R. 2007. Young people's extra-curricular activities: Critical social engagement – Or 'something for the CV'? *Journal of Social Policy*, 36, 417–34.

BUCHANAN, D., ROHR, L., KEHOE, L., GLICK, S.B. and JAIN, S. 2004. Changing attitudes toward homeless people: A curriculum evaluation. *Journal of General Internal Medicine*, 19, 566–8.

BUNDESEN, P. 2003. *Sociale problemer og socialpolitik*. Odense: Syddansk Universitetsforlag.

BURCHARDT, T., LE GRAND, J. and PIAHCAUD, D. 2002. Introduction. *In:* HILLS, J., LE GRAND, J. and PIACHAUD, D. (eds.) *Understanding Social Exclusion*. Oxford: Oxford University Press.

CAMERON, A. 2006. Geographies of welfare and exclusion: Social inclusion and exception. *Progress in Human Geography*, 30.

CAMPBELL, D., MOORE, G. and METZGER, M. 2002. Corporate philanthropy in the UK 1985–2000: Some empirical findings. *Journal of Business Ethics*, 39, 29–41.

CAMPBELL, J.L. 2002. Ideas, politics, and public policy. *Annual Review of Sociology*, 28, 21–38.

CANNON, T. 1992. *Corporate Responsibility*. London: Pitman Publishing.

CARMEL, E. and HARLOCK, J. 2007. Instituting the 'third sector' as a governable terrain: Partnership, procurement and performance in the UK. *Policy and Politics*, 36, 155–71.

CARROLL, A.B. 1999. Corporate social responsibility: Evolution of a definitional construct. *Business and Society*, 38, 268–95.

CARROLL, E. 2002. The impacts and non-impacts of globalization on social policy: Social insurance quality, institutions, trade exposure and deregulation in 18 OECD nations, 1965–1995. *In:* SIGG, R. and BEHRENDT, C. (eds) *Social Security in the Global Village*. New Brunswick, NJ: Transaction Publishers.

CASTLES, F.G. and MITCHELL, D. 1992. Identifying welfare state regimes: The links between politics, instruments and outcomes. *Governance*, 5, 1–26.

CAULKIN, S. 2002. Good thinking, bad practice. *The Observer*.

CBI 2004. DTI international CSR strategy consultation: CBI response. London: Confederation of British Industry.

CHARKHAM, J.P. 1995. *Keeping Good Company: A Study of Corporate Governance in Five Countries*. Oxford: Oxford University Press.

CHRISTENSEN, T. and LAEGREID, P. 2001. *The New Public Management: The Transformation of Ideas and Practice.* Aldershot: Ashgate.

CLARK, J.M. 1939. *Social Control of Business.* New York: McGraw-Hill.

CLARKE, J. 1997. Shareholders and corporate community involvement in Britain. *Business Ethics: A European Review,* 6.

CLARKSON, M.B.E. 1995. A stakeholder framework for analyzing and evaluating corporate social performance. *Academy of Management Review,* 20, 92–117.

CLEMENS, E.S. and COOK, J.M. 1999. Politics and institutionalism: Explaning durability and change. *Annual Review of Sociology,* 25, 441–66.

CLOKE, P., JOHNSEN, S. and MAY, J. 2007. Ethical citizenship? Volunteers and the ethics of providing services for homeless people. *Geoforum,* 38, 1089–101.

COCHRAINE, A., CLARKE, J. and GEWIRTZ, S. 2001. *Comparing Welfare States.* London: Sage Publications.

COLEMAN, G. 2000. Gender, power and post-structuralism in corporate citizenship: A personal perspective on theory and change. *Journal of Corporate Citizenship,* 5.

COLLIER, R.B. and COLLIER, D. 1991. *Shaping the Political Arena.* Princeton, NJ: Princeton University Press.

COLLINGS, R. 2003. Behind the brand: Is business socially responsible? *Consumer Policy Review,* 13, 159–64.

CORBETT, A. 2003. Ideas, institutions and policy entrepreneurs: Towards a new history of higher education in the European community. *European Journal of Education,* 38, 315–30.

COX, R.H. 1998a. From safety net to trampoline: Labor market activation in the Netherlands and Denmark. *Governance: An International Journal of Policy and Administration,* 11, 397–414.

COX, R.H. 1998b. The consequences of welfare reform: How conceptions of social rights are changing. *Journal of Social Policy,* 27, 1–16.

COX, R.H. 2001. The social construction of an imperative: Why welfare reform happened in Denmark and the Netherlands but not in Germany. *World Politics,* 53, 463–98.

COX, R.H. 2004. The path dependence of an idea: Why Scandinavian welfare states remain distinct. *Social Policy and Administration,* 38, 204–19.

CROWTHER, D. 2004. Corporate social reporting: Genuine action or window dressing? *In:* CROWTHER, D. and RAYMAN-BACCHUS, L. (eds) *Perspectives on Corporate Social Responsibility.* Ashgate: Aldershot.

CROWTHER, D. and RAYMAN-BACCHUS, L. 2004. Introduction. *In:* CROWTHER, D. and RAYMAN-BACCHUS, L. (eds) *Perspectives on Corporate Social Responsibility.* Aldershot: Ashgate.

DAVIES, S. 2008. Contracting out employment services to the third and private sectors: A critique. *Critical Social Policy,* 28, 136–64.

DE GEER, H., BORGLUND, T. and FROSTENSON, M. 2009. Reconciling CSR with the role of the corporation in welfare states: The problematic Swedish example. *Journal of Busines Ethics,* 89, 269–83.

DE GILDER, D., SCHUYT, T.N.M. and BREEDIJK, M. 2005. Effects of an employee volunteering program on the work force: The ABN-AMRO case. *Journal of Business Ethics*, 61, 43–152.

DEACON, B. 1993. Developments in East European social policy. *In:* JONES, C. (ed.) *New Perspectives on the Welfare State in Europe.* London: Routledge.

DEAN, J. 2001. Public companies as social institutions. *Business Ethics: A European Review*, 10, 302–10.

DEKKER, P. and VAN DEN BROEK, A. 1998. Civil society in comparative perspective: Involvement in voluntary associations in North America and Western Europe. *International Journal of Voluntary and Nonprofit Organizations*, 9, 11–38.

DENT, M. 2005. Post-new public management in public sector hospitals? The UK, Germany and Italy. *Policy and Politics*, 33, 623–36.

DOH, J.P. and GUAY, T.R. 2006. Corporate social responsibility, public policy, and NGO activism in Europe and the United States: An institutional-stakeholder perspective. *Journal of Management Studies*, 43, 47–73.

DRAKEFORD, M. 2007. Private welfare. *In:* POWELL, M. (ed.) *Understanding the Mixed Economy of Welfare.* Bristol: Policy Press.

DTI 2004. *Corporate Social Responsibility: A Government Update.* London: Department of Trade and Industry.

DUNLEAVY, C.A. 1992. Political structure, state policy, and industrial change: Early railroad policy in the United States and Prussia. *In:* STEINMO, S., THELEN, K. and LONGSTRETH, F. (ed.) *Structuring Politics: Historical Institutionalism in Comparative Analysis.* Cambridge: Cambridge University Press.

DWP 2008. *Working Together: UK National Action Plan on Social Inclusion.* London: Department for Work and Pension.

DWYER, P. 2004. Creeping conditionality in the UK: From welfare rights to conditional entitlements? *Canadian Journal of Sociology*, 28, 261–83.

EBERHARD-HARRIBEY, L. 2006. Corporate social responsibility as a new paradigm in the European policy: How CSR comes to legitimate the European regulation process. *Corporate Governance*, 6, 358–68.

ECONOMIST. 2005. The good company: A survey of corporate social responsibility. *The Economist.*

EDWARDS, B., GOODWIN, M., PEMBERTON, S. and WOODS, M. 2001. Partnerships, power, and scale in rural governance. *Environment and Planning C: Government and Policy*, 19, 289–310.

ESPING-ANDERSEN, G. 1990. *Three Worlds of Welfare Capitalism.* Cambridge: Polity Press.

ESPING-ANDERSEN, G. 2002. Towards the good society, once again? *In:* ESPING-ANDERSEN, G. (ed.) *Why We Need a New Welfare State.* Oxford: Oxford University Press.

ETZIONI, A. 1993. *The Spirit of Community: Rights, Responsibilities and the Communitarian Agenda.* New York: Crown Publishers.

EU-COM 2001. *Green Paper: Promoting a European framework for Corporate Social Responsibility*. Commission of the European Communities.

EU-COM 2002. *Corporate Social Responsibility: A Business Contribution to Sustainable Development*. Commission of the European Communities.

EU-COM 2006. *Implementing the Partnership for Growth and Jobs: Making Europe a Pole of Excellence on Corporate Social Responsibility.* Commission of the European Communities.

EU-COM 2007. *Corporate Social Responsibility: National Public Policies in the European Union*. Employment, Social Affairs and Equal Opportunities, European Commission

EVERS, A. 1993. The welfare mix approach: Understanding the pluralism of welfare systems. *In:* EVERS, A. and SVETLIK, I. (eds) *Balancing Pluralism.* Aldershot: Avebury.

EVERS, A. 2003. Origins and implications of working in partnership. *In:* KJAER, L. (ed.) *Local Partnerships in Europe: An Action Research Project.* Copenhagen: The Copenhagen Centre.

EVERS, A., LEWIS, J. and RIEDEL, B. 2005. Developing child-care provision in England and Germany: Problems of governance. *Journal of European Social Policy*, 15, 195–209.

FAIRBRASS, J. 2008. EU, UK and French CSR policy: What is the evidence for policy transfer and convergence? *Working Paper.* Bradford: Bradford University School of Management.

FARNSWORTH, K. 2004. *Corporate Power and Social Policy in a Global Economy*. Bristol: Policy Press.

FARNSWORTH, K. 2006a. Business in education: A reassessment of the contribution of outsourcing to LEA performance. *Journal of Education Policy*, 21, 485–96.

FARNSWORTH, K. 2006b. Capital to the rescue? New Labour's business solutions to old welfare problems. *Critical Social Policy*, 26, 817–42.

FARNSWORTH, K. and HOLDEN, C. 2006. The business-social policy nexus: Corporate power and corporate inputs into social policy. *Journal of Social Policy*, 35, 473–94.

FERRERA, M. 1996. The 'southern model' of welfare in social Europe. *Journal of European Social Policy*, 6, 17–37.

FLORA, P. and ALBER, J. 1981. Modernization, democratization, and the development of welfare states in Western Europe. *In:* FLORA, P. and HEIDENHEIMER, A. (eds) *The Development of Welfare States in Europe and America.* London: Transaction Books.

FREEMAN, R.E. 1984. *Strategic Management: A Stakeholder Approach*. Boston, MA: Pitman/ Ballinger.

FRIDBERG, T. 1997. Hvem løser de social opgaver? *In:* FRIDBERG, T. (ed.) *Hvem løser opgaverne i fremtidens velfærdssamfund?* København: Socialforskningsinstituttet.

FRIEDMAN, M. 1979. The social responsibility of businesses is to increase its profits. *The New York Times Magazine*, 13 September.

FROSTENSON, M. and BORGLUND, T. 2006. *Företagens sociala ansvar och den svenska modellen*. Stockholm: Svenska institutet för europapolitiska studier.

GAL, J. and BARGAL, D. 2002. Critical junctures, labor movements and the development of occupational welfare in Israel. *Social Problems*, 49, 432–54.

GERMAN FEDERAL GOVERNMENT 2010. *National Strategy for Corporate Social Responsibility: Action plan for CSR of the German Federal Government*. Berlin: The Federal Ministry of Labour and Social Affairs.

GEYER, R. 1998. Globalization and the (non-)defence of the welfare state. *West European Politics*, 21, 77–102.

GIDDENS, A. 1998. *The Third Way: The Renewal of Social Democracy*. Cambridge: Polity Press.

GILCHRIST, V.J. 1992. Key informant interviews. *In:* CRABTREE, B.F. and MILLER, W.L. (eds.) *Doing Qualitative Research*. Beverly Hills, CA: Sage Publications.

GOODIN, R.E. 2003. Democratic accountability: The distinctiveness of the third sector. *Archives Européenes de Sociologie*, XLIV, 359–96.

GOODWIN, M., JONES, M. and JONES, R. 2005. Devolution, constitutional change and economic development: Explaining and understanding the new institutional geographies of the British state. *Regional Studies*, 39, 421–36.

GORE, C., FIGUEIREDO, J.B. and RODGERS, G. 1995. Introduction: Markets, citizenship and social exclusion. *In:* RODGERS, G., GORE, C. and FIGUEIREDO, J.B. (eds) *Social Exclusion: Rhetoric, Reality, Responses*. Geneva: ILO.

GREEN-PEDERSEN, C. 2004. The dependent variable problem within the study of welfare state retrenchment: Defining the problem and looking for solutions. *Journal of Comparative Policy Analysis*, 6, 3–14.

HALL, P. 1992. The movement from Keynesianism to monetarism: Institutional analysis and British economic policy in the 1970's. *In:* STEINMO, S., THELEN, K. and LONGSTRETH, F. (eds) *Structuring Politics: Historical Institutionalism in Comparative Analysis*. Cambridge: Cambridge University Press.

HALL, P. 1993. Policy paradigms, social learning, and the state: The case of economic policymaking in Britain. *Comparative Politics*, 25, 275–96.

HALL, P. and SOSKICE, D. 2001. An introduction to varieties of capitalism. *In:* HALL, P. and SOSKICE, D. (eds) *Varieties of Capitalism: The Institutional Foundations of Comparative Advantage*. Oxford: Oxford University Press.

HALL, P. and TAYLOR, R.C.R. 1996. Political science and the three new institutionalisms. *Political Studies*, 44, 936–57.

HALVORSEN, R. and JENSEN, P. H. 2004. Activation in Scandinavian welfare policy: Denmark and Norway in a comparative perspective. *European Societies*, 6, 461–83.

HANSEN, R. and KING, D. 2001. Eugenic ideas, political interests and policy variance: Immigration and sterilization policy in Britain and the US. *World Politics*, 53, 237–63.

HARDIS, J. 2003. Social multipartite partnerships – When practice does not fit rhetoric. *In:* MORSING, M. and THYSSEN, C. (eds) *Corporate Values and Responsibility: The Case of Denmark.* Frederiksberg: Samfundslitteratur.

HATTAM, V. 1992. Institutions and political change: Working-class formation in England and the United States, 1820–1896. *In:* STEINMO, S., THELEN, K. and LONGSTRETH, F. (eds.) *Structuring Politics: Historical Institutionalism in Comparative Analysis.* Cambridge: Cambridge University Press.

HAY, C. and ROSAMOND, B. 2002. Globalization, European integration and the discursive construction of economic imperatives. *Journal of European Public Policy*, 9, 147–67.

HAY, C. and WINCOTT, D. 1998. Structure, agency and historical institutionalism. *Political Studies*, XLVI, 951–7.

HEMINGWAY, C.A. and MACLAGAN, P.W. 2004. Managers' personal values as drivers of corporate social responsibility. *Journal of Busines Ethics*, 50, 33–44.

HENDERSON, D. 2001. Misguided virtue: False notions of corporate social responsibility. *New Zealand Business Roundtable.*

HENDRY, J. 2001. Economic contracts versus social relationships as a foundation for normative stakeholder theory. *Business Ethics: A European Review*, 10, 223–232.

HILL, M. 2007. The mixed economy of welfare: A comparative perspective. *In:* POWELL, M. (ed.) *Understanding the Mixed Economy of Welfare.* Bristol: Policy Press.

HILL, R.P., STEPHENS, D. and SMITH, I. 2003. Corporate social responsibility: An examination of firm behaviour. *Business and Society Review*, 108, 339–64.

HISS, S. 2009. From implicit to explicit – Corporate social responsibility: Institutional change as a fight for myths. *Business Ethics Quarterly*, 19, 433–51.

HOBBES, T. 1998 (1651). *Leviathan.* Oxford, Oxford University Press.

HOLT, H. 1998. *En kortlægning af danske virksomheders sociale ansvar* København, Socialforskningsinstituttet.

HOWARD, S. 2009 6 February. *Stephen Howard comments on 'The hot air of CSR'* [Online]. London. Available at: http://www.bitc.org.uk/media_centre/ comment/stephen_howard.html [Accessed 18 February 2009].

HUDSON, J., HWANG, G.-J. and KÜHNER, S. 2008. Between ideas, institutions and interests: Analysing third way welfare reform programmes in Germany and the United Kingdom. *Journal of Social Policy*, 37, 207–30.

HUSTED, B.W. and SALAZAR, J.D.J. 2006. Taking Friedman seriously: Maximizing profits and social performance. *Journal of Management Studies*, 43, 75–91.

HUTTON, W. 1996. The stakeholder society. *In:* MARQUAND, D.S. and SELDON, A. (ed.) *The Ideas that Shaped Post-War Britain.* London: New Statesman/ Fontana.

HUTTON, W. 2002. Confronting the Critics, Response to Joseph, E and John Parkinson and to Martin Wolf: Confronting the Critics. *New Academy Review* 1, 66–67.

IMMERGUT, E.M. 1992. The rules of the game: The logic of health policy-making in France, Switzerland, and Sweden. *In:* STEINMO, S., THELEN, K. and LONGSTRETH, F. (eds) *Structuring Politics: Historical Institutionalism in Comparative Analysis.* Cambridge: Cambridge University Press.

JENSEN, B. 1999. *Kan det betale sig at arbejde? Danskernes arbejdsudbud i 90'ernes velfærdsstat.* København: Spektrum.

JENSEN, M.C. 2000. Value maximization and the corporate objective function. *In:* BEER, M. and NOHRIA, N. (eds) *Breaking the Code of Change.* Boston, MA: HBS Press.

JESPERSEN, K. 10 January 1994. Det angår os alle. *Politiken.*

JESSOP, B. 2004. Hollowing out the 'nation-state' and multi-level governance. *In:* KENNETT, P. (ed.) *A Handbook of Comparative Social Policy.* Cheltenham: Edward Elgar Publishing.

JIMENA, J. 2009. What does CSR have to offer in a recession? *Canadian Mining Journal,* May, 11.

JOHNSON, N. 1999. *Mixed Economies of Welfare.* Hemel Hempstead: Prentice Hall.

JONES, C. 1993. The Pacific challenge. *In:* JONES, C. (ed.) *New Perspectives on the Welfare State in Europe.* London: Routledge.

JOSEPH, E. and PARKINSON, J. 2002. Confronting the critics. *New Academy Review,* 1, 48–61.

KATZENSTEIN, P.J. 1996. *Cultural Norms and National Security: Police and Military in Postwar Japan.* Ithaca, NY: Cornell.

KENNETT, P. 2004. Introduction: The changing context of comparative social policy. *In:* KENNETT, P. (ed.) *A Handbook of Comparative Social Policy.* Cheltenham: Edward Elgar Publishing.

KERR, C., DUNLOP, J.T., HARBISON, F.H. and MYERS, C.A. 1960. *Industrialism and Industrial Man.* Cambridge, MA: Harvard University Press.

KING, D. 1992. The establishment of work-welfare programs in the United States and Britain: Politics, ideas, and institutions. *In:* STEINMO, S., THELEN, K. and LONGSTRETH, F. (eds) *Structuring Politics: Historical Institutionalism in Comparative Analysis.* Cambridge: Cambridge University Press.

KING, D. and HANSEN, R. 1999. Experts at work: State autonomy, social learning and eugenic sterilization in 1930s Britain. *British Journal of Political Science,* 20, 77–107.

KINGDON, J.W. 1995. *Agendas, Alternatives, and Public Policies.* New York: HarperCollins.

KNUDSEN, J.S. 2004. Corporate philanthropy and public-private partnerships: Do new approaches to business constitute pitfalls for corporations and society? *The Ethical Wealth of Nations. Values and Social Development (section on Ethics, Business and the Economy).* Barcelona.

KORPI, W. 2002. *Velfærdsstat og socialt medborgerskab. Danmark i et komparativt perspektiv, 1930–1995.* Aarhus, Magtudredningen/Institut for Statskundskab.

KRASNER, S. 1984. Approaches to the state: Alternative conceptions and historical dynamics. *Comparative Politics,* 16, 223–46.

KUHN, T. 1970. *The Structure of Scientific Revolutions.* Chicago IL: University of Chicago Press.

LABONTE, R. 2004. Social inclusion/exclusion: Dancing the dialectic. *Health Promotion International,* 19, 115–21.

LANE, J.-E. 2000. *New Public Management.* London: Routledge.

LARSEN, J.E. 2004. *Fattigdom og Social Eksklusion: Tendenser i Danmark over et kvar århundrede.* København: Socialforskningsinstituttet.

LE GRAND, J. 1991. Quasi-markets and social policy. *The Economic Journal,* 101, 1256–67.

LEIBFRIED, S. 1993. Towards a European welfare state? *In:* JONES, C. (ed.) *New Perspectives on the Welfare State in Europe.* London: Routledge.

LEVITAS, R. 2005. *The Inclusive Society? Social Exclusion and New Labour.* Basingstoke: Palgrave Macmillan.

LEWIS, J. 1992. Gender and the development of welfare regimes. *Journal of European Social Policy,* 2, 159–73.

LEWIS, J. 1995. *The Voluntary Sector, the State and Social Work in Britain.* Cheltenham: Edward Elgar Publishing.

LEWIS, J. 2000. Gender and welfare regimes. *In:* LEWIS, J., GEWIRTZ, G. and CLARKE, J. (eds) *Rethinking Social Policy.* London: Sage.

LEWIS, J. 2003. Responsibilities and rights: Changing the balance. *In:* ELLISON, N. and PIERSON, C. (eds) *Developments in British Social Policy II.* London: Macmillan Press.

LEWIS, J. 2007. Gender, ageing and the 'new social settlement'–The importance of developing a holistic approach to care policies. *Current Sociology,* 55, 271–86.

LIEBERMAN, R.C. 2002. Ideas, institutions, and political order: Explaining political change. *American Political Science Review,* 96.

LINDBOM, A. 2001. Dismantling the social democratic welfare model? Has the Swedish welfare state lost its defining characteristics? *Scandinavian Political Studies,* 24, 171–93.

LINDSAY, C. and MAILAND, M. 2004. Different routes, common directions? Activation policies for young people in Denmark and the UK. *International Journal of Socal Welfare,* 13, 195–207.

LISTER, R. 2004. *Poverty.* Cambridge, Polity Press.

LOCKE, J. 1988 (1689). *Two Treatises of Government.* Cambridge: Cambridge University Press.

LØDEMEL, I. and TRICKEY, H. 2001. *'An Offer You Can't Refuse?' Workfare in International Perspective.* Bristol: Policy Press.

LUND, J.E. 2003. Partnerships in practice. *In:* MORSING, M. and THYSSEN, C. (eds) *Corporate Values and Responsibility: The Case of Denmark.* Frederiksberg: Samfundslitteratur.

LYNGGARD, K. 2007. The institutional construction of a policy field: A discursive institutional perspective on change within the common agricultural policy. *Journal of European Public Policy*, 14, 293–312.

MACGREGOR, S. 2003. Social exclusion. *In:* ELLISON, N. and PIERSON, C. (eds) *Developments in British Social Policy II.* London: Macmillan Press.

MACLAGAN, P. 1999. Corporate social responsibility as a participative process. *Business Ethics: A European Review*, 8, 43–9.

MACLEOD, S. and LEWIS, D. 2004. Transnational corporations: Power, influence and responsibility. *Global Social Policy*, 4, 77–98.

MAHONEY, J. 2000. Path dependence in historical sociology. *Theory and Society*, 29, 507–48.

MAIGNAN, I. and FERRELL, O.C. 2001. Antecedents and benefits of corporate citizenship: An investigation of French businesses. *Journal of Business Research*, 51, 37–51.

MAIGNAN, I. and FERRELL, O.C. 2003. Nature of corporate responsibilities: Perspectives from American, French, and German consumers. *Journal of Business Research*, 56, 55–67.

MANOKHA, I. 2004. Corporate social responsibility: A new signifier? An analysis of business ethics and good business practice. *Politics*, 24, 56–64.

MARCH, J.G. and OLSEN, J.P. 1989. *Rediscovering Institutions.* New York: Free Press.

MARGOLIS, J.D. and WALSH, J.P. 2000. *People and Profits – The Search for a Link Between a Company's Social and Financial Performance.* New Jersey: Lawrence Erlbaum Associates.

MARMOR, T.R., MASHAW, J.L. and L, H.P. 1990. *America's Misunderstood Welfare State: Persisting Myths, Enduring Realities.* New York: Basic Books.

MARTIN, C.J. 2004. Reinventing welfare regimes: Employers and the implementation of active social policy. *World Politics*, 57, 39–69.

MARTIN, C.J. and SWANK, D. 2004. Does the organization of capital matter? Employers and active labor market policy at the national and firm levels. *American Political Science Review*, 98, 593–611.

MATTEN, D. and MOON, J. 2004. 'Implicit' and 'Explicit' CSR: A counceptual framework for understanding CSR in Europe. *ICCSR Research Paper Series.* ICCSR, University of Nottingham.

MATTEN, D. and MOON, J. 2008. 'Implicit' and 'Explicit' CSR: A conceptual Framework for a comparative understanding of corporate social responsibility. *Academy of Management Review*, 33, 404–24.

MAYO, M. 1994. *Communities and Caring: The Mixed Economy of Welfare.* Basingstoke: Macmillan.

MAYO, M. and ROOKE, A. 2006. *Active Learning for Active Citizenship: An Evaluation Report.* London: Home Office.

MCGUIRE, J.W. 1963. *Business and Society.* New York: McGraw-Hill.

MCINTOSH, M. (ed.) 1993. *Good Business? Case Studies in Corporate Social Responsibility.* Bristol: Centre for Social Management/ New Consumer/ Policy Press.

MCNAMARA, K.R. 1998. *The Currency of Ideas.* Ithaca, NY: Cornell University Press.

MCWILLIAMS, A. and SIEGEL, D.S. 2001. Corporate social responsibility: A theory of the firm perspective. *Academy of Management Review*, 26, 117–27.

MCWILLIAMS, A., SIEGEL, D.S. and WRIGHT, P.M. 2006. Corporate social responsibility: Strategic implications. *Journal of Management Studies*, 43, 1–18.

MERRIEN, F.-X. 2001. The World Bank's new social policies: Pension. *International Social Science Journal*, 53, 537–50.

MIDTTUN, A., KRISTIAN GAUTESEN AND MARIA GJØLBERG: 2006. The political economy of CSR in Western Europe. *Corporate Governance*, 6, 369–85.

MISHRA, R. 1990. *The Welfare State in Capitalist Society.* Hemel Hempstead: Harvester Wheatsheaf.

MISHRA, R. 1999. *Globalization and the Welfare State.* Cheltenham: Edward Elgar.

MONBIOT, G. 2001. *Captive State: The Corporate Take-over of Britain.* London: Pan.

MOON, J. 2002. The social responsibility of business and new governance. *Government and Opposition*, 10, 385–408.

MOON, J. 2004. Government as driver of corporate social responsibility: The UK in comparative perspective. *ICCSR Research Paper Series.* ICCSR, University of Nottingham.

MOORE, G. 2003. Hives and horseshoes, Mintzberg or MacIntyre: What future for corporate social responsibility? *Business Ethics: A European Review*, 12, 41–53.

MURRAY, C. 1990. *The Emerging British Underclass.* London: IEA.

MURRAY, C. 1994. *Underclass: The Crisis Deepens.* London: IEA.

NETVÆRKSPRISEN. 2009. *De nominerede til Netværksprisen 2008* [Online]. Available at: http://www.netvaerksprisen.dk/34nomin.html [Accessed 18 February 2009].

NEWMAN, J. 2001. *Modernising Governance.* London: Sage Publications.

NEWMAN, J. and MCKEE, B. 2005. Beyond the new public management? Public services and the social investment state. *Policy and Politics*, 33, 657–74.

OHMAE, K. 1992. *The Borderless World: Power and Strategy in the Interlinked Economy.* London: Harper Collins.

ØKONOMI-OG-ERHVERVSMINISTEREN 2008. Forslag til lov om ændring af årsregnskabsloven. (Redegørelse for samfundsansvar i større virksomheder). .

OSBORNE, D. and GAEBLER, T. 1992. *Reinventing Government: How the Entrepreneurial Spirit is Transforming the Public Sector*. Reading, MA: Addison-Wesley Publising Company.

ØYEN, E. 1997. The contradictory concepts of social exclusion and social inclusion. *In:* GORE, C. and FIGUEIREDO, J.B. (eds) *Social Exclusion and Anti-poverty Policy: A Debate*. Geneva: ILO.

PALAZZO, B. 2002. US-American and German business ethics: An intercultural comparison. *Journal of Busines Ethics*, 41.

PALIER, B. 2002. Beyond retrenchment: Four problems in current welfare state research and one suggestion how to overcome them. *In:* CLASEN, J. (ed.) *What Future for Social Security?* Bristol: Policy Press.

PECK, J. 2001. *Workfare States*. New York: The Guilford Press.

PEDERSEN, E.R. 2006. Making corporate social responsibility (CSR) operable: How companies translate stakeholder dialogue into practice. *Business and Society Review*, 111, 137–63.

PEMBERTON, S. and LLOYD, G. 2008. Devolution, community planning and institutional decongestion? *Local Government Studies*, 34, 437–51.

PENG, I. 2000. A fresh look at the Japanese welfare state. *Social Policy and Administration*, 34, 87–114.

PERKINS, D. 2008. Improving employment participation for welfare recipients facing personal barriers. *Social Policy and Society*, 7, 13–26.

PETERS, G. 2001. *Institutional Theory in Political Science: The 'New Institutionalism'*. London: Continuum.

PIERSON, P. 1994. *Dismantling the Welfare State? Reagan, Thatcher, and the Politics of Retrenchment*. Cambridge: Cambridge University Press.

PIERSON, P. 1996. The new politics of the welfare state. *World Politics*, 48, 141–79.

PIERSON, P. 2000. Increasing returns, path dependence, and the study of politics. *American Political Science Review*, 94, 251–67.

PIERSON, P. 2001a. Coping with permanent austerity: Welfare state restructuring in affluent democracies. *In:* PIERSON, P. (ed.) *The New Politics of the Welfare State*. Oxford: Oxford University Press.

PIERSON, P. 2001b. Introduction: Investigating the welfare state at century's end. *In:* PIERSON, P. (ed.) *The New Politics of the Welfare State*. Oxford: Oxford University Press.

PIERSON, P. 2004. *Politics in Time: History, Institutions, and Political Analysis*. Princeton, NJ: Princeton University Press.

PORTER, M.E. and KRAMER, M.R. 2002. The competitive advantage of corporate philanthropy. *Harvard Business Review*, 5–16 December.

POWELL, M. 2007. The mixed economy of welfare and the social division of welfare. *In:* POWELL, M. (ed.) *Understanding the Mixed Economy of Welfare*. Bristol: Policy Press.

PRIETO, M. 2002. Thoughts on feminist action research. *New Academy of Business Working Paper*, 1–13.

PRYCE, V. 2002. CSR – Should it be the preserve of the usual suspects? *Business Ethics: A European Review*, 11, 140–42.

RAJULTON, F., RAVANERA, Z.R. and BEAUJOT, R. 2007. Measuring social cohesion: An experiment using the Canadian National Survey of Giving, volunteering, and participating. *Social Indicators Research*, 80, 461–92.

REGERINGEN 2008. Handlingsplan for virksomheders samfundsansvar. *In:* ERHVERVSMINISTERIET, Ø.-O. (ed.).

REGERINGSKANSLIET. 2011. *Globalt Ansvar* [Online]. Regeringskansliet. Available at: http://www.sweden.gov.se/sb/d/2657.

RODGERS, G. 1995. What is special about a 'social exclusion' approach? *In:* RODGERS, G., GORE, C. and FIGUEIREDO, J.B. (eds) *Social Exclusion: Rhetoric, Reality, Responses.* Geneva: ILO.

ROOM, G. 1995. Poverty and social exclusion: The new European Agenda for policy and research. *In:* ROOM, G. (ed.) *Beyond the Threshold: The Measurement and Analysis of Social Exclusion.* Bristol: Policy Press.

ROSDAHL, A. 2001. *The Policy to Promote Social Responsibility of Enterprises in Denmark.* København: Socialforskningsinstituttet.

ROSE, R. 1986. Introduction. *In:* ROSE, R. and SHIRATORI, R. (eds) *The Welfare State East and West.* Oxford: Oxford University Press.

ROSE, R. 1991. Is American public policy exceptional? *In:* SCHAFER, B.E. (ed.) *Is America Different? A New Look at American Exceptionalism.* Oxford: Oxford University Press.

ROTHSTEIN, B. 1992. Labor-market institutions and working class strength. *In:* STEINMO, S., THELEN, K. and LIEBERMAN, R.C. (eds) *Structuring Politics: Historical Institutionalism in Comparative Analysis.* Cambridge: Cambridge University Press.

ROUSSEAU, J.J. 1998 (1762). *The Social Contract.* Hertfordshire: Wordsworth Editions Ltd.

RUGGIE, J.G. 2002. The theory and practice of learning networks: Corporate social responsibility and the global compact. *Journal of Corporate Citizenship*, 5, 27–36.

SADLER, D. 2004. Anti-corporate campaigning and corporate 'social' responsibility: Towards alternative spaces of citizenship? *Antipode*, 851–70.

SAMFUNDSANSVAR.DK. 2009. *Kort om virksomheders samfundsansvar* [Online]. Available at: http://www.samfundsansvar.dk/sw41314.asp [Accessed 18 February 2009].

SCHMIDT, V.A. 2002. Does discourse matter in the politics of welfare state adjustment? *Comparative political studies,* 35, 168–193.

SCHMIDT, V.A. 2003. How, where and when does discourse matter in small states' welfare state adjustment? *New Political Economy*, 8, 127–46.

SECRETAN, V.A. 1998. *What Do Companies Risk in Not Being Socially Responsible? A Risk Management Perspective of Corporate Social Eesponsibility.* University of Bristol

SEIFERT, B., MORRIS, S.A. and BARTKUS, B.R. 2003. Comparing big givers and small givers: Financial correlates of corporate philanthropy. *Journal of Business Ethics*, 45, 195–211.

SERBAN, V. and KAUFMANN, M. 2011. Corporate social responsibility: The challenge for medium sized enterprises in the Bamberg-Forcheim region, Germany. *Amfiteatru Economic*, 13, 180–94.

SHAMIR, R. 2008. The age of responsibilization: On market-embedded morality. *Economy and Society*, 37, 1–19.

SILVER, H. 1995. Reconceptualising social disadvantage: Three paradigms of social exclusion. *In:* RODGERS, G. (ed.) *Social Exclusion: Rhetoric, Reality, Responses.* Geneva: ILO.

SKOCPOL, T. 1992. *Protecting Soldiers and Mothers: The Political Origins of Social Policy in the United States.* Cambridge: Cambridge University Press.

SLOTHUUS, R. 2007. Framing deservingness to win support for welfare state retrenchment. *Journal Compilation: Nordic Political Science Association*, 323–44.

SMITH, D.H. 1997. Grassroots associations are important: Some theory and a review of the impact literature. *Nonprofit and voluntary sector quarterly*, 26, 269-306.

SMITH, F., BARKER, J., WAINWRIGHT, E., MANDARET, E. and BUCKINGHAM, S. 2008. A new deal for lone parents? Training lone parents for work in West London. *Area*, 40, 237–44

SMITH, J. and HASNAS, J. 1999. Ethics and information systems: The corporate domain. *MIS Quarterly*, 23, 109–27.

SOCIALMINISTERIET 2006. Handlingsplan om social beskyttelse og inklusion 2006–2008. Socialministeriet, Indenrigs- og sundhedsministeriet.

SØNDERGÅRD, J. 2002. *Danske arbejdspladser – plads til alle?* København: Socialforskningsinstituttet.

STARK, D. and BRUSZT, L. 1998. *Postsocialist Pathways: Transforming Politics and Property in East Central Europe/* New York: Cambridge University Press.

STARKE, P. 2006. The politics of welfare retrenchment: A literature review. *Social Policy and Administration*, 40, 104–20.

STARKE, P., OBINGER, H. and CASTLES, F.G. 2008. Convergence towards where: In what ways, if any, are welfare states becoming more similar? *Journal of European Public Policy*, 15, 975–1000.

STEENSLAND, B. 2008. Why do policy frames change? Actor-idea coevolution in debates over welfare reform. *Social Forces*, 86, 1027–55.

STERN, S. 2009. The deadliest greenhouse gas? The hot air of CSR. *Financial Times*, 3 February.

STEWART, J. 2007. The mixed economy of welfare in historical context. *In:* POWELL, M. (ed.) *Understanding the Mixed Economy of Welfare.* Bristol: Policy Press.

SUREL, Y. 2000. The role of cognitive and normative frames in policy-making. *Journal of European Public Policy*, 7, 495–512.

SWANK, D. and STEINMO, S. 2002. The new political economy of taxation in advanced capitalist democracies. *American Journal of Political Science,* 42, 642–55.

TANZI, V. 2002. Globalisation and the future of social protection. *Scottish Journal of Political Economy,* 49, 116–27.

TAYLOR-GOOBY, P. 1991. Welfare state regimes and welfare citizenship. *Journal of European Social Policy,* 1, 93–105.

TAYLOR-GOOBY, P. 1999. Markets and Motives: Trust and Egoism in Welfare Markets. *Journal of Social Policy,* 28, 97 -114.

TAYLOR-GOOBY, P. 2001. Chapter 1: The Politics of welfare in Europe *In:* TAYLOR-GOOBY, P. (ed.) *Welfare States under Pressure.* London: Sage.

TAYLOR-GOOBY, P. 2005a. Ideas and policy change. *In:* TAYLOR-GOOBY, P. (ed.) *Ideas and welfare state reform in Western Europe.* Basingstoke: Palgrave Macmillan.

TAYLOR-GOOBY, P. 2005b. Paradigm shifts, power resources and labour market reform. *In:* TAYLOR-GOOBY, P. (ed.) *Ideas and Welfare State Reform in Western Europe.* Basingstoke: Palgrave Macmillan.

TAYLOR-GOOBY, P. 2008a. The new welfare state settlement in Europe. *European Societies,* 10, 3–24.

TAYLOR-GOOBY, P. 2008b. Trust and welfare state reform: The example of the NHS. *Social Policy and Administration,* 42, 288–306.

TEEPLE, G. 2000. *Globalisation and the Decline of Social Reform.* Toronto: Humanity Books.

TENGBLAD, S. and OHLSSON, C. 2009. The framing of corporate social responsibility and the globalization of national business systems: A longitudinal case study. *Journal of Busines Ethics,* 93, 653–69.

THELEN, K. 1999. Historical institutionalism in comparative politics. *Annual Review of Political Science,* 2, 369–404.

THELEN, K. and STEINMO, S. 1992. Historical institutionalism in comparative politics. *In:* STEINMO, S., THELEN, K. and LONGSTRETH, F. (eds) *Structuring Politics: Historical Institutionalism in Comparative Analysis.* Cambridge: Cambridge University Press.

TITMUSS, R.M. 1974. *Social Policy.* London, Allen and Unwin.

TORFING, J. 1999. Workfare with welfare: Recent reforms of the Danish welfare state. *Journal of European Social Policy,* 9, 1–31.

TORFING, J. 2001. Path-dependent Danish welfare reforms: The contribution of New Institutionalism to understanding evolutionary change. *Scandinavian Political Studies,* 24, 277–309.

TOWNSEND, P. 1979. *Poverty in the United Kingdom.* Harmondsworth: Penguin.

TREIB, O., BÄHR, H. and FALKNER, G. 2007. Modes of governance: Towards a conceptual clarification. *Journal of European Public Policy,* 14, 1–20.

TRILLINGSGAARD, P. and HOLBECH JESPERSEN, A. 2003. Regulating CSR – A contradiction in terms? *In:* MORSING, M. and THYSSEN, C. (eds)

Corporate Values and Responsibility: The Case of Denmark. Frederiksberg Samfundslitteratur.

UK-GOV 2006. Companies Act 2006. The Stationery Office Limited.

UK-GOV 2010. *Building the Big Society.* London: Cabinet Office.

UN. 2000. *UN Global Compact* [Online]. Available at: http://www.unglobal compact.org/ [Accessed 13 February 2009].

VAN OORSCHOT, W.V. and ABRAHAMSON, P. 2003. The Dutch and Danish miracles revisited: A critical discussion of activation policies in two small welfare states. *Social Policy and Administration,* 37, 288–304.

VFSA. 2010. *Tidligere Vindere* [Online]. Virksomhedsforum for Socialt Ansvar. [Accessed 23 June 2011].

WALKER, A. and WONG, C.-K. 1996. Rethinking the western construction of the welfare state. *International Journal of Health Services,* 26, 67–92.

WALKER, R. 1997. Poverty and social exclusion in Europe. *In:* WALKER, R. and WALKER, C. (eds) *Britain Divided: The Growth of Social Exclusion in the 1980s and 1990s.* London: Childhood Poverty Action Group.

WEIR, M. and SKOCPOL, T. 1983. State structures and the possibilities for 'Keynesian' responses to the Great Depression in Sweden, Britain and the United States. *International Journal of Comparative Sociology,* 24, 4–29.

WHEELER, D. and SILLANPAA, M. 1997. *The Stakeholder Corporation: Blueprint For Maximizing Stakeholder Value.* Harlow: Pearson Education Limited.

WHITEHOUSE, L. 2003. Corporate social responsibility, corporate citizenship and the global compact. *Global Social Policy,* 3, 299–318.

WILDING, P. 1997. Globalisation, regionalism and social policy. *Social Policy and Administration,* 31, 410–28.

WILENSKY, H.L. 1975. *The Welfare State and Equality: Structural and Ideological Roots of Public Expenditures.* Berkeley, CA: University of California Press.

WINDSOR, D. 2006. Corporate social responsibility: Three key approaches. *Journal of Management Studies,* 43, 93–114.

WINTHER, F. 1996. The welfare mix. *European Conference on Social Exclusion.* Aarhus, Denmark.

WITT-HANSEN, L. and ROTHSTEIN, K. 2007 15 December. Bomuld og big business. *Agenda.* Danmarks Radio.

WOLF, M. 2002. Confronting the critics: Response to Joseph, E and John Parkinson. *New Academy Review,* 1, 62–5.

YEATES, N. 1999. Social politics and policy in an era of globalization: Critical reflections. *Social Policy and Administration,* 33, 372–93.

YEATES, N. 2006. The global and supra-national dimensions of the welfare mix. *In:* POWELL, M. (ed.) *Understanding the Mixed Economy of Welfare.* Bristol: Policy Press.

Index

For Product Safety Concerns and Information please contact our
EU representative GPSR@taylorandfrancis.com Taylor & Francis
Verlag GmbH, Kaufingerstraße 24, 80331 München, Germany